THE NEW
VIEW OF SELF

How Genes
and Neurotransmitters
Shape Your Mind,
Your Personality,
and Your Mental Health

LARRY J. SIEVER, M.D.
with WILLIAM FRUCHT

MACMILLAN • USA

DEDICATION

*To my parents, Doris and Ray; my wife, Lissa; my two sons,
David and Daniel; and especially to all the patients
in our program who helped inspire these ideas.*

— LS

MACMILLAN

A Simon & Schuster Macmillan Company
1633 Broadway
New York, NY 10019-6785

Library of Congress Cataloging-in-Publication Data

Siever, Larry J., 1947–
The new view of self: how genes and neurotransmitters shape your mind, personality, and your mental health / Larry Siever, with William Frucht.
p.   cm.
Includes bibliographical references and index.
ISBN 0-02-861544-1 (HC)
1. Biological psychiatry. I. Frucht, William. II. Title.
[DNLM: 1. Neurotic Disorders—etiology. 2. Brain—physiology. 3. Personality—
physiology. 4. Behavior—physiology. 5. Psychiatry—trends. WM 170 S573n 1997]
RC343.S573   1997
616.89—dc21
DNLM/DLC
for Library of Congress   96-46026
CIP

DESIGN BY KEVIN HANEK

Printed in the United States of America

10   9   8   7   6   5   4   3   2   1

CONTENTS

ACKNOWLEDGMENTS   v

PREFACE   vii

CHAPTER ONE
The Soul's Deathly Sleep   1

CHAPTER TWO
Depression as a Physical Disease   27

CHAPTER THREE
The Dramatic Cluster   63

CHAPTER FOUR
Serotonin and Suicide:
The Biology of Impulsive Aggression   89

CHAPTER FIVE
Crossing Reality at an Angle   127

CHAPTER SIX
The Prudent Atom   169

CHAPTER SEVEN
Goodness of Fit   195

CHAPTER EIGHT
From the Individual to the Community   217

NOTES   245

INDEX   253

ACKNOWLEDGMENTS

This book represents the work of many people who were important influences on my own thinking and research. My mentors, some of whom later became collaborators, have included Salva Luria, who introduced me to the excitement of biology at an early age; Keith Brodie and Jack Barchas, who facilitated my entry into the world of clinical psychiatric research while I was still in medical school; John Gunderson, who introduced me to the concept of personality disorders; Dennis Murphy, who gave me encouragement, guidance, and opportunity to conduct biologic research in depression; and Ken Davis, a friend and colleague who helped many of these ideas mature. Special thanks to Emil Coccaro and the late Howard Klar, who worked with me to get the program underway.

This book could not have happened as it did without Bill Frucht, who breathed new life into writing I had perhaps grown too familiar with and who has been a stimulating, thoughtful, and cheerful collaborator. The chemistry worked well.

Special personal thanks to my parents, Ray and Doris Siever, from whom I learned both scientific and humanistic values; my wife, Lissa Weinstein, a psychoanalyst and psychologist who gave many hours to the enrichment of this book as well as tending to its author; and to my two sons, David and Daniel, who came on the scene during the evolution of this book and have been a continuing source of inspiration, delight, and surprise.

— LARRY J. SIEVER

I was brought in on this book some time ago, at what was supposed to be the last minute, to help communicate Larry Siever's fascinating ideas to a general readership. Because career and family commitments dictated a limited writing schedule, because Larry's and my discussions resulted in some fundamental changes in the scope and organization of the book, and because of my excruciatingly slow pace as a writer, the whole project took considerably longer than anticipated. (Readers may judge for themselves whether the effort was worth the time.) I wish to thank everyone involved for their forbearance, especially Larry himself, who has been as patient and responsive a partner as one could wish for.

During much of my work on this book, I was employed by Newbridge Book Clubs, where several of my colleagues provided help and encouragement. I especially would like to thank Arthur Goldwag, who read and commented on several chapters; Lilian Schein, who lent many volumes from her inexhaustible library of psychiatry books and also lent a willing ear on many lonely Sunday afternoons in the office; Jo Ann Winson for her steadfast encouragement; and Ed Renehan for showing that it could be done. My new colleagues at Springer-Verlag, especially Jerry Lyons, Liesl Gibson, and Teresa Shields, also gave me advice and support.

My late father-in-law, Lionel Ovesey, took a strong interest in this book and contributed many valuable insights. I regret that he did not live to see the finished work. My mother-in-law, Regina Ovesey, kindly provided writing space in her apartment after I left Newbridge and has been a good friend in countless ways. I wish to thank my sons, Paul and Craig, for tolerating my regular weekend absences and for letting me make it up to them in other ways. Finally, for love, patience, and help too deep and varied to describe, I wholeheartedly thank my wife, Candy.

— WILLIAM FRUCHT

We both thank our agent, Mike Cohn, and our original editor and now publisher, Natalie Chapman of Macmillan Books, for remaining faithful to this book when others might well have given up. Kelly Franklin referred Larry to Faye Zucker, who had the happy insight to put us together as a writing team. John Michel, Senior Editor at Macmillan, inherited the project and ably shepherded it through to publication. Thanks to him and to the entire Macmillan staff for their competence and professionalism in putting our work between hard covers.

gy of the personality disorders, a new area that until recently has received little attention. In many cases, the distinction between the personality disorders and the major mental disorders is a matter of degree—for instance, there may be no clear line separating the prickly fellow described above from the chronic schizophrenic, even though their ability to function in the world may differ drastically. Looking at these diseases as part of a spectrum implies that that spectrum, along with its biological basis, may extend further into the "normal range" than we had ever suspected.

Does this mean that, in the old "nature vs. nurture" controversy, the nature side has won out? Not at all: it means the controversy itself is obsolete. Psychological makeup is neither formless clay to be molded by circumstances nor a fixed profile predetermined by the genes. [Rather, each person's distinctive ways of experiencing and acting in the world represent the unfolding of specific predispositions in relation to important life events. It is the *interaction* between genetic tendencies and life experience that most strongly defines the new era.]

This interaction also defines how we must begin to think about the issue of personal responsibility. Life's problems cannot be reduced to chemical imbalances, and an increased knowledge of the biology of the brain in no way relieves us of accountability for our actions. Some people recoil from the new knowledge because it seems to reduce us to mere biological machines without autonomy. How can we be responsible for our actions when they are preordained by "bad genes" and "bad chemicals"?

The first answer is that, for someone who is determined to avoid any accountability for his difficulties, "bad genes" is not a markedly better excuse than "bad mothering." Either slogan gets one off the hook about equally well, given a sufficiently credulous audience. More seriously, it is not in the nature of genes to be so rigidly deterministic. Genetic diseases with an unalterable pattern of relentless progression do exist—Huntington's disease, which killed folksinger Woody Guthrie, is one—but much more commonly, genes determine tendencies and leave a great deal of room for environmental forces.

In these cases, far from rendering us helpless, knowledge gives us a measure of control. A diabetic who knows that too much sugar will put him into a coma can avoid sugar. Similarly, someone who knows that certain types of stress can trigger an episode of depression gains, with that knowledge, a better chance of avoiding depression by trying to avoid the stress. With that control comes the obligation to help contain one's own illness. Far from reducing responsibility, the biological view actually increases it by giving us more tools to manage our problems—and the choice of whether or not to use them.

I have been intimately involved, as both observer and participant, in the striking shift that has taken place in psychiatry in the past two decades. With great satisfaction I have watched the enormous growth in our understanding of individual differences in the biology of the central nervous system and how these differences influence the development of personality and susceptibility to emotional disturbance. At the program in Mood and Personality Disorders at Mount Sinai Medical School, my colleagues and I have helped people who have longstanding difficulty in adapting to their world participate in exploring their own biology in an effort to better understand the origins of their problems. We are committed to translating our knowledge of neurobiology into an understanding of the human suffering associated with these disorders so that we may offer better, more certain relief. The stories of patients in our program are fictionalized composites, but they are based on real clinical experience.

The new psychiatry is still in its infancy, and this book reflects that fact. We have many more questions than answers, and some of the most basic questions are the most difficult. We still do not know "what causes" mental disorders, and our grasp of the relationship between specific neurochemical disturbances and specific emotional states is in the best cases only tentative. There are many thousands of brain chemicals, and we have intensively studied only a handful. We cannot fully describe the chemistry of any disease or emotional state—the brain is too complex and our knowledge of it too primitive. Of necessity, then, this book is not a grand overview of settled terrain. It is more like a report from the front. Some of the material offered here represents established findings; other results are preliminary or tentative; other statements represent my own clinical observations or speculations. I have made every effort to be scrupulous in telling readers which is which. The opinions and emphases are mine, and others who are equal-

PREFACE

For the mind of man is far from the nature of a clear and equal
glass wherein the beams of things should reflect according to their
true incidence; nay, it is rather like an enchanted glass. . . .

— FRANCIS BACON

CONSIDER A USUALLY PEACEABLE MAN of sixty-four, happily married for thirty-five years, who starts to hear voices telling him to hurt his wife and, as a result, starts abusing her verbally and physically. After he begins to talk strangely and then has a seizure, his sons take him to a neurologist and he is found to have a brain tumor. A neurosurgeon removes the tumor and the man slowly resumes his customary life. Most people would have no trouble appreciating that his tumor caused his aberrant behavior by disturbing some biological function in his brain.

Now suppose his neighbor has had a lifelong pattern of isolation, mistrust, and occasional belligerence and is described around town as "prickly" or worse. It would not occur to most people that biology plays any role in his personality disturbance, and many would reject the idea that he has a disturbance at all. This resistance to a biological explanation stems in part from the permanence of personality; we tend to search for causes only when something about a person has unexpectedly changed. But it also shows how unaccustomed we are to understanding behavior in terms of altered brain function.

That is the subject of this book: how psychiatrists are beginning to understand behavior—and the mental states that give rise to it—in terms of altered brain function. Such an understanding challenges our notions of free will and individual responsibility. For many people, even to raise these issues in a biological context implies an argument that we are somehow enslaved by our biology. I am not going to make that argument.

Many sciences exist to study the brain and its workings. Psychology studies behavior, cognition, and personality in humans and animals; neurobiology examines the way individual nerve cells function and organize themselves into structures and systems; psychiatry and neurology focus on studying and treating the altered behaviors common to mental and neurologic disorders. While neurologists deal with the results of strokes, tumors, trauma, and other clear physical insults to brain tissue, psychiatrists focus on distortions in feelings and behavior that usually grow out of more subtle causes. More and more, however, we are coming to understand that many of these causes are also physical.

At their extreme, these subtle changes in mental activity can progressively disable a person's capacity to function, as when schizophrenia takes hold in early adulthood and slowly destroys the personality by middle age. Sometimes a mental disease can even be fatal, as when depression leads to suicide. But psychiatrists are not interested only in extremes. The same physical (chemical) mechanisms that cause disease when they go out of control also show quite normal variability that may explain a great deal about the range of human personalities. Some people, for example, are timid and introspective, while others are more outgoing and action oriented. In exaggerated form these variations give us fearful, avoidant personalities on the one hand and impulsive, aggressive personalities on the other. This range of temperaments has long been recognized; what is new is our emerging understanding of the underlying brain mechanisms. We are beginning to know, in a specific and detailed way, that personality styles as well as mental disorders have physical and chemical origins. All are rooted in the biology of the brain. In this sense, even our "selves" are grounded in the brain's biology.

Within the psychiatric community, this is both an old and a new idea. In the 1940s and '50s, psychiatrists in training were taught that their patients' emotional problems were largely grounded in early relationships with the mother or in the family environment. Biological causes were rarely considered—and, when acknowledged, poorly understood. Even as late as the 1970s, when I took my psychiatric residency at McLean Hospital in Boston, psychodynamic mechanisms that often implied early developmental causes were greatly emphasized as explanations for personality disorders. Some of the reluctance to discuss biological causes came from awareness of our own ignorance. Even the most environmentally oriented psychiatrists acknowledged that some illnesses must have biological foundations (Freud himself noted the importance of "constitutional" factors in personality), but until recently no one knew where to begin to identify them.

While my training also reflected the newer psychobiology, it was rooted in psychodynamic and behavioral principles. The psychodynamic approach emphasized the interaction within a person's mind of psychological forces that stem from early, important experiences. These dynamic workings often take place without the person's awareness, as when, for example, a woman is attracted to unavailable men because subconsciously they remind her of her aloof father. Behavioral theories emphasize changing people's behavior, using the principles of psychological conditioning, in order to change their mental states. Both of these approaches have a great deal of validity. They help us understand what is going on with our patients and help them deal with their problems. But they are far from comprehensive: they leave huge gaps in our knowledge that can only be filled by looking at the biology of mental diseases.

The notion of a link between the body and the emotions is antique. Hippocrates wrote more than two thousand years ago that four secretions, variously mixed, determined our dispositions, a theory that still lives in our everyday language. The meanings of the words *sanguine, phlegmatic, choleric,* and *melancholy* reflect the supposed effects of the four humors—blood, phlegm, yellow bile ("cholë") and black bile ("melan-cholë")—on temperament. But this and other early attempts at constructing some systematic biological theory of personality were all based on misunderstandings of the nature of the nervous system. People tried in the nineteenth century to relate temperament to such irrelevant characteristics as the pattern of bumps on a person's skull or their body type. In terms of scientific value—how well they explained observations or predicted new findings—these theories were no better than attributing eccentric behaviors and emotional pain to evil spirits or witchcraft. The rationalism of the twentieth century rejected both the magical notions of earlier times and the systematized pseudoscience of the nineteenth century—and with them the idea of studying the link between biology and human behavior. Environmental influences seemed both more comprehensible and more interesting. Behaviorism, which dominated psychology for much of this century, and psychoanalysis, which dominated psychiatry, both emphasized the role of environmental events in shaping behavior. In fact, the behaviorists considered it illegitimate to discuss internal states at all: only the outward expressions of those states—i.e., behavior—were observable and therefore subject to study.

A focus on the environment also seemed the more optimistic outlook. Before we reached our present (still quite limited) understanding of how genes work, and before there were effective drugs to treat mental illness, biology was seen as final and immutable. There was no appealing the verdict of the genes. The environment, at least, could be changed—and so, therefore, could human behavior. But we are no longer so helpless in the face of biology: we can change the brain's internal chemistry with relative ease, and even our genes are turning out to be less tyrannical than we once thought.

The pendulum is now swinging the other way. Genetic and biological studies of both mental illness and normal personality have shown a crucial role for genetic and biological factors—much greater than had been thought. The spectacular growth of the science of neurobiology has revolutionized our ideas of how the brain works. And the success of drugs to treat mental illness has both confirmed that biology does affect emotional states and spurred us on to try to discover how it does. We are at the edge of a new era in our understanding of human feelings and behavior.

This book comes out of that new era. In it I will describe what the new focus on biology tells us about the major psychiatric diseases: depression, anxiety, obsessive-compulsive disorders, and schizophrenia. We have learned a great deal not only about how these diseases arise and why, but also how susceptible individuals can be identified. We know something about why certain treatments work on some patients but not on others, and how various symptoms are generated. Knowing the biology of these disorders gives us some insight into the experience of people suffering from them. I will particularly emphasize the biolo-

ly expert might approach this material very differently. Many alternative theories exist regarding the biological bases of major mental syndromes, and hundreds of biological measures have been investigated in patients with various disorders. I have been able to discuss only a few. In this way I hope to convey a sense of the excitement and promise that these advances have inspired.

While little consensus exists about specific diseases and mechanisms, there is general agreement about the direction psychiatry is taking. In that broad sense, this book represents the future. This is how we will think about mental diseases and personality in the years to come.

CHAPTER ONE

THE SOUL'S DEATHLY SLEEP

Never let it be doubted that depression, in its extreme form, is madness.

— WILLIAM STYRON

ESPITE MY YEARS OF EXPERIENCE with depression, I found it hard to believe that the man walking into my office was a successful trial lawyer. I couldn't imagine him persuading a jury, arguing a difficult point with a judge, or reassuring a worried client: he looked worn out, hangdog, with heavy bags under eyes that avoided mine. His hair badly needed brushing, and his suit, though clearly expensive, looked as though it had been tailored for someone else—an energetic alter ego who didn't slouch or lean on his elbows quite so much. He introduced himself as Jack; he was thirty-two years old and, as he'd mentioned to me on the phone when we made our appointment, an associate at a large Manhattan law firm. Jack had recently been up for promotion to partner but had been passed over.

"Is that when the trouble began—when you didn't make partner?" I asked.

"No, that just brought things to a head," he replied. "I've known something was wrong for a while, but I couldn't put my finger on it." He'd first begun to worry a few months earlier, when in the middle of a closing summation he was struck by the thought that his arguments were weak. "It was completely irrational, but overwhelming. I've always been a perfectionist—I can't go into a courtroom without being convinced that I've exhausted every possibility and come up with the best possible case for my client. That's why I'm successful. But this time I could look into the jury's eyes and feel their disbelief. It was a case we should have won, too, but here I am giving this presentation, and instead of thinking about what I'm supposed to say next, I'm thinking, 'They're not buying it, it's a sham, I'm a sham, and everybody's finally caught on.'" A failure of confidence at such a crucial moment was devastating. He'd struggled through to the end—"because I had to"—without recovering his usual poise and conviction and lost the case. In thinking it over later, it seemed to him that the entire case had given him more trouble than it should have: his concentration was off and he felt an unaccustomed lack of imagination and legal insight.

His next big case was even worse. He'd been bedridden with the flu for a couple of weeks just before it went to trial, and even though he'd continued to work on it at home, the partner in charge of the case had assigned it to another associate, Barbara, who ended up getting the promotion Jack was hoping for. "What really burns me are the snide remarks she made about all the preparation I did. She was just trying to belittle my efforts in front of the partners—and it worked, too. Couldn't they see I'm better qualified than she is?" I wondered if his emotional condition might have played a role in his not getting the promotion. He had, he acknowledged, sensed a change in people's attitudes toward him—though for a long time his wife assured him he was imagining things. Since his illness he'd been assigned plenty of work, in fact more than he could handle, but no more court appearances. He felt his bosses had lost confidence in him for anything but routine drudgery. At the same time, he was haunted by the thought that they were right to do so. "I should probably look for another job but I can't get motivated to go through the process," he said. "I don't know if I'd hire me right now either."

Ever since his bout with the flu, in fact, he had felt persistently sluggish, with little of his former energy. He had practically given up tending his garden, which he used to enjoy a great deal, and had begun watching TV instead, though with little interest. It was hard to get out of bed in the morning. Yet he slept only fitfully, often waking up at three or four in the morning and lying awake for hours worrying about his job and other problems. Although breakfast used to be his favorite meal, he'd lately begun skipping it because it was all he could do to get himself up and dressed in time to leave for work. He had little interest in food now anyway. "The other night, my wife, Emily, made a special roast, and I couldn't finish one helping. I couldn't even pretend to be enjoying it, even though I knew she was hurt."

"How are things between you and your family?" I said.

"That's the other thing," Jack replied. "Lately Donald (my two-year-old) is constantly getting himself into trouble—climbing on furniture, throwing his toys, breaking stuff. He has to be watched every second. I feel like he's getting all the attention and I'm left on my own. I feel distant from both him and Emily." His older child, Melissa, was much easier, but Donald had been an irritable baby whose frequent ear infections had kept his parents awake many nights. Now he was tearing around the house. It seemed to Jack that whatever time Emily could spare from Donald went to Melissa, leaving none for him.

I asked what feelings or recollections Donald stirred up in him. "Sometimes when I look at Donald, I almost see my younger brother, Craig," he answered. As a boy, Craig had had severe allergies and seemed to consume all of their mother's time. The memory of those years evoked strong feelings of envy and rage. "It's funny you should ask me that," Jack said. "I think about the past a lot these days." He had lately begun reviewing past events over and over, wondering where he had gone wrong and how he could have made them turn out differently.

He often thought about an old girlfriend, Susan, whom he had met shortly after his father died. They began dating the night he scored the winning goal in a big hockey game, during his junior year in college. "It was a really important game to me because after my dad passed away, I kind of immersed myself in hockey. I just didn't want to do anything else. I especially got more and more tongue-tied with girls. Then I'm the school hero and all these people who never knew I existed are suddenly paying attention to me." Susan was beautiful and sophisticated, from a wealthy, old-money family (Jack's parents were immigrants), and when he was with her, Jack felt as if he were living out a Jay Gatsby fantasy. But the romance had gone sour, and lately he had been torturing himself, wondering why. Had he been too diffident? Had he committed some grave social error in front of her rich relatives without even knowing it? Had his controlling, overprotective mother made him too guilt-ridden to hold on to a woman he really desired? He

3

felt comfortable with Emily, but she had never excited him the way Susan did. "I still feel ashamed and humiliated whenever I think about her," he admitted, "almost as if it had happened yesterday."

As Jack related these thoughts, he became aware of being terribly fatigued. The dull, insistent weariness he constantly felt intruded itself again. But it was not just fatigue: his restlessness and constant ruminating on the past made it impossible to stay focused on anything— even something as undemanding as reruns of his favorite TV show.

I asked him what he had done about his condition.

His family doctor had reassured him that there was nothing wrong with him that a long vacation wouldn't cure and had prescribed Valium, which calmed him down a bit but made him feel even more sluggish. So Jack tried telling himself he was basically fine—he had a high-paying job and a good family, after all—and that if he just tried a little harder to get back on track, everything would work itself out. Only it didn't, and Emily was growing increasingly impatient with his unkempt appearance, his pacing in the study each evening, and his poor companionship.

Then a friend gave him the name of a psychiatrist specializing in psychoanalysis. In psychoanalysis, the patient comes to a fifty-minute treatment session four to five times a week, lies on a couch, and talks about whatever comes to mind. The thoughts, feelings, and dreams that emerge in the analysis bring to light emotional conflicts, rooted in childhood, that are outside the patient's conscious awareness. The patient and analyst then proceed to explore these conflicts for the insight they yield about the patient's current problems. Jack's friend had found this psychiatrist's treatment very helpful in alleviating his long-standing shyness and difficulty in relationships.

Jack put off calling the analyst for several weeks, even losing the telephone number at one point, until Emily threatened to leave him if he didn't make an appointment. He recalled approaching the doctor's Park Avenue office with increasingly leaden steps and needing a minute or so to force himself to ring the bell. But the waiting room, with its antique chairs and Oriental rugs, seemed restful enough, and the doctor was a kind, elderly man who encouraged Jack to do most of the talking. He appeared to take a great deal of interest in Jack's recollections of his brother and sister and commented on the tremendous anger he must be feeling toward his son—anger Jack had not been aware of. As the session ended, they made another appointment, but Jack didn't keep it. He couldn't see how this approach would help with his problems at work, and while the psychiatrist had not discussed starting analysis, Jack felt overwhelmed at the prospect of lying on a couch three times a week to pore over his childhood.

Emily, who was growing concerned, had a friend who was helped by an approach called cognitive therapy, and she persuaded Jack to try it. Cognitive therapy works by changing negative self-image and expectations to more positive ones. When Jack visited this therapist, he realized how little he valued himself and how he always expected the worst from every situation. But he wondered how any amount of mere talking could change these basic attitudes.

Then, before his next session with the cognitive therapist, he read a magazine article about a new medication that dramatically relieved symptoms of depression and realized that the symptoms described in the article closely matched what he had been going through. One of the psychiatrists the magazine had interviewed was in New York, so Jack made an appointment. Indeed, he was told, he was suffering from a "biologic" depression that would respond to antidepressant medication, and he was given a prescription for the drug that was featured in the magazine story. But two days after he began taking it, his mouth was dry and he felt mildly queasy all the time, so he threw the rest of the pills away. "I felt like too much of a failure to even call the doctor and tell him what had happened," he admitted.

While pursuing none of the recommended treatments, he continued to brood over his situation, often painfully, and to try to make sense of what was happening. Was it caused by unresolved angry feelings toward his mother and younger brother? Was he burdened with negative thinking patterns that, like bad habits, could somehow be "unlearned"? Was there a chemical imbalance in his brain that might be reversed by the right medication?

He read about our program in a newspaper article. "I said to myself, it just keeps getting worse and worse; I can't go on like this—and suddenly those words had a whole new meaning that really made my hair stand on end." It was, finally, the fear of dying that roused him to try yet another doctor, and to come and see me.

⟡

The beginnings of a depression are often difficult to pinpoint. It can sometimes be brought on by physical stress: starting a new medication, especially steroids or those that treat high blood pressure; childbirth; major surgery; or an acute illness. Depression is often preceded by a change in life circumstances—the loss of a parent, for instance—or a failure or disappointment, such as being passed over for an expected promotion. Sometimes the triggers are less obvious but may have to do with an imagined loss of love or security. For Jack, the birth of his son brought back the jealousy he had felt when his brother's illness dominated their mother's attention, and as Donald required more and more of Emily's care, Jack became increasingly morose. His depression served to restore the attention and concern from his wife that he had been missing. But it would be a mistake either to blame the person who suffers from depression or, at the other extreme, to deny the effects of his behavior on those around him. To take only the most obvious example, Jack's children surely were confused and hurt by his withdrawal—which may partly explain why Donald became so hard to control. Depression has both biological roots and an interpersonal context.

For those of us who have never experienced it, the feeling of a deep clinical depression is difficult to imagine. All of us have periods when we feel "down"—an ambition is frustrated or we have a bad argument with a close friend, and some of the joy goes out of the world. Our pleasure in certain activities is diminished for a time, and we have less energy, optimism, and confidence. Most people recover from such setbacks fairly easily or are able to weather hard times by concentrating on positive experiences or past successes. For people who are susceptible to depression, however, the ordinary stresses of life may serve as the focal point for a far stronger reaction, a truly disabling mood so different in degree as to be almost different in kind. If feeling down is a summer's drought, depression is the Sahara.

Feelings are seldom free-floating or abstract: they often have a trigger and always find something to attach themselves to. Every depression is "about" something in that it refers to the circumstances of one person's life; thus every case of depression is unique. Still, 2,500 years of clinical observation have sufficed to give us a clear picture of the things that all depressed patients have in common. In their comprehensive reference book, *Manic-Depressive Illness*, Frederick Goodwin and Kay Jamison have collected some accounts by patients of what this disease feels like. One wrote:

> *Depression is awful beyond words or sounds or images.... It bleeds relationships through suspicion, lack of confidence and self-respect, the inability to enjoy life, to walk or talk or think normally, the exhaustion, the night terrors, the day terrors. There is nothing good to be said for it except that it gives you the experience of how it must be to be old, to be old and sick, to be dying; to be slow of mind, to be lacking in grace, polish, and coordination; to be ugly; to have no belief in the possibilities of life, the pleasures of sex, the exquisiteness of music, or the ability to make yourself and others laugh.*
>
> *I get enraged when others imply they know what it is like to be depressed because they have gone through a divorce, lost a job, or broken up with someone. Those experiences carry with them feelings. Depression, instead, is truly flat, stale, and unprofitable.*

The inability to feel normal emotions inspires the central metaphor of perhaps the best-known modern depiction of the disease, Sylvia Plath's *The Bell Jar.* The nineteen-year-old narrator, Esther Greenwood, feels closed inside a glass barrier, breathing stale air, in the world but unable to touch it. This feeling of being cut off from the living world is probably at the heart of both the terror and the apathy of depression—apathy because the depressed person is unable to care, terror because this inability is both alien and seemingly irrevocable. The bell jar acts as a barrier in both directions: with lack of feeling comes an overwhelming sense of incapacity. Goodwin and Jamison quote another patient as saying that during a depression,

> *it seems as though my friends require much more from me than I can ever possibly give, I seem a drain and a burden on them; the guilt and resentment are overwhelming. Everything I see, say or do seems extraordinarily flat and pointless; there is no color, there is no point to anything. Things drag on and on, interminably. I am exhausted, dead inside. I want to sleep, to escape somehow, but there is always the thought that if I really could sleep, I must always and again awake to the dullness and apathy of it all.*

This sense of incapacity even extends to the person's own thought processes. Yet another account from Goodwin and Jamison:

> *I doubt, completely, my ability to do anything well; it seems as though my mind has slowed down and burned out to the point of being virtually useless. The wretched convoluted thing works only well enough to torment me with a dreary litany of my inadequacies and shortcomings in character, and to haunt me with the total, desperate hopelessness of it all. What is the point of going on like this; it is crazy. . . . If I can't feel, move, think, or care then what on earth is the point?*

One of my own patients put it this way: "My feelings were overwhelmed so that I couldn't work. I felt tired, overwhelmed. I felt an increasing despair, a feeling of blackness—everything began turning black."

Long-term studies of patients with depression show that about one in five die by suicide. To those of us who treat depression, these deaths are especially tragic because the disease is treatable. I think many people have the misconception that suicide in depression is entirely a sort of artifact of a distorted world view: people with depression do away with themselves because they feel they are sinful and worthless. It is that, but there is more as well. Depression is a very painful disease, and many sufferers think of suicide "rationally," if you will—with the same reasoning that might apply to a terminal cancer patient. Another of my patients wrote,

> *People commit suicide when they're feeling depressed . . .*
> *because they can't tolerate the emotional pain. . . . It is so*
> *severe it is just as if it were an excruciating physical pain.*
> *It is an excruciating emotional pain. You can't deal with*
> *it any more and you just want to end it.*

What makes this affliction still more dangerous is that people may carry such moods around with them and yet maintain an outwardly normal life. It is almost as if, in making its sufferers assign a pervasive unimportance to everything they feel and experience and at the same time often feel deeply ashamed, the disease were employing deliberate camouflage. Goodwin and Jamison quote the Austrian composer Hugo Wolf, a manic-depressive, who wrote in 1891,

> *I have led, truly, the existence of a frog and not even that*
> *of a living one, but that of a galvanized frog. To be sure,*
> *I appear at times merry and in good heart, talk, too,*
> *before others quite reasonably, and it looks as if I felt, too,*
> *God knows how well beneath my skin; yet the soul main-*
> *tains its deathly sleep.*

When Jack told me that suicide had recently for him become a thinkable option in a way it was not before, I knew he wasn't being melodramatic. I had already made up my mind that he was seriously ill.

The program I run at the Bronx VA Medical Center and Mount Sinai Medical School begins with a medical, diagnostic, and family history evaluation, followed by psychologic and biologic testing and finally a feedback session and recommendations for treatment. Jack was an Army veteran and could be admitted to our inpatient unit. When I outlined this sequence and told him I thought he should stay in the hospital for two to three weeks, he first said he didn't know if he had the energy to complete the program. I reassured him he could quit at any time, but I repeated that he did need to come into the hospital for treatment. While recognizing that it would delay relief of his symptoms, he decided to come in for a diagnostic interview and physical evaluation before he entered the inpatient evaluation and treatment program.

§

Depression comes with a well-known cluster of physical symptoms. Jack had already mentioned several of them in our initial visit; one of the tasks of the diagnostic interview is to explore them systematically. Jean, the graduate student who conducted the interview, began by asking Jack about the things he once enjoyed but no longer did, beginning with his morning coffee and his gardening hobby. When she asked him about his sexual activity, he replied that he had really lost interest since his bout with the flu, and in fact he and Emily had not made love in several months—a departure from their previously satisfying sex life. A loss of interest in pleasurable activities is often accompanied by difficulty in concentrating. Depressed people may find themselves distracted by preoccupations; it becomes laborious to read or attend to paperwork, and they lack the energy to complete daily tasks.

Jack had other classic symptoms. His appetite diminished and he began to suffer from constipation. He estimated he had lost about ten pounds in the few months before his admission to the hospital. Loss of appetite is often seen in depression, as is, less frequently, overeating. His sleep disturbances were also typical. Depressed people often have difficulty in both falling and staying asleep. In serious depressions, they may wake up at three or four in the morning, as Jack was doing, and be unable to fall back to sleep. Others sleep too much, up to sixteen hours a day. Jack also felt a persistent heaviness in his arms and legs and moved more slowly than he did when healthy, a condition called "psychomotor retardation" that sometimes precedes by several months any noticeable mood change. One of my patients recalled that the first sign of depression for him was an inability to walk more than a mile on the beach during his summer vacation; his mood change didn't become severe until the following winter. These bodily or "vegetative" symptoms usually indicate that the depression is serious enough to be treated clinically and that it is likely to respond to antidepressant medication.

Alterations in the way a depressed person moves and speaks may parallel his or her thought processes. In an "agitated" depression, these people are in a constant state of motion, pacing back and forth, sitting down and standing up, picking at their clothing, wringing their hands. They often ruminate continuously, thinking the same thoughts and asking the same questions over and over, suffering endless guilt over actions and incidents they have blown out of all reasonable proportion. In a "retarded" depression, the patient is slowed down, moving slowly and laboriously, as if floating in molasses, with a pain that is almost palpable to an observer. These people speak slowly and monotonously, their pitch falling off at the end of each sentence. Before effective antidepressant drugs were developed, patients sometimes suffered extreme psychomotor retardation in which they could not or would not move at all and had to be fed, clothed, and washed like infants. Now that the drugs are available, people almost always receive treatment before they reach this stage.

It is possible to move back and forth from an agitated to a retarded state. Jack's comments about the heaviness of his limbs, and his general lassitude on his first visit to my office, suggested the latter form. But he had also mentioned spending many evenings pacing in his study, and Jean described his state as agitated—an agitation that increased when she asked him what sorts of things he ruminated on or felt guilty about. He replied that he was constantly chastising himself for things he had done even as early as junior high school. He recalled shouting angrily at his sick father a few months before the man died and seeing him visibly hurt. Despite Jean's wish to move on to other subjects, he returned to this incident several times during the interview, seeking her reassurance that he had not done such a terrible thing, but clearly unable to take any comfort when she gave it.

It is possible for depressed people to lose touch with reality: their feelings of worthlessness and guilt may reach such delusional proportions that they think they are responsible for natural catastrophes or wars. Like schizophrenics, they may have auditory or visual hallucinations. They may hear accusatory voices or grow convinced they are physically deformed or suffering from cancer. But these symptoms are rare: most patients, like Jack, are surprised when we ask them if they've experienced such things.

Much more common than outright psychosis, and crucial to the differential diagnosis of a patient's depression, is mania. When Jean probed this subject with Jack, his response was curious but not unusual among depressed patients. She asked whether he could recall several days in a row when he felt elated or irritable, clearly "up" from his normal mood. In fact he counted on such episodes to get work done. Every so often he would go into overdrive—sleeping only a few hours a night, formulating arguments fluidly, speaking rapidly and impatiently to colleagues, charming clients with wit, assurance, and a sure grasp of their legal situation. Jack's symptoms were not severe enough to meet the full criteria for mania, but they did meet the criteria for hypomania, a disorder marked by milder symptoms of the same kind. He hoped for this state of mind whenever he was working on a big case. In effect, he had incorporated his illness into his professional style.

(Jack would also become hypomanic when we began his antidepressant treatment later in his hospital stay. He spoke almost breathlessly, intruded on the business of other patients with unsolicited legal advice, and slept little. This is a common reaction to antidepressants in people with a predisposition to mania. Lithium treats mania very effectively, and when we added it to Jack's medication, he calmed down.)

While depression is the most common mood disorder, affecting about 10 percent of the population, mania affects a much smaller number, perhaps 1 percent. You can get a glimmer of what a manic episode feels like if you recall the elation of falling in love or achieving a significant triumph. In some people, this feeling may become exaggerated into a sense of power and capacity that is frankly unrealistic. A manic episode often brings these people extraordinary bursts of energy, wild optimism, and a sense of heightened urgency about their role in the world. Some become intensely irritable as well. A normally reticent man may grow expansive or vituperative with neighbors; a frugal man may go on a buying spree that drains his life savings; a prudent businesswoman may invest large sums in risky enterprises or fire her entire staff. It is as if the brain systems that motivate us and allow us to assert ourselves in the world have mushroomed out of control, leaving manic people with little appreciation of their own limits or the possible consequences of their actions.

A person in the throes of a manic phase experiences a torrent of ideas, which find expression in rapid, voluble, pressured speech. In its milder forms, this flight of ideas can be highly engaging: a euphoric person possessing boundless energy, libidinous and funny, free-associating rapidly, making unexpected connections unconstrained by logic but often based on puns or double entendres, can be the life of the party. Manic people are easily distracted, constantly starting up projects and dropping them for other, newer ones. They may feel an intensified sense of arousal and purpose so different from their normal experience that they believe they possess extraordinary powers, carry a special message for humanity, or are destined to play an exalted role in the universe. They place themselves centrally in the scheme of the world and experience life on a grander scale.

Robert Lowell was subject to manic episodes that would gradually build up for weeks or months. In his recent biography, *Lost Puritan*, Paul Mariani describes the poet's tour through Latin America in 1962. After several stops in the Caribbean and Brazil, the original large group had been pared down to Lowell and Keith Botsford, a host from the Cultural Congress, which sponsored the tour.

> *On the 4th [of September] he flew to Buenos Aires with Botsford in attendance as his "lieutenant," treating him as a flunky, making him pay for everything, and calling him a homosexual. He was drinking constantly now and even managed to get Botsford drunk. He insulted the U.S. Ambassador to Argentina by bringing along a group of Communists to a party in his honor, and then—more dangerously—tweaked the general who was about to become Argentina's president. He accused the cultural attache of being an illiterate. He waxed eloquently on the*

subject of Hitler. He decided he would not teach that fall at Harvard, but stay on in Buenos Aires for another month. . . . He read the entire volume of Life Studies *to an audience, without a single comment. On a boulevard in the capital, he undressed and climbed up onto an equestrian statue. He threw away his antimanic pills. He began asking for his old girlfriend, Sandra Hochman, again.*

Botsford, "exhausted," flew back to Rio for a few days and then, at the urging of Lowell's wife, returned.

Cal [i.e. Lowell] meanwhile was partying (and arm-wrestling) with the exiled left-wing Spanish poet Rafael Alberti somewhere in Buenos Aires. When Botsford tried to contact Cal, Alberti's friends hid him from what they saw as a CIA attempt to kidnap their friend. Finally, when Cal returned to his hotel with an Argentine woman named Luisa, an ambulance was called. In his full-blown manic state, it took six paramedics to wrestle him into a straitjacket. Then he was taken to the Clinica Bethlehem, where his arms and legs were strapped and he was injected with 2,000 milligrams of Thorazine four times a day until his blood once more turned to lead. As he lay there, struggling helplessly, confused and afraid, he begged Botsford to help calm him by whistling.

The aftermath of such attacks was devastating and humiliating. After another episode some fifteen years later, Lowell wrote to a friend, "I got well shortly after your visit, and wish to God it had been sooner so that you would have been spared my antics."

Not surprisingly, people in the grip of mania may become paranoid. Their sense of having special powers may carry with it a feeling that they are being persecuted for their gifts or being thwarted from saving the world. Sometimes these delusions involve elaborate networks of people and events, woven together into a complex drama with the manic individual at the center. These linkages add an element of myth to the manic's personal narrative, an element often enhanced by their attraction to religious or mystical pursuits.

The distinction between mania and hypomania rests on how they affect a person's social and occupational functioning. The combination of energy, conviction, and self-assurance in hypomanics can make such people highly effective. Jack felt, probably with good reason, that his hypomanic episodes helped him win cases. But the intensity and pressure of mania often lead to disorganization. When hypomania fades into full-blown mania, the bonds of logic slip further, thoughts and speech come faster still, links between successive ideas grow more tenuous and finally disappear altogether, and charm gradually fades into incoherence, first to others and then, frighteningly, to oneself.

As the two poles of bipolar affective disorder, mania and depression constitute one of the major categories in the American Psychiatric Association's classification system. Bipolar I disorder is diagnosed when the patient meets the full criteria for both manic and depressive episodes. Bipolar II disorder describes people like Jack, with at least one major depressive episode alternating with hypomanic, but not manic, states. People who develop manic or hypomanic episodes only on antidepressant medication have bipolar III disorder. The four-fifths of depressive patients who have no manic symptoms at all, but who may have recurrent and frequently severe episodes of depression, are classified as having unipolar major depressive disorder.

While these four represent the classic mood disorders, psychiatrists have identified several other syndromes that undoubtedly share the same physiological basis. Cyclothymia may be thought of as an attenuated form of bipolar illness, with mood changes that are briefer and less severe. Though they don't meet the criteria for a major affective disorder, these episodes, which often begin in childhood and recur throughout life, still profoundly color the personality. People with cyclothymia go through periods when they feel a lowered sense of self-worth, inattentiveness, social awkwardness, and difficulty in being productive at work. They need more sleep and tend to withdraw from many activities. At other times they are expansive, optimistic, unrealistically self-confident, and extroverted; they find that thoughts come lucidly and effortlessly, and they have a lot of well-focused energy and need less sleep. I briefly considered classifying Jack as cyclothymic but decided that his high periods were more discrete and severe, as well as less frequent, than is characteristic of cyclothymia.

Dysthymia corresponds to unipolar depression in the same way that cyclothymia does to bipolar illness. It is an attenuated form of depression, with dejected feelings that persist for long periods but never reach the intensity of a major depression. Many people with dysthymia also periodically suffer from major depressive episodes, a syndrome called double depression. Researchers are now finding that many dysthymic patients respond to the same antidepressants that are used to treat the major affective disorders.

We can cast our net wider still. One current area of debate concerns the relation of dysthymia to "depressive personality disorder." This diagnosis refers to people who are chronically gloomy and irritable. Do they suffer from a dysthymia so constant and of such early onset that it has completely colored their personalities—and can they be treated with antidepressants as well? Or are such wide-ranging personality disturbances partly or wholly distinct from the mood changes that characterize the classic depressive disorders? I served on the committee that prepared the personality disorders section of the latest version of the psychiatric diagnostic manual, *DSM-IV*. After much discussion we decided to put "depressive personality disorder" into the appendix, meaning it is not now considered an official diagnosis but needs further research.

It's not immediately obvious that this classification scheme, which covers diseases experienced at one time or another by perhaps a quarter of the entire population, is at all justified. Why do we think depression is a single disease or group of diseases—instead of, for instance, a common symptom that can arise from any number of underlying causes? Even the fact that many depressions respond to the same medications is not conclusive. Most fevers, after all, respond to aspirin, but we don't consider fever a disease. Why lump all depression together?

One answer is that depression runs in families.

๑

This has been known, somewhere on the border between medicine and folklore, for centuries. In the great seventeenth-century work *Anatomy of Melancholy,* Robert Burton cited a host of classical and contemporary writers in support of his assertion that "I need not . . . make any doubt of Melancholy, but that it is an hereditary disease." Lord Byron, Winston Churchill, Robert Schumann, Henry and William James, and many others knew they had inherited a temperament that included bouts of mania, despair, and, often, suicide. Emil Kraepelin wrote in *Manic Depressive Insanity and Paranoia* that "*Hereditary taint* I could demonstrate in about 80 per cent. of the cases observed in Heidelberg." But despite this long tradition of folk wisdom supported by scientific observation, until a generation ago psychiatry could not really address the most important genetic question of all: *why* does depression run in families?

Family members may eat the same food, breathe the same air, live in the same place (sometimes for many generations), speak the same language, and be exposed to the same germs. They share a common culture. Children and grandchildren often enter the same occupation as their forebears and follow their parents' examples in countless other ways as well. Any one of these factors may cause a pattern of inheritance. Black lung disease, for instance, may run in a family of coal miners and even seem at first glance to be a sex-linked disorder if it primarily strikes males—but it is clearly an environmental disease. The Hapsburg family of Austria famously passed down both political power and a protruding lower jaw, the "Hapsburg lip"; one inheritance was sociocultural and the other genetic. Which kind of inheritance is depression? Until recently it was fashionable for psychiatrists to posit elaborate sociocultural mechanisms to explain its inheritance pattern. Even though we can assign a number to the extent to which depression runs in families (one recent study showed that 25 percent of the relatives of patients with bipolar disorder had some affective disorder themselves, versus 20 percent of the relatives of unipolar patients and 7 percent of the relatives of healthy controls, though these percentages can vary with the diagnostic criteria the researchers use), it is very difficult to tease out the genes from amid all the other possible causes of inheritance. But thanks to the tendency of mothers sometimes to produce twins, it is not impossible.

Twins come in two varieties. Identical twins develop from a single fertilized egg and share all of their genes. Fraternal twins develop from two separate eggs, fertilized at the same time, and share no more of their genes than any other pair of siblings—on average, 50 percent. In scientific jargon, the synonyms for *identical* and *fraternal* are, respectively, *monozygotic* and *dizygotic*—that is, from one zygote (fertilized egg) or two. Identical twins are always the same sex; fraternal twins, like other siblings, are the same sex exactly half the time. Identical and fraternal twins both usually come from the same family surroundings, neighborhood, schools, and so on. Unlike siblings born separately, they share the same place in the birth order (the few minutes' age difference seldom affects how they are treated, except among royalty), and any important family events will happen to both twins at the same age. Geneticists thus consider that they share substantially the same environment. The difference between identical and fraternal twins reduces to just one: the number of genes the twins share. Identical twins share the same environment and the same genes; fraternal twins share the same environment but have different genes.

Thus if genes affect depression, their influence should show up as a difference in the frequency with which identical and fraternal twins of the same sex share affective disorders. This is precisely what psychiatric geneticists have found. In one large study in the 1960s, using the Danish Twin Register, researchers sent questionnaires to every set of twins born in Denmark between 1890 and 1920. They found fifty-five pairs of identical twins in which at least one twin had manic depressive illness; the other twin was also manic depressive in 67 percent of the pairs. For fraternal twins of the same sex, the concordance rate was only 20 percent. Later studies have supported these findings: on average, the concordance rate is 60 to 70 percent for identical twins and 14 percent for fraternal twins. The more severe the illness, the more likely it is to affect both twins rather than just one.

There are other ways to approach this question, and all support the position that at least some of the inheritance of depression is genetic. Families of depressed patients have been found to have a higher than normal incidence not only of depression but also of anxiety disorders, panic attacks, and eating disorders, all of which respond to antidepressant drugs. In people who have been adopted and who develop depression, there is a much greater chance that the *biological* family, rather than the adoptive family, also has a history of depression. In the 1960s a British psychiatrist, J. Price, combined these approaches, combing the psychiatric literature for scarce reports of affective disorder in identical twins who had been raised apart. Of the twelve such reports he found, eight showed that both twins were affected, a 67 percent concordance rate. Twelve pairs is a tiny sample, and it is probably only coincidence that the concordance rate for identical twins reared apart was exactly the same as that for identical twins raised together, but the results agree with other studies in suggesting that genes play an important role in the predisposition to depression.

Research on identical twins has shown how strong a role genetics can play in personality generally. A series of studies by Jack Bouchard and Auke Tellegen at the University of Minnesota suggested that identical twins reared apart are more alike than most of us could have imagined. Many of the twins they studied, who had not been together since infancy, not only showed similar personality traits but similar hobbies, hairstyles, and even tastes in clothing. (This fascinating research has implications for a number of psychiatric diseases, and I will treat it more extensively in Chapter 3.)

Ironically, much of this work rediscovered what Robert Burton knew, in a less systematic way, in 1621. Even the most interesting result—that while it is indeed genetic, depression appears only sometimes, and unpredictably—only confirms centuries of clinical observation. "And that which is more to be wondered at," Burton wrote, "it skips in some families the father, and goes to the son, or takes every other, and sometimes every third in a lineal descent, and doth not always produce the same, but some like, and a symbolizing disease." Put into modern prose, this thought would fit comfortably into any current medical text. But why should it be true at all? What exactly is being inherited? Clearly, what the genes carry is not a certainty of depression, in the same way that they carry, for instance, a certainty of brown eyes or red hair, but something more indeterminate: a predisposition. Whether the disease is expressed or remains latent is up to the environment. But "environment" in this sense can mean anything from a person's life experiences to his or her physical health to the way the expression of a gene for affective disorders is promoted or suppressed by the action of other genes. One of the purposes of understanding the genetic mechanisms of depression is to better identify the environmental factors that influence them.

The fact that much of depression's inheritance is truly genetic and not cultural or occupational means that it resides in the genes: something physical is passed on in the genetic material from one generation to the next. The genetic material, deoxyribonucleic acid, or DNA, consists of two molecules—each a long chain of similar segments—laid next to each other and twisted into the famous double helix discovered by Watson and Crick in 1953. If you can imagine a tremendously long, thin zipper in which the teeth meet end to end instead of overlapping, you can not only get the general structure but also understand why this structure is ideal for passing along information. Unzip the zipper, lay alongside each chain a new partner chain made up of individual teeth you have handy, and when you're done you have two chains where one existed before. When a cell divides into two cells, its entire complement of DNA replicates in this way.

When it was first shown, in 1944, that you could use purified DNA to transfer heritable traits from one group of bacteria to another, many geneticists refused to believe it. DNA was too simple, they thought, to carry such complex information. The importance of the double helix was not so much the structure itself but that the structure showed how the DNA molecule *could* carry information. This is possible because the individual links in the chain, called nucleotides, are not identical but come in four varieties: adenine (A), cytosine (C), guanine (G), and thymine (T). When chains are assembled, an A nucleotide will pair off only with a T, and vice versa, and a C only with a G. A year after Watson and Crick published their discovery, the physicist George Gamow declared that the four varieties of nucleotides must form a kind of alphabet—which could be strung together into something like words.

A chain with, for instance, the sequence GATGAT will pair up with the sequence CTACTA and no other; the CTACTA, in turn, can create a new partner chain with the sequence GATGAT. Thus the *information* GATGAT can be re-created, in theory, infinitely many times. With this insight, molecular biologists could begin to understand the relationship between molecules and genetic traits.

Each of the forty-six chromosomes of a human cell can be thought of as a single DNA molecule millions of nucleotides long. Together they contain the template for everything the cell is able to do. The replication that occurs en masse when a cell is dividing also goes on, on a more selective scale, during its entire life. Small segments of DNA are being unzipped, transcribed, and zipped back up thousands of times each second. The products of these transcriptions, a slightly different molecule called RNA, travel outside the cell nucleus into the surrounding cytoplasm, where they in turn serve as the template for the creation of proteins. Proteins are also chains—of amino acids—and each possible set of three nucleotides codes for one of twenty amino acids. The sequences GAG and GAA, for instance, code for glutamic acid; CCA codes for alanine. (There is some duplication because the sixty-four combinations of nucleotides need to account for only twenty amino acids.) Proteins range in length from a few to thousands of amino acid units.

If DNA and RNA are a cell's managers, proteins are its labor force. They maintain its structure, move materials into and out of the cell, move the cell itself, send and receive messages, make chemical reactions happen, go off-site to handle special jobs like digestion, care for the DNA and oversee its replication, and everything else. Whatever needs doing is done by proteins.

When we speak of depression as a genetic disease, unavoidably we are speaking on this level. Specific pieces of DNA code for proteins whose functioning is just abnormal enough to somehow have a subtle effect on the overall activity of the brain. But there are somewhere between 10,000 and 100,000 human genes, of which about a quarter are involved in some aspect of brain structure and function, and they interact in uncountable numbers of ways. That word "somehow" is a fine thread stretched across a canyon of ignorance.

§

DNA replication is not one hundred percent reliable: sequences are sometimes copied inaccurately, resulting in a mutation. These mistakes occur spontaneously but may be promoted by radiation or carcinogens—substances that increase the error rate of gene copying and thus increase the likelihood of cancer. Most of the variations thus created either are inconsequential or contribute to healthy individual differences such as hair or eye color. In fact these variations are the basis of evolution. Species change and give rise to new species through the continuous production and selection of different varieties of genes. It doesn't take much variation in the genes to create a noticeable difference: evolutionary biologists estimate that the difference between a human genome (the entire complement of genes) and that of a chimpanzee is about 1 percent. Between any two human genomes, the difference is far less than that. Sexual reproduction is a means of merging two different genomes to create a new one containing some genes from both. Successive generations receive different combinations of chromosomes and different arrangements of genes within each chromosome. Some evolutionary biologists think that the reason sex is so widespread among plants and animals is precisely that it permits genes to mix and diffuse rapidly through a population.

Some genes code for key proteins, and if they are seriously altered, the fetus carrying the mutation may not survive until birth. Other genetic abnormalities may result in serious illness but do not prevent those carrying them from growing up and reproducing. If an abnormality affects a neuronal system involved in the regulation of feelings and thoughts, it may be expressed as a severe and impairing disorder such as depression or schizophrenia, or as a variant in personality style. The outcome will depend on interactions with many other genes, as well as on circumstances ranging from the chemical environment in the womb to how the child relates to his or her parents. But although a single gene abnormality can have many outcomes, the reverse is not true: if members of the same family all share the same genetic disease, there will not be a wide variety of genetic causes. With rare genetic diseases, almost certainly the affected members of a single family will share the same defective gene or genes. With more common diseases, there may be a number of gene defects in the population at large that have the same end result—in this case, depression. But any one family is likely to carry only a very small number of them.

Thus we can use "linkage" studies to find a gene for bipolar disorder. Relatives of a patient with bipolar disorder who themselves have the disease should carry the same gene for bipolar illness as the patient—but their unaffected relatives may lack it. Until recently a major limitation to this strategy was the difficulty of identifying genetic differences among family members. But molecular genetics has given us a new and powerful approach to this problem.

There are enzymes, called restriction nucleases, that cut DNA in very specific ways. If you think of the structure of DNA as a necklace with four different-colored beads—say, red, green, blue, and orange, corresponding to the base pairings A-T, T-A, C-G, and G-C—then a restriction nuclease is equivalent to a knife that will cut the necklace only in very specific places: for instance, wherever a green bead follows three red ones, and nowhere else. The number and length of pieces the knife makes will depend on the distribution of this particular sequence on the necklace. If, in one of these sequences, a red bead is replaced by a blue one, the knife will no longer cut the necklace there. We will now have one longer piece where two shorter pieces would have been. Two necklaces that have identical sequences, except at that one point, could be distinguished by the length of pieces this knife produces.

If specific gene sequences differ between two family members, the fragments of DNA that remain after incubation with a restriction nuclease will differ in size. You can compare them by placing each sample at one end of a gel preparation and applying a small electric current; this makes the DNA migrate through the gel in the direction of the current. The smaller the fragments, the farther up the gel they will travel, so that fragments of different sizes will sort themselves out quite visibly. It's easy to compare the relative fragment lengths of any number of samples simply by placing them side by side; the differences are known as restriction fragment length polymorphisms, or RFLPS.

This method has been extremely powerful. It has already helped geneticists find markers—not necessarily the genes themselves, but nearby sequences that are closely associated with the genes—for

Huntington's Disease, some forms of epilepsy and cancer, and a growing list of other diseases. With some diseases, such as cystic fibrosis or
Huntington's Disease, the altered gene itself has been identified.
Molecular geneticists hope to find a marker that the affective-disor-
dered members of a single family all share and that the unaffected family members mostly lack. If they can do this, then they will be close to
a gene for depression.

At first the results appeared to be negative. There was a report of
linkage to a site on chromosome 11 among the Amish of Pennsylvania,
who are a good group to study because their insularity and large family size make it easy to find large groups of relatives with well-known
pedigrees. But this finding could not be replicated either in other families or even in an extension of the original families in which the linkage was first identified. It seems to be only a tantalizing mirage. A new
finding, however, of a linkage on chromosome 18 has been reported by
Wade Berritini, Elliot Gershon, and colleagues and appears to have
been partially replicated by other groups. Linkage to chromosome 21
has been reported as well.

But molecular genetic analysis grows more sophisticated all the
time. Indeed, methods using restriction nuclease have been almost
entirely supplanted by newer technologies. One new technique,
called gene amplification, lets biologists create thousands of copies of
specific gene sequences in order to study them more closely and is the
predominant molecular genetic analytic technique used currently. It
is based on initiating a chain reaction using an enzyme that synthe-
sizes new DNA (DNA polymerase) and thus is called PCR (polymerase
chain reaction). Once a gene is identified, we now have techniques
for inserting it into cultured cells in such a way that they will create
massive amounts of whatever protein the gene codes for. Thus we will
quickly be able to find out what the gene does and relate it to our
knowledge of the biochemistry of the disease. Other techniques now
being developed, utilizing matches and mismatches between strands
of DNA, promise even faster ways of finding genetic variations
between family members. So we keep looking: we know the genes are
there to be found.

Still, it's a mystery why they should exist at all. Evolutionary theory holds that genes survive and flourish in a species' gene pool to the extent that they increase the likelihood that the bearer will reproduce. The more offspring, the more copies of the gene are passed on to the next generation, and so on to successive generations. A gene that *decreases* the likelihood of reproduction—by making its bearer prone to inactivity, suicide, unattractiveness, and lack of sexual appetite— should, in theory, die out. Why, then, are the genes for depression so widespread?

Part of the answer may lie in mania. If people who are sometimes depressed are also sometimes abnormally energetic, aggressive, and sexually promiscuous, then their manic phases may have enough of a counterbalancing effect to account for the spread of the gene. But this easy answer may not be the correct one. Perhaps the gene that predisposes to depression has other functions as well, functions we know nothing about, that may even be completely unrelated to the nervous system. Perhaps the "gene" is really a constellation of smaller genes, each in itself neutral or even slightly beneficial, and trouble arises only when certain varieties are thrown together in combination. Almost certainly, we will not fully understand the genetics of depression until we have a better grasp of its biology.

CHAPTER TWO

DEPRESSION AS A PHYSICAL DISEASE

The gaps in our knowledge keep roaming.

— ELIAS CANETTI

WHEN SOMEONE'S MOODS, thoughts, or behavior cause so much suffering or disruption that the person cannot function effectively in the world, we say that he or she has a mental or psychiatric disorder. But where do we draw the line? How do we distinguish between the suffering associated with acute grief—say, the death of a child—and a major mood disorder? Both the inward feelings and the outward symptoms may be very similar, yet by psychiatric definition the depressed person is ill while the grieving person is not.

One way of addressing this ambiguity is to say that "mental disorders" don't exist. All of the enormous range of human experience, from the melancholic moods of depression and the hallucinations of schizophrenia to the everyday joys and frustrations of ordinary life, are simply different but comparable aspects of the human condition. When I was in college in the 1960s, this view was actually quite popular. Thomas Szasz argued that the diagnosis of a psychiatric disorder often serves as a means to push difficult people to the margins of society rather than as part of a genuine effort to provide help. R. D. Laing even romanticized the "journey" of the psychotic individual, whom he considered to have transcended the constraints of ordinary consciousness—usually in response to parents who made ambiguous or impossible demands.

More recently, in his best-selling book, *Listening to Prozac*, Peter Kramer also addressed the issue of drawing boundaries, but from a different perspective. The psychiatric tradition of using drugs to "dissect out" specific syndromes from large, vague diagnostic categories, he wrote, has led to "'diagnostic bracket creep'—the expansion of categories to match the scope of relevant medications." The temptation to think that "if we can treat it, it's a disease" has led psychiatrists to reclassify as pathological some syndromes that once were thought of as normal personality variations—or that, at least, were not well enough defined to merit a diagnostic category. In some cases these redefinitions were clearly a good thing—for example, the widespread recognition of panic anxiety as a behavioral syndrome after a drug, imipramine, became available to treat it—but others raise complex ethical and social issues.

I will return later to the ways the revolution in psychopharmacology has altered the terms on which we understand illness, normality, and the boundary between them. For now, I want to make a point that Szasz might not acknowledge but Kramer clearly would: that we are justified in drawing the boundary at all. There are mental states that entail a great deal of unwanted suffering, and with help this suffering can be eased. Some human conditions are treatable conditions.

The medical model that underlies my field of research, biological psychiatry, relies on defining clear criteria by which we can decide whether a given person is ill. This is the approach I learned in medical school. It explicitly leads us to think of a mental disease the way we think of a physical disease: as an abnormal, harmful condition with clear diagnostic criteria, such as we saw in the last chapter; a common natural history (the way the disease usually develops over time); and a standard set of treatment strategies. This approach has become so well accepted that some people now consider the term "biological psychiatry" redundant; they prefer to say "clinical neurosciences" instead. This progression in terminology reflects the medical model's increasing sophistication.

We invoke the traditional medical model whenever we say someone "has" a disease: it's an either-or proposition. Either you are infected with the influenza virus or you are not; either your leg is broken or it's not. Many genetic diseases follow this pattern: either you have the gene or you don't. While intelligent doctors have always known that things are not so clear-cut, medicine's traditional emphasis on diagnosis—and thus on placing patients in a diagnostic category—has led to a great preoccupation with these in-or-out decisions. Doctors honor this tradition every time they fill out an insurance form, where their reimbursement is governed by the diagnostic category in which they place the patient.

While I couldn't imagine a system of scientific medicine (let alone a system of health care reimbursement) in which diagnostic categories didn't have a fundamental place, modern medical research has moved a good deal beyond the either-or approach. In the *biological* model, which as its name implies deals with the underlying biological processes that bring about disease, susceptibility to a disease may be as important as having the disease itself. At the frontiers of medical research we are often less concerned with dividing the population into the sick and the well than we are with the more-susceptible and the less-susceptible. Depression, in this view, is a disease much like heart disease.

Few recent messages about health have been broadcast more widely and insistently than that cholesterol is bad. In fact this isn't quite true: cholesterol is present in our bodies all the time and is necessary for life. What is true is that too much cholesterol in the bloodstream in the long run is bad for your heart, and this well-known connection provides a good example of the biological model of disease at work.

Normally, cholesterol bound to protein circulating in the bloodstream is taken up by proteins called cholesterol receptors on the body's cells, which use it to renew cell structures. The amount circulating at any one time is closely regulated—when too much is in the bloodstream, the receptors remove and inactivate it, restoring cholesterol levels in the blood to normal. But some people's cholesterol levels are chronically too high. They may have a genetic disorder that renders their cholesterol receptors ineffective, or the receptors are suppressed because of high fat intake. More likely, there may be a combination of factors. The excess cholesterol forms deposits, called plaques, along the inner surfaces of these people's arteries, resulting in a disease called atherosclerosis. One common place for plaques to form is in the coronary arteries, which supply blood (and the oxygen and nutrients blood carries) to the heart muscle. When the coronary arteries grow narrow and stiff with plaques, less oxygen gets to the heart muscle, which may have trouble responding when it needs to pump harder. A person with this condition may feel chest pain when he is angry or needs to run for a bus—his heart cannot cope with the demands life has placed on it. If the heart muscle grows too damaged from chronic lack of oxygen, it may one day suddenly lose its ability to maintain the intricate rhythm by which it pumps blood throughout the body, a medical crisis that is a feature of a "heart attack."

Modern medicine thinks of heart disease as an illness to which genetic susceptibilities and environmental influences both contribute. Some people—the very small minority whose cholesterol receptors are genetically defective—have extraordinarily high concentrations of cholesterol in their bloodstream and are innately very susceptible to heart disease. Only by sticking to a very restrictive diet and taking cholesterol-reducing medications can these people hope to avoid or at least postpone the prospect of heart disease. For others the genetic influence is less powerful, and environmental factors such as diet, smoking, exercise, and stress play the major role. While everyone develops some degree of atherosclerosis as they age, many do not develop heart disease. In some people, severe atherosclerosis may considerably reduce the amount of blood reaching the heart muscle and yet remain "silent"—i.e., without symptoms—but detectable through medical or radiologic examination. By a variety of means, including laboratory tests, physical examination, and asking about daily habits and family history, a physician can assess a patient's risk of heart disease. And by interventions ranging from counseling to prescription drugs to surgery, depending on the degree of atherosclerosis, both healthy and ill patients can be helped to reduce their risk of having heart trouble in the future.

Many psychiatrists view depression in a similar way. Susceptibility to depression appears to run in families and be genetically based. But like heart disease, it does not follow a simple, predictable pattern of inheritance. A large study by Ken Kendler recently demonstrated that both genetic and environmental factors play significant roles in the development of depression. Some people who are susceptible to depression never actually become clinically depressed, just as some who are susceptible to heart attack never have one. Environmental factors, such as the loss of a loved one or the disappointment of expectations, seem to play a role in the expression of susceptibility to the disease. Like heart disease, a predisposition to depression may be "silent" until acute symptoms break out under stressful circumstances. And like our colleagues in internal medicine, we psychiatrists have devised an array of clinical tests for assessing who is at risk for depression and a range of treatment strategies for helping these people gain some control over their illness.

But unlike heart disease, depression is not obviously a physical problem; it's a disease of mood and behavior. In a society in which it's not uncommon to hear it said that "depression is just a form of unhappiness" and where mental illness is often either stigmatized or dismissed, biological psychiatry has a special need to explain its goals and methods to the public. We need to show that the biological model is not just a metaphor—we're not just saying that it's "as if" there were a physical disease—but rather that there are real chemical differences distinguishing people at risk for clinical depression from those who are not, and that we can say what those differences are and how they work. Because they occur in the brain, they are expressed as problems in thought and feeling. This idea is no less sensible than that a disease in the stomach should be expressed as a problem in digestion, but many people find it foreign and difficult to accept. As a psychiatrist I'm interested in both the chemical differences and their expression: not simply the body or the mind, but how body and mind interact in psychiatric illness.

The site of that interaction is an organ of staggering complexity about which our rapidly growing knowledge is still massively outweighed by our ignorance. To understand some of what we *do* know, we need to look at the workings of the nerve cell and especially at the junction between cells, a space that has been a subject of endless fascination to scientists since its discovery late last century: the nerve synapse.

⑤

The brain, the executive center of the nervous system, takes in and analyzes data from the world through our senses. These perceptions are ordered into patterns that are evaluated in relation to our memories of past experience, form the basis of our decisions and actions, and are themselves stored for future reference. Everything that makes us individual, our memories, hopes, emotions, talents, ideas—our entire personality and identity—is contained in the brain. The brain also organizes behavior, both conscious and unconscious. Whenever we speak, scratch an itch, sneeze, or glance up in surprise at some interruption, the impulse to do so originates in the brain. We can think of the brain as an organ for dealing with information—sensory data in, behavior out, ourselves in between.

The cells that perform this function, the nerve cells, or neurons, are specifically adapted for receiving and transmitting information in the form of chemical and electrical signals. The brain contains approximately ten million million of them, all interconnected in a network far more complex than the telephone network of a major city. There may be as many as a thousand different kinds of neurons, each specialized for a particular role in transmitting and processing data. For example, the receptive apparatus of a muscle sensory neuron responds to the stretching of the muscle; a skin sensory neuron may respond to the pressure of touch. This mechanical stimulus is translated into electrical signals in proportion to the strength of the stimulation. The more the muscle is stretched or the stronger the pressure on the skin, the more often the cell will fire off a signal.

Although neurons come in many shapes and sizes, most share a similar organization. The cell body, or soma, contains the nucleus, where the cell's genetic material is stored, as well as the organelles that keep the cell alive and synthesize the various molecules needed for its special functions. A network of branching filaments, called dendrites, connects to the cell body and receives information from surrounding neurons. The neuron's transmitting function is usually taken care of by the axon, a long, narrow, cylindrical structure that is often sheathed in an insulating substance called myelin, which improves electrical conduction. As the axon extends away from the cell body, it arborizes into multiple branches, which end in terminals. These are the points from which chemical signals are released to send messages on to other nerve cells. The gap between a terminal from a transmitting cell and a terminal on a receiving cell is the synapse.

Within a single nerve cell, signals are transmitted electrically, as impulses traveling along the cell's outer membrane. A neuron carries a positive electrical charge on the outside and a negative charge on the inside; this difference in charge is called the resting potential—because it is the potential energy stored by the cell, as in a battery, when it is at rest—and it amounts to about 60 millivolts. If you place an electrode inside the cell and another just outside, you can record this difference. The cell membrane can be thought of as a dam. The greater the difference in water level, the more energy will be generated when the dam opens—but the higher the dam, the more energy is needed to make it open. When the nerve cell fires, the dam opens, literally. Large protein structures called ion channels open up, permitting positive ions to rush in and negative ions to rush out. This process of depolarization travels along the nerve cell in a wave until it reaches the axonal terminals, where it stimulates the synaptic vesicles to open and dump neurotransmitters into the synapse. These chemicals travel across the tiny gap between neurons and bind to receptors on the other side. Each receptor is specifically tailored to a specific neurotransmitter, like a lock that will open only to the correct key.

What happens next is not simple. The binding of neurotransmitter to receptor begins a cascade of chemical reactions in the postsynaptic neuron. Synapses may be either excitatory or inhibitory. Neurotransmitters released at excitatory synapses decrease the membrane potential of the receiving cell (i.e., make the dam lower), making the nerve more likely to fire. Chemicals released across inhibitory synapses have the opposite effect. Other chemical changes may affect the activation of specific proteins or genes that play important roles in memory or learning. At any moment, the postsynaptic neuron is receiving messages from hundreds and perhaps thousands of synaptic inputs, both excitatory and inhibitory, that combine to determine whether or not it will fire. This process occurs millions of times each second in an infinite variety of patterns throughout the central nervous system.

The constantly changing patterns of excitation and inhibition along networks of neurons are how we store, represent, and act on information about the world. These patterns depend in large part on the signals passed across synapses. And the transmission of signals depends a great deal on alterations in the formation, release, and potency of neurotransmitters at receptor sites. This is why psychiatrists study neurotransmitters and their receptors.

᯽

We can see, then, that a lot of things have to happen correctly for a signal to pass properly from one neuron to the next. The nerve cell has to synthesize the correct amounts of neurotransmitter—neither too much nor too little—and release it into the synapse at the right time. The neurotransmitter has to bind to the receiving cell's receptors, which must be appropriately sensitive; and it can't linger in the synapse after that but must be reabsorbed. And the transmitting neuron must know when to stop releasing the neurotransmitter. If any one of these functions is disrupted, then something will change in the way signals move through the nervous system; they will be distorted or poorly regulated.

Some neurotransmitters are modulatory: that is, they fine-tune or modulate the activity of other neurotransmitters. They do not change the pattern of information but may alter its persistence, intensity, and impact on other brain systems. In this way, modulatory neurotransmitters may affect the emotional coloring, evaluation, or tone of external events being processed by the brain. They are of particular interest to psychiatrists, since it is often the evaluation and emotional impact of events that are disturbed in psychiatric disorders, rather than the sensory perception of events themselves.

One important system of modulatory neurotransmitters is the catecholamines. At one time researchers thought catecholamines might provide the entire explanation of the chemical basis of depression. We now know that they are only one of several neurotransmitter systems that are involved, but they do make an important and unique contribution. The two main catecholamines, norepinephrine and dopamine, play an activating or energizing role. They serve as alerting signals to the brain that say, "This is important: pay attention!" When the norepinephrine system is more active, our experience of our surroundings becomes more vivid. Much as turning up the contrast control intensifies the image on a television screen, making the dark colors darker and the light colors lighter, norepinephrine increases the excitation of the excitatory synapses and the inhibition of the inhibitory synapses. The norepinephrine neurons extend widely throughout the brain and, in monkeys, become more active when an unknown or threatening event occurs nearby—when the animal's attention needs to be focused outward. When its attention turns inward, during feeding, grooming, and sleep, the system quiets down. Thus, the norepinephrine system seems to regulate how attuned an animal is to its environment. It shifts attention toward changes in the environment and readies the body to respond quickly.

When you encounter an unfamiliar, potentially dangerous situation—say you are driving on a dark, rainy night, and something large suddenly darts in front of your headlights—the norepinephrine system goes into action. Your senses are heightened as you scan the situation for the most effective response; you determine that the form is a deer crossing the road, that if you swerve the car to the right you will miss it, and you do it, as you might tell friends later, "without thinking." Some people also notice a change in their awareness of time—"it's as if everything was happening in slow motion." This is our subjective experience of the way a sudden activation of the noradrenergic system can change the brain's processing of information.

Outside the brain, norepinephrine neurons form a special network called the sympathetic nervous system. When this is activated in an emergency, it tells the heart to start beating faster and more powerfully, the little muscles around your hair follicles to contract (you feel your hair stand on end), the capillaries in your skin to constrict (with the increased heartbeat, this raises your blood pressure dramatically), and the sweat glands to pump (you break into a cold sweat). Your limb muscles receive more blood and react more quickly and powerfully, and your gut and other nonessential systems shut down, since you don't need to be digesting food or making urine while you're fighting for your life. It is no coincidence that norepinephrine's effects on the body so perfectly complement its effects on the brain. What animal could survive for long if it were otherwise?

When there is no emergency—which is most of the time—the sympathetic nervous system does not simply fall silent. It works with its opposite number, the parasympathetic nervous system, to keep many of the body's involuntary functions at the right level. The parasympathetic nervous system stimulates the gut, slows the heartbeat, lowers blood pressure, and generally prepares the body for feeding, resting, and other inward-directed activities. These two systems thus maintain a balance between attending to the outside world and seeing to the body's internal requirements—between catching one's food and eating it, in other words, or between fighting and retiring to lick one's wounds. The parasympathetic nervous system is mediated by a different neurotransmitter, acetylcholine, and the balance between acetylcholine and norepinephrine may also play an important role in mood distortions—as we shall see in Chapter 4.

Julius Axelrod, who won a Nobel Prize for this work, showed that dopamine and norepinephrine are both made from tyrosine, an amino acid, one of the building blocks of proteins. Tyrosine is found in a variety of foods; after it is absorbed from the gut, the bloodstream carries it to dopamine and norepinephrine nerve cells, where it is converted to L-dopa and then to dopamine. In the norepinephrine cells, dopamine is further modified to norepinephrine. Norepinephrine, in turn, is in some cells turned into epinephrine, which when released as a hormone by the adrenal glands is also called adrenaline.

"Prepare to act" and "execute the plan" are messages of the dopamine system. Dopamine helps us plan, start, and maintain our thoughts and movements, in part by reinforcing behaviors that are rewarded. Dopamine is believed to play a key role in the reward centers of the brain. In the movement centers, it helps initiate complex motor patterns, while in more executive centers it aids in planning future actions. Too little dopamine will result in sluggish thoughts and movements, while too much may lead to exaggerated thoughts and movements. The movie *Awakenings,* in which Robert De Niro played a man with Parkinson's disease, dramatically illustrated the effects of the dopamine system. Parkinson's disease is marked by deficiency of the dopamine cells in the brain; rigid postures, a slow, shuffling walk, and a masklike face result. You can see patients with Parkinson's disease literally frozen in midgesture. Oliver Sacks, the neurologist who wrote the classic book on which the movie is based, treated these patients with L-dopa. As L-dopa is converted to dopamine in the brain, it dramatically relieves the symptoms of Parkinson's disease. But with continued treatment, the main character became paranoid and suffered exaggerated writhing movements. This reaction, a sign of too much dopamine, resembles the behavior of longtime abusers of amphetamine, which also releases dopamine.

The idea that spurred the development of L-dopa—that Parkinson's disease could be explained relatively simply as a problem of too little of a single chemical—resembles the way psychiatric researchers were thinking about the relation between norepinephrine and depression when I arrived at the National Institute of Mental Health as a staff fellow in 1978 to study depressive diseases. NIMH has a venerable history: it was one of the first centers in the country for studying the biology of depression, and the first biological theory of the disease had been proposed by three prominent NIMH researchers, Joseph Schildkraut (who by this time had moved to Harvard), as well as William Bunney and John Davis. Their idea was very compelling. Manic depressive disease is a bipolar disorder, so it made sense to think it represented a pair of biochemically opposite states. Too much catecholamines, and you got mania. Too little—depression. This was called the catecholamine hypothesis, and in 1978 it had been the dominant way of thinking about the biology of depression for the past decade. In fact the theory had been around long enough to grow badly frayed at the edges.

The catecholamine hypothesis had some strong evidence to recommend it. Schildkraut, as well as Bunney and Davis had been intrigued by the fact that many drugs with a profound effect on people's behavior were found to act directly on the norepinephrine system, and vice versa. They had observed that psychoactive drugs such as cocaine and amphetamines, which increase the amounts of catecholamines in the synapse, often produce a "high" that strongly resembles clinical mania. Dennis Murphy, with Fred Goodwin, Keith Brodie, William Bunney, and other colleagues at NIMH had shown that high doses of L-dopa, the precursor of both dopamine and norepinephrine, can bring on a manic episode in a manic depressive patient. Reserpine, on the other hand, which depletes stores of norepinephrine, can lead to depression. Moreover, two important groups of drugs used to treat depression were both shown to increase norepinephrine levels. Tricyclic antidepressants slow the reabsorption of norepinephrine once it is released into the synapse—meaning that at any one time, more of the chemical is present, because it takes longer to go away. Another group of antidepressant drugs, the monoamine oxidase inhibitors (or MAOIs), inhibits the breakdown of norepinephrine into waste molecules. During the late 1960s and early 1970s, exciting findings like this had drawn many of the brightest young psychiatrists to come to NIMH to help unravel the mystery of depression.

The hope was that they might close in on a single chemical—perhaps an enzyme—that formed a weak link in the whole catecholamine system, and whose absence or malfunctioning explained at least a large fraction of cases of depression. We know of a number of diseases of this type, and they make up some of the classic success stories of modern medicine. Phenylketonuria (PKU), for instance, which leads to severe mental retardation and early death if untreated, is caused by the liver's inability to manufacture a single chemical, phenylalanine hydroxylase, which it needs to break down tyrosine. Now that we know this, pediatricians can screen infants for PKU and through severe dietary restrictions prevent the worst effects of the disease. Was depression caused by an equally simple defect, somewhere in the long biochemical chain connecting tyrosine and norepinephrine?

Sadly, the answer so far appears to be no. The catecholamine hypothesis was a great advance—the first theory that conclusively tied depression to a biochemical system—but by the time I got to NIMH it was becoming clear that this was not the whole story. For one thing, we know that tricyclic antidepressants and MAOIs work on the nerve cell to increase norepinephrine levels relatively quickly—in a matter of minutes. But they take weeks of repeated doses to lift a patient's depression. What's happening in the meantime? Moreover, some very potent drugs that increase norepinephrine levels, such as cocaine, have no real antidepressant properties, while others that are effective antidepressants, such as the selective serotonin reuptake inhibitors, don't work directly on the catecholamine system at all.

Finally, you can measure the amount of norepinephrine's waste products, or metabolites, in a person's blood or urine or in the fluid surrounding the brain and spinal cord. Norepinephrine is recyclable. After it binds to a receptor and is released again, it can be absorbed back into the presynaptic terminal and placed into short- or long-term storage for future use. But a certain percentage of it is constantly being broken down by an enzyme, monoamine oxidase, and these breakdown products make their way from the nervous system to the bloodstream to the urine, and so out of the body. Thus the level of metabolites gives a good indication of the level of norepinephrine production and indirectly of the amount available for use in the nerve cells. But when researchers measured norepinephrine metabolites in both depressed and healthy people, their results didn't always correspond to what the catecholamine hypothesis led them to expect.

The early studies went according to plan: depressed patients did indeed have lower levels of noradrenergic metabolites than healthy controls. These studies, done before lithium became popular, mainly involved severely and, as far as was then known, incurably manic depressive patients. But since NIMH largely admits "treatment refractory" patients—those who are not responding to treatment—they stopped seeing so many cases of bipolar disorder once lithium's effectiveness became known and it was widely prescribed. The patient population at NIMH shifted toward anxious depressed patients, most of whom had never experienced a manic episode—they were "unipolar"—and whose disease usually could not be treated with any of the antidepressants then available. When the same studies were done on this group, the result was a surprise: their norepinephrine levels were often *higher* than the controls'.

Perhaps these patients were fundamentally different from the patients in the earlier studies. Perhaps the unipolar patients suffered from increased noradrenergic activity and needed higher doses of antidepressants than they were currently getting. But if that was true, then what exactly was the abnormality in the noradrenergic system that united the two groups? Interest shifted from the pre-synaptic neuron, where norepinephrine is produced and released, to the receptors on the post-synaptic neuron and the relationship between the two. In the lock-and-key mechanism that lies at the heart of synaptic transmission, people began to think the problem was not so much with the key as with the lock.

🌀

I arrived at Dennis Murphy's laboratory at NIMH, fresh from my psychiatric residency at McLean Hospital in the Boston suburbs, just as this shift was taking place. My first year was spent on the research unit, taking care of patients who were participating in our clinical investigations. First-year associates were also expected to start developing their own research protocols, which they would begin to implement at the end of the first year and then continue throughout their careers at NIMH. It was an exciting place to be. Investigators were crammed three or four to an office; the hallways were cluttered with filing cabinets, spare equipment, and extra furniture; and nobody worked regular hours. The files went back to the days when Biff Bunney, John Davis, Herb Meltzer, and other leaders of the field had themselves been research associates there, giving us a sense of the place's history. At any hour of the day or night, scientists were bumping into each other in the hallways, exchanging ideas and advice, gossiping and complaining, and thinking up new protocols. There was a sense that we were doing pioneering work.

People are often surprised to hear me say that working with depressed patients is not always depressing. We can offer much more help than our colleagues could a generation ago. I certainly saw some very ill patients at NIMH; like all physicians, psychiatrists see humanity at some of its most vulnerable moments. At times it seemed like our unit was permeated with suffering. One woman I worked with, Jean, would shift back and forth from a depressed state, when she was unkempt, wore old clothes, and stared at the floor, to an "up" period, when she would be hyperactive and talkative and appear in new clothes and heavy makeup. Every day I sat with her and heard her history of painful losses and family difficulties. Some patients came because they had heard of some new antidepressant we were trying out. Jim felt that the only time he had felt good was on a new monoamine oxidase inhibitor, but the effect had not lasted and he hoped to get a more sustained reaction from one of our new medications. Phil was a loner who led a life of quiet misery and had never really responded to any antidepressant treatment. But at the same time, NIMH was a source of hope to these people, and our unit was a place where our patients could at least share their experience. Each morning, all the patients, doctors, and nurses would gather for a meeting in which we would get a sense of how the patients were doing and monitor any shifts in their clinical state. The patients monitored our progress as well. Since they had such a personal stake in it, many of them were intensely interested in our research. We were all in it together.

There are many windows onto brain function, and each laboratory selects those few that will give it the best view of whatever aspect of the brain it is studying. One of the windows we found most useful was the "challenge" paradigm, which had been used with great success in neuroendocrinology, the study of hormones in the nervous system. We would see patients who had not responded to conventional antidepressant treatments in their communities, and either measure the levels of different brain chemicals in their bloodstreams or subject them to chemical challenges that perturbed their neurotransmitter systems. This involved giving them single doses of one medication that would target a specific brain chemical system, and then evaluating the challenge's effect on hormones that we could measure in the blood. We would then place the patients in double-blind studies to test new medications—studies in which no one, not the patients, nurses, or physicians, knew who was receiving the drug and who was getting a placebo, until after the protocol was completed. The idea was to look for correlations between the neurochemical changes we induced and the behavioral changes we observed in our patients. One of the second-year associates, Dave Pickar, had devised a protocol to look at the effects of tyramine, a neurotransmitter related to norepinephrine, in people before and after treatment with two new antidepressants, clorgyline and deprenyl. These were monoamine oxidase inhibitors that were supposed to avoid one of the most serious side effects of this class of drugs: when people on MAOIS eat food containing tyramine, their blood pressure can rise drastically. The main purpose of Dave's protocol was to test whether patients on these new drugs were indeed less susceptible to this effect.

At the same time, however, the study gave us the chance to directly evaluate the noradrenergic receptors' responsiveness to tyramine. A stronger response (i.e., a greater jump in blood pressure) would suggest that the receptors were more sensitive, while a weaker response would suggest the opposite. Biff Bunney had recently proposed that receptor responsiveness might vary in manic depressive disorder, with decreased sensitivity in depressed states and increased sensitivity in manic periods. When we gave the tyramine test repeatedly to Jean, we found exactly this pattern: during depressed periods her blood pressure response was diminished, but just before and during a hypomanic episode, her response increased. Once it even seemed that the tyramine test triggered a hypomanic episode. The day after she received a tyramine test, she came to our morning meeting wearing heavy makeup and looking animated—signs I knew well from having worked with her. That her blood pressure response the day before had been higher than usual reinforced the idea that receptor changes precede clinical changes.

This study opened up the question of how receptors were regulated. Normally, receptors become less sensitive when bombarded with increased levels of neurotransmitter, and more sensitive when they are exposed to reduced levels. If reduced norepinephrine was associated with depression, receptors might "up-regulate"—become more sensitive—causing a switch to mania in a susceptible person like Jean. But if her receptors could change their sensitivity, why couldn't they find an equilibrium level that would allow her to function normally?

As we looked at the relationship between plasma norepinephrine levels and receptor responsiveness in a number of studies, we frequently saw different patterns in depressed patients than in our normal volunteers, suggesting that the relationship between norepinephrine released into the synapse and the response of receptors was somehow different in depressed patients. But these different relationships kept recurring in different ways. When confronted with these paradoxical results, we would shrug our shoulders and say, "It's dysregulation." But no one was quite sure what "dysregulation" was or how we could even define it well enough to study it. We needed something to compare it to. In scientific jargon, we needed a model.

৯

More and more, depression was looking to us like a well-known receptor-mediated disease, type ii diabetes.

Diabetes' symptoms have been known since antiquity: excessive thirst and hunger, a great deal of urine, fatigue, weight loss. Sometimes the disease progresses rapidly to coma and death; in chronic cases one sees the effects of gradual destruction of the blood vessels: gangrene, blindness. It is the leading cause of blindness in the United States and the third leading cause of death by disease. The classic sign, the accumulation of sugar in the blood and urine, reflects the essential nature of diabetes, an inability to process carbohydrates into a form that the body's cells can use for energy. You can detect the disease at an early stage with the glucose tolerance test. Patients are given a fixed dose of glucose (a kind of sugar) in a drink, and then the level of glucose in their blood is tested periodically to see how long it takes them to return to normal. A person without diabetes gets back to his or her baseline level in 120 minutes with a delay in the reburn to baseline indicates mild diabetes, and when the fasting level is elevated, overt diabetes is present.

Type i diabetes is caused by the pancreas's inability to manufacture insulin, a crucial hormone involved in carbohydrate metabolism. This form is called juvenile-onset diabetes because it is the kind that strikes in childhood, although it may occur up to age forty. Normally, when a person eats, the sugar absorbed from the gut stimulates the pancreas to secrete insulin, which transports sugar across cell membranes and into the cell's interior. Without insulin, sugar cannot get into the body's cells and builds up in the bloodstream. Type I diabetes has recently been shown to be an autoimmune disease, like arthritis—the body's own immune system attacks and gradually destroys the pancreatic cells that produce insulin. The disease is defined by the result: too little insulin in the bloodstream. If you give a person with type I diabetes regular injections of insulin to make up the deficit, the symptoms may clear up. Several genes have recently been shown to contribute to susceptibility to this disease—some related to the immune system and some to insulin production.

Type II diabetes is a different story. Although it shares many of the symptoms of type I, as well as high blood sugar, the defining characteristic—too little insulin—is absent. People with type II (also called adult-onset) diabetes may have high, low, or normal insulin levels, depending on the individual or the phase of the illness. If you looked only at measures of circulating insulin in patients with type II diabetes, you might conclude that insulin was not involved in the disease at all— yet we know that it is. This similarity to our problem with norepinephrine levels in depression led us to look at the disease closely.

One indication of the link between type II diabetes and insulin is that it is *insulin resistant:* unlike healthy people, patients with the disease do not respond to an injection of insulin with a decrease in blood sugar. Rosalyn Yalow and Solomon Berson at the Bronx VA Medical Center developed the insulin challenge test to distinguish type I from type II diabetes based on the patient's response to insulin. Later, Jesse Roth and his colleagues at the National Institute of Health showed that patients with type II diabetes have abnormalities in both the number of insulin receptors and in how those receptors respond to changing insulin levels. Some forms of adult-onset diabetes appear to be caused by a gene that produces a defective insulin receptor, preventing insulin from acting effectively on the cell. The body's cells become starved for sugar. Since these receptors also regulate the pancreas's production of insulin, they may respond to the cells' sugar starvation by calling for more insulin, even though the problem is not insufficient insulin at all but the receptors' own inability to use what's available. Thus you can have the symptoms of diabetes even with high insulin levels. In other cases the problem is not a genetic defect but an environmental influence. Obesity, for instance, may upset the regulatory mechanism, making the pancreas produce insulin in amounts that bear little relation to the body's real needs. Or the two factors may combine: a moderately inefficient receptor, adequate for normal needs, may prove unable to cope with increased stress in the form of sudden weight gain or a change to a sugary diet. The illness may be controlled, particularly in its early stages, by diet and weight reduction.

The lock-and-key binding of chemicals to receptors is one of the body's fundamental biological mechanisms. Receptors help regulate energy production, growth, and resistance to infection, as well as information processing. Taken together, they arguably make up as important an information-carrying system as the genes or the nervous system. Receptors serve as signals attaching to and altering the activity of crucial enzymes, proteins that speed up chemical reactions in the cells; on the cell membrane they regulate which substances go into or out of the cell; and they regulate the action of genes in producing the information or models needed to construct the building blocks of the cells. They are essential links in the feedback loops that control homeostasis, the maintenance of the body's chemical equilibrium.

If we compare the receptor's homeostatic function to a rather sophisticated thermostat, we can see that it maintains equilibrium (or fails to do so) on a variety of levels. The simplest is for our thermostat to maintain a set temperature: we set it at 72°F, and whenever the room temperature falls enough below that, a switch closes inside the thermostat, signaling the furnace to turn itself on and send up some heat. When the room temperature rises again to 72°, the switch opens, the signal stops, and the furnace shuts off. But suppose our thermostat is becoming corroded inside, so that the switch no longer makes contact reliably. Sometimes it sends the "on" signal to the furnace at the right time and sometimes it doesn't. We might notice that the house is sometimes cooler than we like, and respond by changing the thermostat's temperature setting—or we might try to repair the furnace. Alternatively, suppose the corrosion were so severe that the thermostat effectively recalibrated itself. It works fine around 72°, but the switch breaks contact at 65° and doesn't reestablish a complete circuit again until the temperature falls to 50°. This can, under certain conditions, become the new "set-point." If you accidentally leave a window open one winter day and the thermostat cools down too far, eventually the whole house is maintained at 50°.

Let's make our thermostat more sophisticated. Suppose it has a clock. Now we can set two or more temperatures: we want to wake up in a warm room, say, 75°F, have the room a little cooler during the day (once we're up and dressed), perhaps 70°, and let it cool down to 60° at night. So we set it as follows: 6:00 A.M. – 9:00 A.M., 75°; 9:00 A.M. – 9:00 P.M., 70°; 9:00 P.M. – 6:00 A.M., 60°. The only trouble is that the thermostat is not all that well made. The clock is too sensitive to power fluctuations, and whenever we run our toaster and electric hair dryer at the same time, it switches to the next temperature setting and gets out of rhythm. Before we know it, we are getting 75° heat at midnight, making us throw our blankets on the floor, and we have to wear sweaters during the day.

We could make the thermostat considerably more sophisticated (and less plausible)—make it responsive to light levels, noise, the presence of people in the room, and any number of other conditions—without beginning to approach the complexity with which receptors control the myriad functions of the living body. But the basic idea of keeping things close to an equilibrium point applies to both.

The idea that depression might involve a defect in the way receptors regulate the norepinephrine system clearly suggested a more complex disease than the original catecholamine hypothesis did. It implied a failure of one or more homeostatic mechanisms. The consequence, as with our various annoying thermostats, would be an inappropriate response to the person's needs. The norepinephrine system would be unstable and would not react correctly to the environment. As "dysregulation" became a buzzword in our seminar rooms and scholarly publications, we began to investigate specific receptors in the noradrenergic system.

The receptors in this system are classified as alpha-adrenergic or beta-adrenergic according to their binding properties and physiologic effects. The beta-adrenergic receptor allows the postsynaptic neuron to become more responsive to repeated incoming stimuli. Gene Redmond at Yale found that he could make monkeys aroused and fearful by electrically stimulating their locus ceruleus, which in turn releases norepinephrine, activating beta-adrenergic receptors in the brain; but when he dosed them beforehand with a chemical that binds to the receptor without activating it, they responded to the stimulation much more calmly. The alpha-adrenergic receptor comes in two varieties. Alpha-1 seems to be primarily excitatory and to increase the efficiency of other neuronal systems, and some evidence links these receptors with reward-seeking or motivational behavior.

Alpha-2 is an inhibitory receptor. It is found on the cell bodies of noradrenergic neurons and inhibits their firing. One form of the alpha-2 receptor is located on the presynaptic terminal, close to where norepinephrine is stored and released, a position that suggests its primary job is to provide negative feedback. This receptor, called an autoreceptor because it allows the cell to receive its own chemical signals, is the main thermostat control for noradrenergic activity. When it becomes too high, the alpha-2 receptors inhibit further release of the chemical from the nerve terminal and bring the system back into balance. While it is not the only influence on norepinephrine levels and interacts with other neurotransmitter systems as well, it serves as a central link in the control of noradrenergic activity. Alpha-2 appeared central to the dysregulation hypothesis.

One way to test a biological system is to put it under stress. In diabetes, this is done with the glucose tolerance test. One of the advantages of this test is that it can detect diabetes at an early stage of development, before any symptoms have appeared, as well as after the disease has gone into remission. This was important: if dysregulation was truly involved in depression, then like the broken thermostat in summertime, it should be detectable even when there were no outward symptoms—if you looked in the right place.

With this in mind, many of us looked for new agents to challenge receptor systems in the brain. We were hoping to find an agent that, unlike tyramine, got into the central nervous system and acted directly on the central noradrenergic receptors. Clonidine, one of the few agents that is able to do this, had been bandied about as a possible probe. Clonidine acts directly on the alpha-2-adrenergic receptors. In the hypothalamus, a part of the brain that oversees the endocrine system, stimulation of these receptors prompts the release of growth hormones. If adrenergic receptors were abnormal in depressed patients, that fact should show up as an abnormality in the amount of growth hormone they produced in response to clonidine. I learned of a study in Germany that suggested this might indeed be the case. When Tom Uhde came to Bethesda from Yale, where he had been studying clonidine's use in opiate addiction, we began to collaborate in looking at clonidine's effects on growth hormone production in depressed patients at NIMH.

This study, which has since been repeated many times, gave us our first clear link between depression and an adrenergic receptor. We found that depressed patients did in fact produce less growth hormone in response to clonidine than our healthy controls did—even those who had a history of depression but no current symptoms. I still use this test today in my research evaluation program at the Bronx VA Medical Center to help me assess patients' long-term risk of depression.

By the 1980s, different research groups were looking for other correlations. The clonidine/growth hormone test measures the activity of post-synaptic receptors. We later developed a test to measure the activity of autoreceptors using levels of a chemical called MHPG, again in response to a clonidine challenge. Since it is a metabolite of norepinephrine, changes in the MHPG levels we measure in the blood should reflect changes in the amount of norepinephrine released into the synapse. Here again we found that clonidine produced less effect in depressed patients than in normal controls—suggesting that the pre-synaptic receptors, like the post-synaptic ones, were less responsive in depressed patients—consistent with the notion of a faulty thermostat. When we looked outside the nervous system, we saw that alpha-2-adrenergic receptors on the platelets, a kind of blood cell, were less responsive in depressed patients. When other researchers looked at depressed patients' blood cells, they found similar abnormalities in the beta-adrenergic receptors.

It isn't enough, of course, just to demonstrate these lovely correlations; I was pursuing an overarching idea that would both guide our research and give us some help in treating patients. In 1984, by which time I had moved to Mount Sinai Hospital and the Bronx VA, my colleague Ken Davis and I were ready to propose a general hypothesis of how dysregulation of neurotransmitter systems brings on and sustains depression. We used the norepinephrine system as a case study, as it were, to illustrate general principles, but the hypothesis was meant to apply to all neurotransmitter systems. We proposed six criteria:

- *A neurotransmitter system is impaired in one or more regulatory mechanisms.* In other words, the thermostat is broken—which implies that there is a thermostat to *be* broken and that we can say what it is and what is wrong with it. This is very likely not a single defect; disturbances at any number of molecular sites involved in neurotransmission could yield a common final pathway of dysregulation leading to depression.

- *Basal output of a dysregulated neurotransmitter system is erratic.* We can think of basal output as the thermostat's temperature setting. Another phrase I often use is "set-point." Neurotransmitter systems have certain resting levels that are appropriate for normal function in unstressful circumstances. In a dysregulated system, the set-point is either inappropriate or, like a badly tuned radio (to mix metaphors), keeps drifting off the correct setting.

- *Normal periodicities, including circadian rhythms, are disrupted.* The thermostat's built-in clock is not working properly. We can show in primates and cats, as well as people, that the norepinephrine system's normal pattern is a stable daily cycle: relatively quiescent when the animal is not aroused, markedly reduced during sleep, higher during active periods, and showing only occasional spikes of activity when the animal is presented with some unexpected stimulus. In depressed patients this circadian cycle is disrupted. They may be out of phase, usually "phase-advanced," or be in a twelve-hour cycle, or show no circadian rhythm at all. This disruption accounts for one of the classic symptoms of depression: tiredness during the day coupled with insomnia at night.

- *A dysregulated neurotransmitter system is less selectively responsive to environmental stimuli.* The thermostat has trouble switching on. This is the main lesson of the clonidine/growth hormone test. When presented with stress in the form of a sudden rush of chemicals binding to them, the receptors of depressed patients responded sluggishly compared to those of normal controls. They appear to be as inefficient responding to natural challenges as to manmade ones, reacting too sensitively to less relevant stimulation and less efficiently and robustly to specific stressors.

- *A dysregulated neurotransmitter system returns more slowly to basal activity following a perturbation.* The thermostat also has trouble switching off. The clonidine/MHPG test, which measured the activity of autoreceptors, suggested that these receptors in depressed patients were sluggish in recognizing that "enough" norepinephrine was in the synapse. The stress systems regained normal activity more slowly after the stress.

- *When a drug works, it does so by restoring effective regulation to the dysregulated system.* Antidepressant drugs seem to stabilize erratic or dysregulated neurons by blocking the reabsorption of neurotransmitter or its breakdown by enzymes. They thus make more neurotransmitter available to send the message when the system is stimulated, with less of the chemical lingering when the system is not aroused. The result is a higher "signal-to-noise ratio": a stronger signal against a quieter background, leading to a more efficient system.

✿

Why does dysregulation make people feel depressed? How does norep-inephrine explain why Sylvia Plath's heroine felt imprisoned in a bell jar? It doesn't, not entirely, but it explains some of the symptoms.

If the alpha-2-adrenergic receptor doesn't bind to norepinephrine efficiently or is somehow desensitized (perhaps through chronic stress), it will be less responsive to norepinephrine levels in the synapse and will be unable to shut off synthesis and release at the correct time. The result will be chronically high levels of norepinephrine—which may further desensitize the receptors and further limit their ability to shut off norepinephrine release. The healthy cycle of negative feedback will have turned into a malignant one of positive feedback: more norepi-nephrine leads to more desensitization leads to more norepinephrine. If this cycle goes on long enough, the system will start to be regulated by other, less environmentally sensitive mechanisms. The nerve cell could simply keep on manufacturing and releasing norepinephrine until it runs out of raw materials. Alternatively, if noradrenergic nerve firing slows down, the norepinephrine could stay locked inside the vesi-cles for a long time before it is once again released in an unregulated rush. Cycles of such alternations cascading through the nervous system may be one of the components of bipolar disorder: a state of exagger-ated arousal followed by a prolonged quiescence. (None of these sce-narios is documented, but our knowledge of the norepinephrine system in depression suggests that something like this is taking place.)

Less critically, a norepinephrine system that can neither turn on fully nor turn itself down—like a badly tuned engine that can neither idle nor race but only sputter with the gas pedal pressed halfway to the floor—may explain what we see in patients with agitated depression. These people live in a constant state of semireadiness, able neither to relax nor to arouse themselves to the point of action. So they fret. They pace, wring their hands, pull their hair, rub their skin, pick at their clothing. Yet they cannot direct this energy toward constructive behav-ior: the smallest task seems difficult or impossible.

We don't know nearly enough about the brain to be able to con-struct physical models of emotional states. But we can observe correlations and suggest plausible connections. The noradrenergic system is an arousal system. It prepares us to focus on important aspects of our environment and to act on them. But it doesn't do this at a purely mechanical level—it's part of us and we sense it working. Changes in brain activity may be expressed as changes in the way we feel and think. If we look at emotions as having specific functions in the brain's overall task of managing our relationship with the world, then it makes sense that the *ability* to focus on certain aspects of the environment and the *feeling* of caring about those aspects may be more than closely related. They may be one and the same. Just as we cannot focus on anything for very long or very intently if we don't care about it, so we cannot care without focusing. The depressed patient's loss of interest in the world—in the flavors of food, in sex, hobbies, work, friends, and loved ones—may be the conscious expression of how it feels to be unable to pick out the aspects of these things that used to give pleasure. It's as if the patient has become blind to differences that matter. Everything is gray.

By the same token, the urge to take action to control our environment and the feeling of the *capacity* to act may be two sides of the same coin, and if one is diminished, the other necessarily is too. A sense of incapacity may be the depressed person's emotional awareness of an inability to rouse himself to action—in which case the incapacity, though not apparent to others, is not illusory. Is a sense of incapacity to control one's environment so far removed from a general feeling of inadequacy?

ら

The link between norepinephrine and depression is only one wall of a much larger structure, encompassing the contribution of other neurotransmitter systems to depression as well as norepinephrine's contribution to other diseases. In depression, norepinephrine is particularly important in melancholic states whose physical disturbances—disruptions in the sleep-waking cycle, loss of appetite and sexual interest, anxiety, and an inability to focus one's attention—reflect this system's role as an arousal mechanism. Other neurotransmitters, such as serotonin, are equally or perhaps more important, as we shall see. Depression may be the final common pathway of disturbances in a number of related brain systems, interacting in ways we are only beginning to comprehend.

One system that is clearly involved in depression is the hypothalamic-pituitary axis, or HPA, which is the primary link in the brain's intimate relation with the endocrine system. The hypothalamus is an organ at the base of the brain that secretes hormones that stimulate various endocrine functions. It is connected to the pituitary gland, the endocrine organ just below it, by a special blood supply called a portal vein, one of only two blood vessels in the body that do not lead directly to or from the heart (the other portal vein connects the small intestine to the liver). The pituitary can be thought of as the body's master gland. Many of its products are called releasing factors or releasing hormones because they cause other glands to release their products. The pituitary plays a key role in growth, reproduction, and many other body functions, including the response to stress.

When a stressful event occurs, such as a near-accident on the road, the hypothalamus releases corticotropin releasing hormone (CRH), which travels down the portal vein to stimulate the pituitary to release adrenocorticotropic hormone (ACTH). (CRH can also stimulate the locus ceruleus, the center of noradrenergic activity in the brain.) ACTH, in turn, causes the adrenal glands to release epinephrine, with the results I described earlier in this chapter, as well as cortisol, one of the body's most important means for responding to stress. Cortisol's many actions include altering the body's metabolism, mobilizing energy from fat cells and the liver, and suppressing immune function and other systems not needed for immediate survival. (It also, as I will discuss in Chapter 7, may destroy certain brain cells.)

Charles Nemeroff and his colleagues, currently at Emory University, have found that CRH concentrations may be increased in patients with a major depressive disorder. Several studies have also shown not only that cortisol concentrations are increased in depression but that they lose their normal daily rhythm. Under normal circumstances, high concentrations of cortisol serve as a feedback control on

HPA activity by inhibiting the release of ACTH from the pituitary, but this mechanism seems not to work well in people with depression: cortisol is less effective in inhibiting ACTH secretion in these people. This finding is the source of a proposed diagnostic test for major depressive disorder, the dexamethasone suppression test.

Dexamethasone acts like cortisol in inhibiting the pituitary's release of ACTH and thus usually suppresses the body's natural secretion of cortisol. It is only partially effective at this in depressed patients: their suppression of cortisol on administration of dexamethasone is significantly weaker than in nondepressed control subjects. While this effect is not limited to people suffering from depression, it certainly suggests that HPA abnormalities and alterations in the capacity to handle stress play some role in the disease—what role we can't yet say. On a biological level, we seem to be looking at another dysregulated receptor with an altered setpoint.

We can try to reproduce in animals the altered responses to stress that we think are important in depression. The most important and remarkable of these attempts is Martin Seligman's "learned helplessness" model. In these experiments, one group of rats was exposed to a series of electric shocks that they had no hope of escaping, while a second group was exposed to the same shocks but could, with effort, escape. The first group soon stopped trying to get away—and with this behavior came a host of other symptoms resembling depression. These animals slept less, ate less, groomed themselves less, and moved more slowly. Using a similar paradigm, Jay Weiss, one of Seligman's colleagues, showed changes in the sensitivity of the noradrenergic receptors and activity of the locus ceruleus in the animals' brains, changes that could be reversed by antidepressant drugs. Weiss also found that some strains of rats appeared to develop the behavioral and biological signs of learned helplessness more readily than others, suggesting that susceptibility to this syndrome may have a genetic component.

The learned helplessness environment, in which the animal has no control over the stress to which it is exposed, parallels the experience of the depressed person, who feels inadequate to the task of controlling the events in his or her life. Stressful events over which we have no control are most likely to make us feel hopeless, and if prolonged and severe, these stresses may result in depression. Some people may have a genetic susceptibility to depression in the face of an inability to control important aspects of their lives. There is also an element of learning in the human equivalent of learned helplessness: someone who has been trained to be ineffective in the face of minor stresses may develop depression when faced with a major stress that is not, in fact, beyond his or her power to change.

§

Just as the biological path to depression differs from one person to the next, so does the biological path to recovery. The history of antidepressant drug development is one of increasing specificity in targeting individual neurotransmitter systems. The first effective drugs for depression, introduced in the 1960s, were the tricyclic antidepressants, which block the reuptake of norepinephrine and serotonin into the neurons that released them. Monoamine oxidase inhibitors, or MAOIS, which block the main mechanism for breakdown of these neurotransmitters, were also used at this time. Though often effective, neither class of drug is very specific by today's standards, and they tend to disrupt the functions these neurotransmitters must perform outside the brain. The tricyclic antidepressants' side effects include dry mouth and blurred vision, and they may interfere with electrical conduction in the heart, resulting in arrythmia—weak heartbeats caused by incoordination among different parts of the heart. With MAOIS, patients have to observe strict dietary rules: even small amounts of foods containing tyramine can bring about dangerous rises in blood pressure.

The newer antidepressants are much more finely tuned. The selective serotonin reuptake inhibitors (SSRIS), such as fluoxetine (Prozac), sertraline (Zoloft), paroxetine (Paxil), or fluvoxamine (Luxox), leave many patients virtually free of side effects (a substantial minority experience nausea, decreased libido, or delayed orgasm). Venlafaxine (Effexor) targets both norepinephrine and serotonin and so could be useful in patients with disordered regulation in either or both systems. Netazadone (Serzone) also enhances serotonergic activity but blocks specific serotonin receptors and is less likely to produce sexual side effects. Buproprion (Wellbutin) blocks reuptake and stimulates release of dopamine and norepinephrine.

These new drugs have brought a number of changes to the treatment of depression. First, they have largely eliminated a major argument against the widespread use of antidepressants. As the risk of side effects diminishes, more patients, and more highly functional patients, are being prescribed these drugs than ever before. Second, they make an understanding of the underlying mechanisms increasingly relevant. When the only available antidepressant drugs were the MAOIs, tricyclic antidepressants, and lithium, it made little difference from a clinical point of view whether norepinephrine or serotonin or some other brain chemical was the main culprit in depression, since all of the known drugs were going to affect them all about equally anyway. Now that we can target specific systems and even combinations of systems, it becomes important to know exactly which neurotransmitter systems are disordered in each patient. Because we cannot yet predict which patients will respond to which antidepressant, most doctors still approach this question by trial and error: they keep changing medications until they find one that works. The kind of extensive pretreatment testing that we do at the Bronx VA and Mount Sinai is still limited to a few major research centers and is still at the experimental stage. As our research teaches us better ways of speeding effective treatment, these tests may become more widespread.

ⓢ

A week after he had completed our testing program, Jack was ready to be admitted to our inpatient unit and start antidepressant treatment. He settled in with an attitude of hopeless acquiescence, as if too despairing even to be skeptical. I got the impression that Emily, nearly at wits' end with the worry and family disruption Jack's illness had caused, would have forced him into the car at knifepoint if necessary to get him to the hospital, and that he came because he hadn't the will to resist her.

Since both his growth hormone and MHPG responses to clonidine were blunted, we started him on desipramine, a medication that makes more norepinephrine available in the synapse. Within a week he was clearly improved: talking more cheerfully to the staff, chatting with the other patients, brightening visibly when his family came to visit. After three weeks he became hypomanic, so we added daily doses of lithium. As he improved, I made arrangements to send him home and treat him in the outpatient clinic.

I also began to see him in psychotherapy. Jack was angry at his mother for being overprotective for selfish reasons ("using me for her own needs") and for giving his younger brother both more real attention and more freedom. "She spent more time talking to me," he once said, "but she actually *listened* to him." He was angry at his father for dying and for the long illness that led up to his death. Jack felt he would have had more confidence if his mother had given him more leeway to develop and assert himself, and if his father had maintained a stronger presence to loosen her suffocating embrace. He was later able to see how his dependence on his mother conflicted with his resentment of her. These conflicts affected his relations with his wife and even with me in treatment; but with continued psychotherapy and antidepressant treatment, he slowly grew more comfortable with his own internal contradictions and thus more self-confident. After his release and a few weeks' rest at home, he returned to work—if not quite triumphantly, at least with more of his old spark than his colleagues had seen for many months. A year later we both agreed that his recovery seemed complete, and he stopped taking the medication.

Jack kept coming in as a recovered patient. He attended group therapy sessions and participated in research as part of our cohort of remitted depressed patients. Even though he was in fine health, he still presented abnormal responses to our pharmacologic challenges, characteristic of people with depression. These blunted responses do not represent the state of being depressed but rather are long-term properties of the brain's emotional centers that confer a vulnerability to depression. It was this kind of finding, in fact, that led us to the dysregulation hypothesis in the first place—that a persistent disturbance at a regulatory site may underlie the pathogenesis of depression. Whatever the keys to depression ultimately turn out to be—perhaps altered regulation of the receptors themselves, or maybe mistranslation within the nerve cells of the signals that affect information transmission, or even the expression of certain genes—they leave clues in the form of abnormalities farther downstream. It is up to us researchers to find ways to detect these abnormalities and puzzle out what they mean.

I have never managed to lose sight of how hazardous this enterprise is. If you consider the common scientific view of the world as a hierarchy ranging from simple systems to complex ones—physics at the simplest level, moving up through chemistry, biology, cognition and behavior, society and ecology, and finally such extremely complex systems as our entire planet considered as a living unit—you can see that the effort to link biochemistry to behavior bridges two widely separated levels of the hierarchy. Many people argue that attempts like this are pointless: that each level obeys its own laws and no level can be understood completely in terms of the laws of the levels below it. You cannot hope to explain evolution, for instance, solely by applying the laws of physics. The behavioral sciences seem especially prone to this kind of criticism, since their history is littered with dead theories that tried to explain complex events through oversimplification.

Still, every so often we scientists are lucky enough to get a little encouragement along the way, some bit of reassurance that our search is not quite hopeless and that some connections can in fact be understood. We treasure these little epiphanies. Jack provided me with one. He did it by demonstrating, quite by accident, an amazing confluence of two well-known ideas in psychology: the concept of schemas and the phenomenon of state-dependent learning. Let me digress a bit to explain what these are.

There is a complicated relationship between our state of feeling, our experience of ourselves, and our representation of the world. One way to think about these relationships is to say that we process different experiences in terms of different schemas. Each schema consists of a representation of ourselves and of other people and events, as well as an emotional coloring to the whole memory. If the experience is falling in love, the schema may include a self who is treasured and powerful, while the immediate surroundings and especially the beloved are seen as sources of pleasure that we wish to visit again and again. The experience of failing an exam may be accompanied by a re-emergence of low self-confidence resonating with other personal failures, along with a view of our teacher and those who passed the exam as objects of envy or resentment. The affective coloring is disappointment and anger. You can grasp the idea of a schema by revisiting the scene of some important period of your life: as soon as you set foot in the place and breathe the air, you'll probably find yourself having feelings, thoughts, and memories you thought you'd forgotten. (In fact, the purpose of college reunions is precisely to induce this state in alumni.) Our self-image, feelings about the world, and narrative memories all serve as contexts for one another; each is an aspect of the organization of our memory of the other two. The bundling together makes the schema.

We have schemas covering all kinds of large and small experiences—not just places but also the people we know, our hobbies, driving a car, eating an ice-cream cone, the phrase "Go ahead, make my day," and anything else we can name. Each carries its own network of remembered feelings, self-image, and narrative memories. These in turn intersect, overlap, and connect with all the others. The product of all these schemas contributes ultimately to our sense of who we are.

State-dependent learning is a psychological event that has been repeatedly demonstrated in animals. Representations learned in a specific state of the central nervous system are more easily elicited when the animal is again in the same state. When rats learn a maze after being dosed with amphetamine, for example, they will not navigate through it as well when the amphetamine wears off. But when the amphetamine is readministered, they run easily through the maze. This effect has nothing to do with increased alertness due to the amphetamine: other drugs have precisely the same effect, and amphetamine does not help rats that learned the maze when not drugged. An animal that learns a task in a specific drug-induced state recalls the task better in the same state.

State-dependent learning may occur in humans as well. Some studies have shown that college-student volunteers, when asked to remember a face while in a sad or apprehensive mood, recall the face better when the mood is reinduced (for example, after they have watched a sad movie). Many people have had similar experiences. For instance, a person met at a cocktail party is easier to recognize at another cocktail party. If we meet the same person in a different environment—such as a business meeting—we may find them only vaguely familiar or even be embarrassed to learn that we didn't recognize them at all.

Two years after his hospital stay, Jack continued to thrive. His antidepressant medication had made his moods steadier and more consistent, an effect that seemed to last even after we discontinued the treatment, and the insights he gained from psychotherapy gave him more depth than he had had before. His firm made him a partner. He grew attentive to his whole family and took special pleasure in his new relationship with Donald. At the weekly group therapy sessions, I often marveled at the transformation that had occurred since I first saw him: he was confident, articulate, and kind to others in a way that showed abundant self-esteem. But we both knew he carried a vulnerability.

Even after a person has recovered from an acute episode, the experience of being depressed is extremely demoralizing. Most people who go through it never forget the way they felt and the things they thought about themselves. Severe or frequent episodes color a person's entire life. Someone who is depressed much of the time may develop a negative self-image in which she continually anticipates failure and discouragement. Even if her mood brightens, her feelings about herself are so ingrained that she enters any situation expecting the worst, or doesn't enter it at all. Pessimism becomes a self-fulfilling prophecy, worsening her mood and reinforcing her negative self-image—a vicious cycle.

Others, more fortunate, recover fully—usually those who have had long periods of health without a depressed mood, or who had better developmental histories before their depressive episodes began and are therefore able to maintain an optimistic view of life between episodes. But even in these people, the memories and the possibility of a relapse remain.

Two years after his hospital stay, Jack's internist changed his blood pressure medication. Even though I was told of this change (I keep abreast of all medical treatments my patients receive, especially any changes in drug therapy), I was unprepared for what ensued to unfold with such unmistakable clarity. Jack began saying things he hadn't said for years.

Depression carries its own corrosive schema—for each sufferer, a specific set of feelings about the world and oneself, and characteristic memories. One by one, Jack's depressive worries and complaints returned. Emily had no time for him any more; Donald, now a delightfully madcap four-year-old, had grown uncontrollable and troublesome; his partners in the law firm no longer had confidence in him. He fretted that he had lost his edge as a litigator and felt the new associates were trying to avoid working with him. Susan reappeared as a theme in our discussions, as did his bout of anger at his dying father. Then it emerged that he was having trouble sleeping and was once again pacing in his study each night, torturing himself over past mistakes, and that he'd let his garden go to seed. We had to readmit him to the hospital for a short stay, and needless to say his doctor stopped the new medication.

I think this was a case of state-dependent learning in humans. By changing a single neurochemical system—the norepinephrine system—the new drug brought back with full force the entire depressive schema that Jack had successfully kept at bay for two years. The disruption of a chemical state perfectly replicated the old disruption of his affective state. I have never seen a more compelling demonstration that depression is, at bottom, a physical disease.

CHAPTER THREE

THE DRAMATIC CLUSTER

She fights because thereafter she is better able to weep. He fights because thereafter he is all the more strongly aroused.

— ELIAS CANETTI

I FIRST MET NANCY IN HER ROOM at Mount Sinai Hospital, where she'd been admitted as an emergency patient the night before. She made a striking, almost glamorous impression: a thin, dark-haired young woman whose exceptional paleness was enhanced by the greenish cast of light that comes into the patient rooms overlooking Central Park on rainy days. She'd changed out of her hospital-issue nightgown into one of her own, and put on rouge, lipstick, mascara, and eye shadow. But her elaborate makeup did not hide the extraordinary weariness around her eyes (referring to those eyes, a psychiatric resident who worked with Nancy later described her as "twenty-eight going on sixty-two"), and her perfectly polished fingernails made a jarring contrast with the bandages on her wrists and the IV tube taped to one forearm. Nancy's attention to her appearance put me on guard. Was this a way of coping with what had happened, a way of denying it, simply a way of passing the time in the hospital, or something else?

When I asked her how she had come to be there, she cooperatively described what she had done and felt over the past few weeks. "I could feel it coming on just like before," she said: a familiar yet still terrifying feeling of being dead inside. She had felt like a circuit slowly becoming overloaded, until the only way she could shut out the pain was to disconnect. First there had been the brush-off by Jerry, her most recent boyfriend. He worked for the same firm as Nancy, was a bit younger, and had a *savoir faire* that she found very charming. "He also drinks like a fish, flirts constantly, and loses interest after two months," she added. "Everybody in the office warned me about him. I don't know why I thought he'd be any different with me, but I did. He was such a gentleman at first, so attentive . . . he made me feel safe and valuable, like I was a rare orchid."

This ended quickly. Jerry grew more and more distant and critical of her, Nancy became angry and demanding, and several of their dates ended in fights. They would always forgive each other after a day or so, however, and mark their reconciliation with a session of blissful lovemaking. Then, after one especially bad fight, they didn't make up. "We were at a party somewhere in New Jersey, and Jerry spent the whole evening carrying on with my friend Suzy. Finally I threw my plate on the floor and stalked off. I took a train home that night. I thought it was just another of our fights, you know? And that we'd make up. But after Jerry didn't call for a week, I called him. He said he didn't want to see me anymore; I was 'jerking his chain too much' and he 'needed his own space.'

"I was shocked. I spent a whole weekend doing nothing but crying. I blamed myself for the whole fiasco. Why did I have to make such a scene? Why do I only feel better after some kind of blowup? Why do I constantly feel betrayed by the men I'm attracted to?"

The next week Nancy's therapist began their session by announcing he would soon take a month's vacation. "Sometimes he's so useless. I'm going through a crisis and he's thinking about Aruba. He always leaves town just when I need him the most. I really felt like he did it deliberately, to punish me for blowing another relationship or maybe just to show how much I needed him." It was just such incidents, she said, that made her unwilling to trust him completely. Sometimes he was so sympathetic and understanding that it was hard to leave his office when the session ended; at other times, like her last visit, he seemed so critical and uncaring that he made her furious. It was hard to remember that she had felt so differently only a week earlier.

After a couple of agonizing weeks during which she called in sick at work several times "just because I couldn't face going," Nancy continued, "I told myself I had to face facts: I was totally alone and abandoned." Jerry had been gone a month; her therapist was unavailable, having given her, in case of emergency, the number of "some stranger" whom she had no intention of calling. "At first, I thought the tension and futility would drive me up a wall. Then I started to feel disconnected, like I was just operating my body the way you would drive a car—it wasn't really part of me anymore." Returning home from work one day, she made herself a large gin and tonic and used it to wash down a Valium. The tension in her stomach began to ease a bit and it seemed like a good idea to go to a popular new singles' bar that had opened a few blocks uptown. She ran into Rick, an old college friend. Though they had never dated, they had belonged to the same crowd and she found him surprisingly warm and reassuring. They had several drinks together, and then she invited him back to her apartment.

When she heard Rick leave the next morning, she couldn't recall what had happened. A couple of hours later, filled with rage and self-loathing, she got out of bed. It had been almost two years since she had last cut herself, and she had vowed never to do it again. She took a bottle of white wine out of her refrigerator and broke it against the side of the kitchen sink. Watching the last of it bubble down the drain, she began to feel calmer. As she drew a piece of glass along her wrists, a slight tinge of pleasure overtook the more familiar anesthesia.

"I awoke in this bed and realized I was back in the hospital. It's like a recurring nightmare."

Later, after she agreed to be part of a study I was starting up and had participated in several group therapy sessions, it emerged that Nancy's entire life was an emotional roller coaster. "I've always been like this: high-spirited, sensitive, either really up or really down—a hysterical female." She had been very close with her father, an alcoholic, but when she turned eleven their relationship became disturbingly sexualized. To an outsider, perhaps, some of his behavior could be explained away as the mistakes of an affectionate but bumbling dad, doing his best to cope with an overly sensitive teenager: remarks about her clothes or developing body that were a little too personal, fatherly hugs that were a little too intimate and went on a little too long, forcing her to push him away. "A few times he came into the bathroom while I was taking a bath, saying he was 'looking for his razor' or some crap like that. When I screamed, he'd say, 'Don't be silly, I used to change your diapers.' It was always worse when he'd been drinking."

Only twice had he done something undeniably abusive. Both times, coming home at night and finding her alone in the kitchen, he'd tried to fondle and kiss her. He was falling-down drunk and she escaped him easily. "I'm sure he'd have had me right there on the kitchen floor if I'd let him." Nancy had never forgiven her mother for refusing to intervene. "She said he was drunk and didn't know what he was doing. And as for the rest of it, she denied everything. She said I was getting hysterical and exaggerating, like always. And what I'm most angry about is that I thought, she's right. Here I have this wonderful father and I'm such a little bitch I can't even forgive him if he crosses the line once in a while."

She and her mother fought often. Nancy perceived her as distant, unloving, and hypercritical, and many of Nancy's comments in therapy, such as that her mother sometimes spent an entire day without dressing or leaving the house, made me think the woman may have been subject to depression. Much of Nancy's anger at her father wound up being directed at her mother—an easier and less dangerous target. "Despite everything, I always felt that Daddy was the one who really loved me. He was the one I could talk to. We were *simpático*, you know?"

〽

There are some clear differences between Jack's illness and Nancy's, the most obvious of which is that Jack's can be considered an isolated event in an otherwise generally healthy life. He maintains stable attachments, has a satisfactory career, and has ways of relating to the world that are largely separate from his rare bouts of depression. Nancy's problems, on the other hand, reflect a long-term difficulty with her relationships and her capacity to modulate her self-esteem. It is hard for her to keep feeling good about herself because she is so completely dependent on the comings and goings of important people in her life. She also has a tendency to take drastic measures in response to frustration—the most agonizing frustration of all being real or threatened abandonment by others. After a separation, Nancy feels rage toward both herself and the person who has left her. This may be directed outward, as an angry outburst, or inward, as a suicide attempt or other self-mutilation.

People like Nancy are often considered "difficult." They are flagrantly moody. They can be manipulative as well: in their desperate efforts to control the people around them, they often neglect the feelings of others, even those on whom their own sense of well-being so vitally depends. They thus frequently drive away the very people they need most. Nancy's adult life was a junkyard of short affairs, most of which had ended with her in a jealous rage. Her three suicide attempts all came after traumatic breakups.

At the same time, such people seldom understand why life is so hard for them or why they constantly feel victimized. Their problems are part and parcel of their characteristic ways of coping with the world around them. Although personality clearly plays a huge role in determining individual success and happiness, most people regard it as a given and seldom think about why one person's personality differs from another's. But when a person's ways of coping with the world are clearly maladaptive and cause chronic distress to herself or those around her, we are justified in calling that personality "disordered" and in asking what the causes are, and what can be done.

Why do unstable personalities develop? What does it mean when we say that the causes are partly inborn and partly environmental? It is often assumed that personality is entirely a product of deeply ingrained habits learned over a lifetime. For many years, personality disturbances were thought to be the result of faulty parenting—with the implicit assumption that if parenting had been adequate, the personality disorder would not have developed. Traditional psychoanalysts emphasized early childhood relationships, especially the early awakenings of sexual feelings, while more behaviorally oriented psychologists focused on repeated reward for maladaptive behaviors. But again, as with mood disorders, we are beginning to recognize the role of genetic factors in personality.

I have already mentioned the study by Tellegen and Bouchard of the University of Minnesota, in which researchers gave a questionnaire to more than two hundred sets of identical twins raised apart and more than one hundred sets of fraternal twins, measuring personality traits along three dimensions, which they labeled positive emotionality, negative emotionality, and constraint. (Note that positive and negative emotionality are not simply opposites but at right angles to each other on the three-dimensional grid. It is possible to have a high score in both areas.) A shared family environment significantly affected only positive emotionality—pleasurable engagement with one's environment—and especially a subset of it labeled social closeness (closeness to other people). For every other trait the researchers addressed, the family environment's contribution was negligible.

Oskar Stohr and Jack Yufe, two of the study participants, are a striking example of identical twins reared apart. Jack was raised as a Jew by his adopted father in Trinidad, while Oskar was raised as a Catholic in Germany. Despite growing up in different cultures, they dressed similarly, had similar grooming habits, grew similar mustaches, wore similar glasses, and even shared a quick temper and similar senses of humor (both found it funny to surprise people by sneezing in elevators). They were a surprising reminder of the famous Charles Addams cartoon in which two identical twins separated at birth meet accidentally in a patent attorney's office; on their laps are identical inventions. The existence of pairs like Stohr and Yufe calls into question simplistic environmental theories; they are much more compatible with models that emphasize how genetic factors may influence the perception and internalization of experiences. In another study, Robert Plomin compared temperament, behavioral problems, and cognitive processes of adopted children with those of both their natural and adoptive mothers. His results, too, suggest that traits that appear to be environmentally influenced may in fact be genetically mediated.

Other studies suggest that personality is remarkably constant over a lifetime. Paul Costa and Robert McCrae of the National Institute of Aging, in Baltimore, interviewed a group of individuals at age twenty-five and again at sixty-five, looking for changes in such traits as emotional volatility, agreeableness, anxiety levels, and novelty seeking. In forty years these basic elements of personality changed little. Jerome Kagan and his colleagues at Harvard have found that shyness and inhibition may be detected in early infancy and seem to last throughout childhood. These two studies, taken together, hint at a continuity of temperament from infancy to old age. The person who wished to test this proposition with a single group of subjects would be in the position of the ancient Japanese makers of exquisite lacquered boxes that took many decades to finish: he or she could only start the project and trust that later generations would find the effort worth continuing.

The relationship between genes and environment in personality development can be compared to the formation of a crystal. You can grow crystals, for instance table salt, in a glass by dissolving a great deal of salt in water and then adding small formed crystals of salt. These provide "seeds" around which other salt molecules can come out of solution and add to the original crystals. The different shapes these growing aggregates of crystals can form are practically infinite, and each is unique—yet their structure is constrained by certain rules. Because sodium chloride molecules bond to each other at right angles, they form cubic structures. Any crystal made from pure table salt will be an assortment of cubic structures stacked in various ways. Table salt will not form needles or flat plates or tetrahedra or hexagons. You need different molecules for those shapes. Water ice, which forms six-pointed snowflakes, will not form cubes (unless constrained by the tray in your freezer). Crystals also have characteristic cleavage planes: those formed from the same substance have the same weaknesses and will break in similar patterns.

How does this analogy relate to personality development? All behavior is ultimately mediated by brain chemical systems. In newborns, who by definition have not had much time to learn behaviors from their environment, differences in brain chemistry probably account for much of the difference we can see in temperament. Some babies draw back from new stimuli, while others are more active and responsive to cues. Some are irritable and fussy; others are more placid. There is now experimental evidence to support what any experienced maternity-ward nurse will tell you: much of this variation is innate.

The habits people develop depend not only on what happens to them but also on what they bring to their experiences. A baby's temperamental style influences how it will experience its mother, father, siblings, and others, as well as how they will react to it. One who is not easily soothed will give his parents a hard time, making them feel frustrated, angry at the child, and perhaps guilty at their own failure to keep him happy. As he grows older, he may continue to feel distress more deeply than other children. He may have temper tantrums that do not let up easily and continue to have them long past the age when tantrums are considered developmentally normal. The adults around him, desperate to meet his difficult-to-comprehend needs and hoping to calm him by indulging his wishes, may unintentionally train him that tantrums are a legitimate way to get what he wants. Over time, this child may adopt his parents' view of him as his own: he will internalize an image of himself as "angry and needy." His image of his parents, on the other hand, will be colored by his frequent bouts of distress, when he sees them as the malevolent or uncaring people who withhold what he wants. His relationship with them may come to center around conflict and be charged with negative feelings.

Other children may be anxious. They resist separation, are frightened of being alone at night, and have difficulty adjusting to being in school without a parent nearby. They cling to their mothers in situations where other children are off happily exploring new surroundings, and they have trouble relating to playmates. Still other children have a hard time making sense of the varied sights, sounds, and smells of their world. They may find paying attention in school difficult and their peers confusing and uncontrollable.

The ways in which parents deal with a child's temperamental style depend on their own personalities. To a large extent, the successful development of a personality depends on a good fit between parents and child, where the parents enable the child to develop her strengths and minimize her vulnerabilities. When this process goes awry, it is because even unusually empathetic parents could not help the child compensate for her inborn weaknesses, or because the parents' own problems left them unable to adequately address the child's needs. Anxious parents who tend to deny their own anger, for example, may find an active, aggressive child threatening. The child, in turn, may come to see himself as threatening or destructive. With a fearful child, the same anxious parents might reinforce in the child their own apprehensions about the world. Parents whose behavior varies widely from one day to the next will naturally be erratic in responding to their child, making it hard for the child to know how to behave and ultimately hindering his development of a secure sense of himself.

Nancy's childhood environment worked against her chances of developing a healthy personality. Her exhausted mother, withdrawn and often depressed, was able neither to satisfy Nancy's incessant demands for attention nor to provide the steady reassurance that would have been required to bolster Nancy's fragile self-esteem. She could not supply the brake Nancy needed for her impulsive, frequently outrageous behavior, because these outbursts were often necessary just to get her mother's attention. Her father, though affectionate, was hardly a steady figure either: often absent, often drunk, sometimes abusive or irrationally angry when he was present. He, like Nancy, had trouble controlling his impulses, and he allowed his sexual feelings toward his daughter an unhealthy expression. The final irony was that, when he began his abuse, she had (and knew she had) by then developed the kind of personality that to many people almost demands disbelief: histrionic, overemotional, prone to exaggeration. Her father found pleasure in and reinforced her dramatic, seductive style and even felt encouraged in his transgressions. For Nancy's part, stopping the abuse would have jeopardized one of the only, albeit unreliable, sources of security in her life.

Nancy's adult life clearly reflects her conflicted feelings toward her father. By the time she was grown, love, sexuality, insecurity, and rage were inseparable elements of the only kind of intimate relationship she knew how to have.

Treatment for people like Nancy may involve medications that stabilize mood and dampen impulsivity if the symptoms are severe enough (which, given her history of suicide attempts, I felt they certainly were). But in contrast to Jack, Nancy's depressions are deeply ingrained in her character. Her impulsivity, self-defeating attachments, and rages are very much who she is. Although these traits may have partly grown out of her underlying neurochemistry, they are now woven into a larger system of self-images, memories, wishes, and fantasies. In short, they have acquired meaning. Furthermore, her impulsive acts, particularly her self-destructive episodes, have a function—they soothe her. It would take Nancy a long time to be able to understand and change these patterns of behavior and to substitute more adaptive responses. Thus one difference between depression and personality disorders is the relative autonomy of the episode of depression from the overall personality. The less autonomous the episode, the more essential it is that the patient receive other forms of treatment besides medication.

With psychotherapy, Nancy may learn to compensate for her vulnerabilities, to recognize that not every frustration is a crisis, and to reflect and plan how she will respond. Coping strategies such as temper tantrums and manipulative behavior, which in Nancy's childhood may have seemed like the only way she could survive, can be replaced by more mature ways of handling frustration. The old strategies may be based on unconscious beliefs such as, "If I take charge of my life, I'll be abandoned and feel overwhelmed." The helpless feeling of victimization, and the many issues that arise from it, play an important role in the psychotherapy of people like Nancy. By understanding her vulnerabilities, her beliefs about herself, and the maladaptive coping strategies she has carried over from childhood, someone like Nancy can take more responsibility for her own behavior, as well as grow more wary about getting into situations that will cause her misery later. Treatment for such people has to address both the biological and psychosocial aspects of their problems.

᠙

Nancy's illness belongs to a subset of personality disorders defined in the *Diagnostic and Statistical Manual* (*DSM-IV* in its latest edition) as the "dramatic cluster," after the theatrical behavior people with these syndromes exhibit. She is unusual in that she actually sought and cooperated with therapy; many people with personality disorders, even severe ones, see nothing wrong with their behavior and refuse treatment. The dramatic cluster comprises four distinct (but often overlapping) entities: histrionic, narcissistic, antisocial, and borderline personality disorders.

HISTRIONIC PERSONALITY DISORDER. Although people with histrionic traits are highly excitable, the emotions they express are often stereotyped or greatly embellished, so that the histrionic person may seem to lack depth. In the hospitals where I work, for instance, a woman may come to the emergency room complaining of severe abdominal pain. Although X-rays are negative and she has no fever, she is crying and saying the pain is so bad she can't stand it. It turns out she has just broken up with her boyfriend. After he visits her in the hospital and they make up, her pain miraculously disappears; the next morning, preparing to leave, she is full of praise for the handsome doctors and how much they helped her. She flirts with every male who enters the room. We never see her again.

This combination of rapidly shifting and exaggerated emotions leads many people to dismiss the histrionic person as someone not to be taken seriously. But people with these traits experience these dramatic presentations of their emotions as authentic, even if outsiders do not. The more muted ranges of feeling may not be available to them.

Persons with histrionic personalities characteristically seek approval from others, particularly authority figures such as doctors and teachers, and sometimes become sulky or demanding when their needs for approval are not met. Their self-esteem depends on a steady stream of positive feedback. To get the attention they need, they often flaunt their sexuality, wearing provocative outfits, flirting in the most inappropriate situations, going to great lengths to maintain their looks, and growing profoundly distraught at what they perceive to be imperfections in their appearance. This behavior is often appealing at first, but when it becomes overly provocative, it puts people off.

Histrionic people are often seen as shamelessly self-centered, as they put their needs and wishes ahead of the concerns of others. They are easily frustrated and show little tolerance for any delay in getting what they want. But they often have little sense that others see them as insensitive. They tend to rationalize their self-serving behavior, seeing themselves as helpless victims of the demands others place on them. Their self-centeredness and inconsistency prevent their many superficial love affairs from developing into deeper, more enduring relationships, yet they experience even slight criticism as a wholesale rejection.

The possibility of losing their romantic partner often leads to frantic efforts to hold on, which may appear manipulative or controlling.

Like the rest of the dramatic cluster, a histrionic personality often includes a hunger for novelty. New hobbies and relationships are taken up with boundless enthusiasm, then quickly abandoned. A histrionic man may decide to take up skiing, buy a complete set of new and fancy equipment, and then get out on the slopes only twice before switching to some other, trendier hobby. These people are easily influenced by fashion and gravitate toward seductive figures who project an authoritative knowledge of the "right way" to act. They may be exceptionally gullible. Their appraisals of situations are intuitive rather than analytic and are reflected in an ostentatious speaking style that lacks specifics. A histrionic woman, if asked about her new boyfriend, is likely to exclaim "he's fabulous" but be unable to provide any clear details to support this global assertion. In fact, an effort to glean more precise information may be perceived as an attack and be tearfully rebuffed. Even in less personal areas, histrionic people may develop strong convictions without being able to describe what led up to them; it seems hard for them to know when they should make tentative judgments and when to be decisive. Their firm insistence on momentary convictions belies a deep-seated insecurity about their own intellectual or evaluative powers.

For histrionic individuals, the body and its sensations are a sensitive medium through which to communicate psychic pain. They complain of headaches, dizziness, and other aches that often—but don't always—lack physical foundation. In Freud's time, people with this disorder commonly developed what he called "hysterical conversion" reactions: parts of their bodies would become numb or paralyzed, with no apparent neurological cause. They were not consciously faking. Freud reasoned that these symptoms were related to an underlying psychic trauma that, when resolved, would bring about their reversal. In investigating the unconscious processes that led to these symptoms, he and his followers focused on forbidden sexual wishes. For instance, a young woman whose hand accidentally brushed against her fiancé's genital might forget the incident, but the next morning might find that hand numb from the wrist down.

The histrionic person's distress may also find expression in feelings of unreality. They may have the experience that their body no longer exists (which is called depersonalization) or that the world is dreamlike and unreal ("derealization"), as if a fog had rolled in and left them cut off from their surroundings. These symptoms embody the sense of helplessness these people have in confronting their world and cut them off from immediate sources of pain. For instance, I once was asked to consult on a patient who was in a troubled marriage with an abusive man. She frequently complained of headache and weakness while denying her husband's behavior. When doctors could find no medical basis for her complaints, she was referred to a counselor who began to ask her about her marital situation. Unable to deny the actual facts of her marriage any longer, the woman began to feel that her body was evaporating. Her symptoms waned only after she began to come to terms with reality and make efforts to cope with her situation.

NARCISSISTIC PERSONALITY DISORDER. The hallmarks of narcissistic personality disorder are the belief that one is special and the expectation of being treated accordingly. This grandiose sense of self contrasts sharply with the narcissist's sensitivity to criticism and constant need to replenish his feeling of self-worth through the admiration of others. Narcissists frequently boast of their talents and achievements. They seldom understand the bad impression this creates because they have difficulty identifying with others. Other people largely function as mirrors whose job is to reflect back an unblemished image of the narcissist's projected glory. But this grandiosity is a house of cards, easily toppled by a snort of derision or a rebuff from the opposite sex. In their exhibitionism, need for attention, and lack of concern for others, people with narcissistic personality disorder resemble those with histrionic personality disorder. But the latter is marked more by dramatic expressiveness and is more often diagnosed in women; the core of narcissistic personality disorder is the inflated self-image requiring constant refueling from the approbation of others, and it is more often seen in men. It may be that both disorders arise from similar underlying causes but, due to a combination of biological, psychological, and cultural factors, are expressed differently in the different sexes.

Everything the narcissistic person experiences is evaluated according to whether it increases his sense of importance. He insists that people know he gets the best, whether it be investment counseling or pizza. A narcissist may spend unreasonable sums of money on an eye-catching car or massive stereo components, not because he has any appreciation for music or fine machinery but because being seen with them makes him feel important. While most people strive for success and its trappings, narcissists are set apart by their total absorption with image. At the same time, they anticipate that others will appreciate their specialness without their having ever to prove themselves, and they become angry and despondent when placed in situations that do not support this hope. Constantly preoccupied with shoring up their precarious self-esteem, narcissists are forever hungry for praise and become enraged when others seem scornful of their great gifts. Their fury is fueled by a powerful sense of humiliation and shame, a fear that perhaps they are really not so special as all that and that others see through their pretense. Often this sense of shame is disguised by an air of calculated indifference.

When narcissistic people seek psychiatric help, it is often because they cannot develop satisfying relationships. They tend to choose romantic partners for their superficial traits. Sometimes they seek to make up for their own perceived shortcomings: a short, plain-looking journalist, for instance, may marry a tall, strikingly beautiful model, or a wealthy real-estate magnate from a poor background may look for a wife from "old money." In other instances, a narcissistic person may marry someone who mirrors his special attributes—such as the body builder who marries a cover girl or the aristocrat who chooses a spouse based on lineage. These often joyless and short-lived unions present a facade to the world, a mutual admiration society, that masks the absence of any deeply shared values, respect, or intimacy between the partners.

Because the narcissist is so completely absorbed in protecting his self-esteem, he never develops the capacity to imagine himself in the place of another. Lacking this crucial empathy, narcissists can be ruthlessly exploitative. They are often astute at finding and taking advantage of other people's weaknesses. For instance, an artist may wish to bring his attractive and articulate wife to a gallery opening, even though she is recovering from the death of a close friend and is in no mood to go anyplace, because several important art-world figures will be there and he wants to use her to impress them. He may make her feel guilty, telling her she doesn't support his career, and ultimately bully her into going. He feels little compassion for what she is going through, instead rationalizing that he is specially talented but undervalued, so he needs to maximize every opportunity to increase his exposure. Narcissists are consumed with envy of people they see as (always undeservedly) more successful than they are. This resentment poisons their relationships with coworkers and even social acquaintances.

Psychiatrists consider a certain level of narcissism a good thing, even necessary—you have to love yourself, in a healthy way, to have any success at work or in relationships. To those who feel about others' triumphs the way an oyster feels about a grain of sand in its shell, even a strong dose of arrogant self-regard may ultimately help, not hinder, their success and happiness. (Being in good mental health does not imply that someone is admirable or even terribly likable.) At what point, then, does narcissism become pathological? Only when it is based on an unrealistic or exaggerated sense of one's importance and carries an oversensitivity to the perceptions of others, who then become serious threats to one's emotional balance. Often there is some real talent or gift around which the narcissistic self-image crystallizes; the narcissist may build his entire sense of self-worth around this ability, often mirroring the desires of one or both parents. For instance, a mother who wanted to be a singer may cultivate her daughter's vocal skills, encouraging a feeling of specialness around that talent but never acknowledging the whole range of the girl's personality, including her desires and fears. The daughter, if talented, may go on to become a professional vocalist, but will suffer the scars of never having been fully acknowledged as a person by her mother. Narcissists with outstanding talent or the good luck to become celebrities may find more opportunity to realize their fantasies. But even in these cases, no amount of success or recognition satisfies a narcissistic personality for long, and they end up feeling empty and desolate.

Because they are so vulnerable to deflation of their self-esteem, narcissistic individuals may become dejected or even depressed. They seldom develop the classic features of the major depressive disorders, instead becoming preoccupied, dejected, and demoralized. Chronic depressive symptoms often develop with age, as the narcissistic person becomes aware of his limitations and failure to achieve the bright fantasies of his youth. Narcissists may find old age, with its loss of power and looks, particularly stressful, and they sometimes cannot shift their sources of satisfaction to developing and appreciating the successes of offspring, apprentices, students, or younger coworkers.

ANTISOCIAL PERSONALITY DISORDER. The defining feature of antisocial personality disorder is a lifelong tendency to commit crimes and other acts forbidden by society. These behaviors often begin in childhood, and the current diagnostic criteria require a history of disordered behavior beginning before age fifteen. Though not synonymous with criminal behavior, antisocial personality may be diagnosed in up to 75 percent of the prison population.

In childhood, a persistent pattern of antisocial behavior may be diagnosed as "conduct disorder." Children with conduct disorder persistently violate the rights of others or disregard age-appropriate social norms and rules. They start fights, occasionally using weapons, and are often gratuitously cruel to other children, especially those who are social outcasts—mocking them mercilessly, tripping them, or sticking gum in their hair. They sometimes destroy the property of others and may rip the cover off a classmate's book or gleefully shred the papers of a successful student. As they get older, they become sexually aggressive or coercive. They may run away from home, stay out all night in defiance of their parents' orders, or engage in fire setting, vandalism, theft, and mugging.

This pattern usually continues into adulthood. The antisocial person is not able to maintain a responsible position in society and frequently stays unemployed for months at a stretch. Even when he gets a job, he frequently fails to show up or may quit on a moment's impulse with no realistic future plans. Antisocial persons do not follow through on their financial obligations and often default on debts or fail to make child support payments. To cover up their past failures and irresponsibility, they move frequently and may disguise their identities.

Like the conduct-disordered child, antisocial adults may have a pattern of recklessness and aggression, getting into frequent fights, assaulting people, sometimes beating a spouse or child. They take little care of their own or other people's safety and may drive while intoxicated or speed recklessly with family members in the car. They are usually impulsive in a variety of spheres, living largely for the moment, learning little from their mistakes, and seldom anticipating the consequences of their behavior. This impulsivity and irresponsibility also show up in an inability to form long-term relationships. While an antisocial person may be married for a time and even have children, they are rarely faithful. Most never have a serious relationship, drifting from one casual romance to another. They often exploit those they are involved with. They make unreliable parents, with consequences for their children that include poverty, illness, malnutrition, and delinquency. They may leave toddlers alone in the house, sometimes for days—in extreme cases the child is entirely dependent on neighbors or relatives. Money that could be spent on household needs goes instead to liquor, gambling, or extramarital affairs. Like narcissists, antisocial people lack empathy and use others for their own ends. Like people with borderline and histrionic personality disorders, they need constant novelty and have difficulty controlling their aggressive impulses.

Antisocial disorder is not always expressed violently. It also takes the form of deception. Antisocial people seem less to experience emotion than simulate it, as an actor would. They make gifted swindlers, engaging in elaborate confidence schemes or starting romantic relationships with women, sometimes even marrying them, in order to steal from them. The superficial charm characteristic of the classic psychopath seduces others into accepting their grand visions and their fast-talking excuses for questionable behavior. Many are extremely glib; they lie earnestly, with an open-faced innocence that deceives victims, police, and therapists alike. The classic work on this disorder, written by Hervey Cleckley and published in 1938, reflects its deceptive character in its title, *The Mask of Sanity.*

It is as if the antisocial person has never learned to feel bad when he has injured another person or broken a societal rule. Although he can objectively perceive the difference between right and wrong, he lacks any internalized standard of behavior. The part of the mind that prohibits destructive behavior and signals an alarm when those prohibitions threaten to be violated is, of course, the conscience, and it must be active if adults are to maintain lawful and responsible behavior.

Failure to develop a conscience is one of the hallmarks of the antisocial personality.

BORDERLINE PERSONALITY DISORDER. Borderline personality disorder, whose name comes from the boundary between neurosis and psychosis, may be the prototype of the dramatic personality disorders because it incorporates so many features of the entire dramatic cluster. Borderline individuals live in an unstable world of chaotic relationships, shifting moods, oscillating self-esteem, fragmentary or diffuse identity, and impulsive, erratic behavior. Their turmoil and instability are most evident in their attempts to form intimate relationships, which they seek desperately and intensely, because they are so frightened of being abandoned and left alone with their feelings of emptiness and rage. They are perhaps most comfortable, if they are ever comfortable, at the beginning of a relationship, when they can idealize their partner as a powerful figure who can make them feel "held," providing a sense of security and nurturance. They often feel extreme attraction at this stage, being more involved with their fantasy of their partner than with a realistic or discriminating evaluation of their qualities.

As, inevitably, the partner's limitations become apparent, the person with borderline disorder grows disillusioned. The fall from the pedestal is swift and far: both partner and relationship are seen as worthless, and the borderline person is filled with fury and disappointment at the relationship's failure to provide the contentment and nurturance they need. This oscillation between idealization and contempt, from the romantic glow of a crush to cruel dejection, is a hallmark of borderline disorder. The character played by Glenn Close in *Fatal Attraction* presents a stereotype of this personality. She became intensely attached to a married man with whom she had an affair; then, when he withdrew from the relationship, she first turned her rage inward by cutting her wrists, then wreaked revenge on the man and his family. In all the borderline's relationships, romance, rage, and yearning vie for dominance.

I felt that Nancy's relationship with Jerry, and her recurrent pattern of similarly brief, violent affairs, fit this description: early idealization, swift disillusionment, later contempt—she spoke of Jerry now as someone completely worthless, with no redeeming features whatsoever. This habit of borderline personalities is called splitting. Individuals are seen as either all good and nurturing, or all bad, depriving, and frustrating, and they make quantum leaps from one state to the other without crossing through any middle ground. Important people in the borderline person's life may make this transition frequently. With Jerry, Nancy was always either fighting or head-over-heels in love. Her therapist came in for the same treatment: a benevolent, fatherly figure one week, disdainful, uncaring, and selfish the next. Borderline people attempt to keep these disparate images of the same person separate, to the extent that they find it hard to imagine that they once felt exactly the opposite way about them.

In group sessions Nancy was astonishingly mercurial. She could be cruelly dismissive one moment, hilariously catty the next, in tears the next. It was as if the videotape of her emotions were stuck on fast-forward. This instability, and the unstable self-image that gives rise to it, is the driving force behind the maladaptive traits of borderline personality disorder. Borderline people tend to react impulsively and with wild extremes to events that frustrate, disappoint, or excite them. They have short, volatile tempers and are easily drawn into fights, whether in a domestic squabble or with strangers in a bar. At times they will turn this aggression against themselves in direct self-destructive behavior, such as Nancy's repeated suicide attempts. Wrist cutting is remarkably common in borderline individuals, either as an actual suicide attempt or as a deliberate effort to relieve stress. Many report that the pain breaks through their psychological numbness and gives them a sense of relief.

Aggression is only one of the many impulsive activities borderline personalities exhibit. Others may react to abandonment with shopping sprees, binge eating to the point of vomiting, gambling, drinking, drug abuse, or promiscuous sex. The last four activities, especially, perform the dual roles of buffering these people against failure and satisfying their hunger for novelty and excitement.

Under extreme stress, borderline personalities may suffer psychotic symptoms, though these are both more transient and more closely connected with actual experiences than the hallucinations of schizophrenia. For instance, a person with borderline personality who feels wrathful after a perceived abandonment may read her own anger in the eyes of strangers. Or she may engage in magical thinking, nurturing the idea that if she concentrates hard enough on the boyfriend who left her, he will call and end her distress. Rarely, borderlines may have actual hallucinations—seeing creatures crawling up their arms or faces staring out from the wallpaper—but these usually disappear once the immediate crisis has passed.

§

One of the many striking aspects of the dramatic cluster is how frequently people with these disorders seem to associate with other mentally ill people, with diseases either within or outside this cluster. Some pairings almost seem made for each other, coexisting in a strange counterworld whose peculiar logic parodies sanity. Antisocial personalities, for instance, find each of the other three easy prey because of their vulnerabilities and need for attention; histrionic personalities, with their gullibility and attraction to a strong, self-assured image, are often drawn to narcissists. Narcissists, in turn, find that the overt sexuality of histrionic persons both bolsters their own self-image and makes them attractive ornaments. This tendency, which is part of a larger phenomenon geneticists call assortative mating—the tendency of like to mate with like—leads to situations in which personality disorders affect, to greater or lesser degree, entire extended families and persist undiluted for generations. It is often impossible to tell how long this condition may have continued: every family member in living memory may have been affected. In these instances it is clearly futile to try to show that the transmission of the disease is either all environmental or all biological. The most likely possibility is that environmental effects reinforce an inborn tendency, which in turn influences the choice of partners and the temperament of future generations.

Nancy's family fit this pattern well. Her father had been an alcoholic with antisocial traits. After he lost a succession of sales jobs because of his drinking, he became more aggressive and abusive, both at home and at neighborhood bars, where he would get into fights.

His sister was described as impulsive and subject to eating binges. She died when she drove her car into a tree. Nancy's mother appears to have had a serious depression soon after Nancy was born, as well as a number of milder ones throughout Nancy's childhood. Her brother, Nancy's uncle, unexpectedly committed suicide while away at college. Nancy's grandfather on her mother's side was known to be moody and frequently angry. So she had a family history of impulsivity, especially on her father's side, and affective instability and suicide on her mother's side.

A woman who is chronically depressed, like Nancy's mother, may become attracted to the glib charm of a man with antisocial traits, such as Nancy's father. His alcoholism may encourage her desire to care for him and thus to feel needed, and his abuse may serve to confirm her low self-esteem. Thus their relationship provided precisely the contradictions Nancy's mother needed in order to feel secure: she was at once despised and indispensable. (In this position she would have had neither the necessary self-assurance nor anything to gain by intervening on Nancy's behalf against her father.) Nancy's father, for his part, exploited and manipulated her mother's low self-esteem to keep her bound to him and meet his needs. Nancy, too, seems to have sought out partners who resembled her father, though here the mix was more explosive: her latest boyfriend Jerry's reputation as a callous womanizer constantly after his next conquest, as well as his drinking, suggest (but hardly prove) antisocial traits. And what are we to make of Nancy's comment that she and her father were *simpático*? This seems less a statement of affection than a recognition that they were birds of a feather.

Still, despite inborn and environmental influences being so closely interwoven, certain genetic factors in the dramatic cluster have been shown beyond much doubt. Borderline personality disorder patients frequently have a family history of depression. Antisocial disorder is more common in the blood relatives of criminals who have been adopted than in their adoptive relatives; antisocial disorder and alcohol abuse often coexist in families; histrionic disorder is associated with somatization disorder, the chronic suffering of varied symptoms of physical illness without any recognizable medical cause. Other such correlations undoubtedly remain to be found. (One correlation that probably does not exist is between the dramatic cluster and major psychiatric disorders such as schizophrenia. Even borderline disorder, despite having been called "ambulatory schizophrenia" in the past, is not related to true schizophrenia.) But these broad strokes of the geneticist's brush can take us only so far: they are of little help in differentiating one disorder in the cluster from another, in telling us why men are more frequently diagnosed as antisocial or narcissistic while women are more often seen as histrionic or borderline, or in guiding us toward appropriate treatment. What, then, can a biological approach bring to our understanding of these disorders?

As I pointed out in the last chapter, the "one neurotransmitter–one illness" idea, which looked so attractive in the early days of biological research on depression, is proving unsatisfactory in explaining neurotransmitter abnormalities in psychiatric diseases. We need another approach. One alternative has been to try to correlate specific neurotransmitters not with specific diagnoses but rather with personality traits. This has been one of my long-term interests, both at NIMH and at Mount Sinai, and it was the focus of the study that I was eager to have Nancy join.

❧

The tradition of studying personality traits, as opposed to diseases, in psychiatry again extends back to Hippocrates, whose humoral theory remained the foundation of thought about mental diseases for over two thousand years. The humoral theory specifically relates bodily fluids to character types. In nineteenth-century England, personality differences were attributed to the size or shape of the skull. Early in this century, Shelton classified temperaments according to body types: the mesomorph was active, athletic, and outgoing; the ectomorph frail, introverted, and often eccentric; and the endomorph heavy, slothful, and body-oriented. Kretchmer, a German psychiatrist, proposed a classification of personality types that included the schizotypic, marked by eccentricity and social withdrawal, and the cyclothymic, marked by mood swings and emotional reactivity. All of these schemes have been abandoned or substantially modified, although Kretchmer's models have remained influential.

Sigmund Freud, discussing patients who were "resistant" to the interpretations of classical psychoanalysis due to deeply ingrained characterological problems, wrote in *Analysis Terminable and Interminable* that "each ego is endowed from the first with individual dispositions and trends, though it is true we cannot specify their nature or what determines them." Psychoanalytic theory has never succeeded in defining these foundations of character. The last comprehensive psychoanalytic theory of character, Karl Abraham's scheme of oral, anal, and genital character types based on the maturational phases of the libido, lives on in the popular culture (mainly in the "anal-retentive personality") but is widely regarded in the profession as, in Elizabeth Auchincloss and Robert Michels's phrase, a "brilliant failure." Beyond the absence of a specific theory, however, there is a deeper conceptual problem. As "the individual's habitual modes of bringing into harmony his own inner needs and the demands of the external world" (Moore and Fine, *A Glossary of Psychoanalytic Terms and Concepts*, 1968), character takes in instincts, Freud's "constitutional factors," environmental influences, learned responses, and almost everything else that is a legitimate subject of psychiatric inquiry: critics complain that the term is so broad as to be meaningless. E. G. Glover, in a 1966 paper called "Metapsychology or Metaphysics," wrote, "No term that involves such a complicated interaction of factors and phases of development can lay claim to the status of a basic mental concept." Character has no clear relationship to health or disease but is common to both. One author, writing in 1982, counted 810 different personality types "identified" by one psychiatrist or another. Given these problems with "character" as a concept, can anything meaningful be said about a character "trait"?

One approach to this dilemma is to turn it around and ask whether we can understand what personality is before we know what it's made of. We can start by trying to identify dimensions of personality that are likely to have underlying biological bases. The purpose of doing this is not to oppose the schemes that emphasize developmental influences but rather to complement them. Until we know what aspects of personality are innate, we will have a very hard time understanding (or even rigorously identifying) environmental influences on personality, because their effects will be obscured by their interaction with such a wide variety of innate temperamental styles. Sorting out the discrete aspects of personality and where they come from may be a prerequisite to any grasp of the whole.

We have now reached a point where we can begin to identify the basic building blocks of the predisposition to character type. It appears that disturbances in a few psychologic domains play an important role in personality development. The psychologist Hans Eysenck emphasized three central factors: an extroversion factor, characterized by outgoing, sociable behavior, and its opposite, introversion, characterized by a more self-contained style; neuroticism, characterized by anxiety and emotionality; and psychoticism, characterized by eccentric, unconventional, and occasionally antisocial behavior. Recently, Eysenck has added a fourth factor, impulsivity. He and his colleagues and students have extensively documented the presence of these factors in normal populations and have attempted to establish their biological correlates.

Others have modified or challenged Eysenck's system. One of his former students, Sir Jeffrey Grey, a neurochemist who studies pharmacology and behavior in both animals and humans, has suggested that these dimensions may be more accurately conceived as impulsivity, anxiety, and psychoticism. McCrae and Costa, using their studies of the continuity of personality over lifetimes as well as their work with personality-disordered patients, argue for three additional dimensions: agreeableness, openness to new experience, and conscientiousness—all of which show great stability throughout development. Finally, Cloninger has developed a theory of personality traits based on three factors: "novelty seeking," a tendency toward exploratory activity and reactivity to novel stimuli; "harm avoidance," an intense response to aversive or negative stimuli, with a strong capacity to learn to avoid punishment; and "reward dependence," a strong response to reward and a tendency to maintain behaviors that are rewarded. He has shown all of these factors to be strongly heritable. Cloninger has since expanded his theory to include such factors as self-directedness and transcendence.

There is little agreement on what the basic components of personality are or even how many there are. But all of these schemes converge in suggesting three to five major dimensions of temperament related to the quality of thinking about the world, the regulation of emotions, the capacity to contain aggressive impulses, and anxiety—the reaction to potential future punishment. These are the domains of personality that seem most likely to have a strong biological basis. They are also the domains that, when disturbed, are implicated in a variety of personality disorders.

CHAPTER FOUR

SEROTONIN AND SUICIDE: THE BIOLOGY OF IMPULSIVE AGGRESSION

No neurotic harbors thoughts of suicide which he has not turned back upon himself from murderous impulses against others.

— SIGMUND FREUD

ONE OF THE DIFFICULTIES with the "one neuro-transmitter–one disease" model was that mental diseases do not always fit neatly into the categories we have devised to label them. The precedent of mental retardation associated with phenylketonuria, a single gene defect causing a single metabolic defect leading unmistakably to a severe mental disorder, inspired hope that some other simple genetic defect might similarly be found to work through a single, clear pathway to yield a psychiatric disease such as depression. But this scheme tried to compare apples to oranges: neurotransmitter systems are physical systems, while mental diseases are complex amalgams embracing biological, psychiatric, and social definitions. There is no obvious reason for assuming a one-to-one correlation between them. The variability of depression, the waxing and waning of its symptoms, and the complexity of brain circuitry compel more intricate explanations.

We can look at this problem another way, however, and ask whether there are behavioral attributes that do correlate with brain chemicals. One of the strongest and, to me, most interesting links is between serotonin and aggression.

Serotonin's name comes from its first known biological role, as a substance in the blood that causes contraction of smooth muscle (*sero,*

89

from "serum"; *tonin,* from "tone" or "tension"). In fact most of the body's serotonin lies outside the central nervous system, in the circulatory system or the gut; only about 1 to 2 percent actually resides in the brain. This small quantity plays a major role in the regulation of mood, temperature, appetite, sleep, sexual behavior, and pain. Clusters of serotonergic neurons (nerve cells whose primary neurotransmitter is serotonin), located in the brainstem, have axonal branches extending throughout the brain.

As a modulatory neurotransmitter, serotonin has effects that are generally inhibitory. It has been shown to diminish appetite and sexual behavior and to suppress the perception of pain. When it is absent, there is a marked increase in aggression. Surgically destroying the serotonergic centers of laboratory rats turns these normally placid animals into aggressive killers that will mercilessly attack mice that are placed within reach. (But when the rats have been raised with the mice before surgery, they don't attack. It appears that serotonin doesn't modulate the systems that decide whether a stimulus is a novelty or a threat, only the aggressiveness of the response.) These rats also become less capable of suppressing behaviors that will result in punishment. For instance, an investigator may train a rat to press a bar to receive a food pellet, and then change the rules so that pressing the bar now delivers an electric shock instead. A rat with an intact serotonergic system will quickly learn to stop pressing the bar, but one whose serotonergic system has been destroyed takes much longer to unlearn the response despite repeated punishments. Serotonin's message to the brain seems to be "hold back, slow down, or something bad will happen." It inhibits destructive behaviors, especially those that may have negative consequences.

Barry Jacobs of Princeton University has measured the serotonergic activity of cats by implanting electrodes in their serotonergic centers and then observing them in their cages. When the cats were engaged in rhythmic self-directed activities such as eating or grooming, their serotonergic neurons were relatively active. But a situation requiring alertness, heightened sensory processing, and possibly an aggressive response, such as the opening of the door to their cage, quickly suppressed these neurons. This pattern, of increased firing during self-directed activity and decreased firing in response to a challenge from outside, is exactly opposite to the one we saw in the noradrenergic system in Chapter 2. We can think of these two systems, along with others such as the dopamine system, as regulating attention to our inner and outer worlds.

As one of a class of neurotransmitters called biogenic amines, which includes norepinephrine and dopamine, serotonin has been studied in connection with depression for several decades. In fact the "indoleamine hypothesis"—that depression was caused by a serotonin deficiency—competed with the catecholamine hypothesis for many years as an alternative explanation for the biological basis of depression. Much of the supporting evidence was similar. Drugs that increase serotonin levels in the synapse, such as monoamine oxidase inhibitors, are effective antidepressants. (Prozac, or fluoxetine, one of the first new antidepressants to catch the public's attention, is an SSRI, a "selective serotonin reuptake inhibitor," meaning that it selectively inhibits the reentry of serotonin into the neuron but not norepinephrine or dopamine.) Chemical precursors of serotonin, i.e., drugs that the body transforms into serotonin, also relieve depression. Depressed patients have lower levels of serotonin breakdown products in their cerebrospinal fluid than normal volunteers. Herbert Meltzer and colleagues at Case Western Reserve Medical School have found evidence of reduced serotonin reuptake sites on the blood cells of depressed patients, suggesting that if the same abnormalities exist in the brain, these patients' serotonergic systems may be less active than normal. When researchers such as Charles Nemeroff at Emory University have monitored the binding of antidepressant drugs to neurons at a site close to the serotonin reuptake site, they have noted that depressed people seem to have fewer such sites than normal—again suggesting reduced activity of the entire system.

The contradiction in the fact that both the catecholamine and indoleamine hypotheses work, in the sense that both have led to moderately effective treatments for depression, has not been lost on psychiatric researchers. At the very least, neither hypothesis offers a complete explanation. To further confuse the issue, serotonin has also been implicated in obsessive-compulsive disorder, panic disorder, schizophrenia, eating disorders, and impulsive aggressive disorders. Noradrenergic dysfunction has been suggested in anxiety disorders and schizophrenia.

The first clue that serotonin might be associated with aggression came from studies in depressed patients. Although depressed patients were shown to have a diminished concentration of a serotonin metabolite called 5-HIAA in their cerebrospinal fluid, this finding was not uniform—some had it, some didn't. Further research showed that the lowered concentrations were associated with a history of suicide attempts and could even be used to predict future suicide attempts. Marie Asberg of Stockholm, who had made some of the original discoveries of serotonin abnormalities in depression, suggested that these suicide attempts were a form of self-directed aggression. Studying criminals, soldiers, and other volunteers, Asberg and others both here and in Europe found a clear link between decreased concentrations of 5-HIAA and a penchant for arguments, fist fights, and violent crime. In effect, Asberg gave a modern biological foundation to the Freudian concept of suicide as aggression turned inward.

When I arrived at NIMH to work with Dennis Murphy, he was also studying serotonin, looking for ways of challenging the serotonergic system in order to produce a measurable response, much as he was doing with norepinephrine. The standard means of measuring serotonin activity at that time was simply to follow its normal metabolic pathway to its endpoint. Serotonin is synthesized from tryptophan, an essential amino acid—"essential" because the body cannot manufacture it, and therefore we must get it in our food. Milk, red meats, and bananas are high in tryptophan. (Since serotonin is thought to be involved in sleep maintenance, it may be the tryptophan in milk that makes so many people like to drink it at bedtime.) Brain levels of serotonin can be significantly reduced if tryptophan is eliminated from the diet, and in fact Pedro Delgado and his colleagues at Yale found that when depressed patients on medications like Prozac, which increase serotonin activity, were put on a tryptophan-free diet, their depressive symptoms returned or worsened.

After it is taken up into a neuron, tryptophan is converted by the enzyme tryptophan hydroxylase into 5-hydroxytryptophan. The activity and amounts of this converting enzyme are regulated by feedback control, so that a high serotonin level inhibits the enzyme's activity. Another converting enzyme turns 5-hydroxytryptophan into 5-HT, the chemical name for serotonin, which is then packaged and stored in preparation for release into the synapse. When it is released, it acts on both pre- and post-synaptic receptors: the former serve as autoreceptors to control subsequent release of the neurotransmitter, and the latter excite or inhibit the post-synaptic neuron. Serotonin is removed from the synapse in the same way as the other biogenic amines, by being reabsorbed into the nerve cell, where it is packaged for reuse. But, also like the others, a certain amount is steadily metabolized by monoamine oxidase, or MAO. It turns into 5-HIAA, which shows up in the cerebrospinal fluid. An abnormality along any part of this pathway—synthesis, release, inhibition, inactivation, metabolism—should presumably affect the concentration of 5-HIAA found in the spinal fluid. Most studies of this system relied on measuring 5-HIAA to determine serotonin levels.

But we were looking for ways to evaluate serotonergic activity that didn't involve a spinal tap. If we were going to do repeated testing with many volunteer subjects, we needed something simpler and less painful. And we wanted to be able to measure the system's reactivity— not just overall serotonin levels but how quickly and sensitively they could change on demand.

The test Dennis devised used fenfluramine as a probe. Originally developed as a treatment for obesity, fenfluramine is chemically similar to amphetamine. It stimulates serotonin release, blocks its reuptake, and directly stimulates the serotonin receptors. Serotonin in turn stimulates the pituitary gland to release prolactin, the hormone that promotes milk production and release (this is one reason mothers need to be relaxed before they can nurse their babies), and prolactin levels can be measured by a simple blood test. Rather than targeting one specific aspect of the system, then, fenfluramine gives us a general picture of its capacity. The greater the system's capacity for activation, the larger the prolactin peak in response to fenfluramine. A reduced prolactin response would indicate a less active serotonin system.

A good probe like this has several uses. One is that you can use it to monitor the action of drugs on the serotonergic system: drugs that enhance serotonin's effects enhance the prolactin response to fenfluramine. You can also use it to study the serotonergic system itself in health and disease. When we tried the fenfluramine probe in volunteers with depression, we found reduced, or "blunted," prolactin responses, which fit with the idea that serotonin capacity was reduced in depressed patients.

Marie Asberg's work and the American research that followed it, including some important studies at NIMH conducted by Markku Linnoila, Gerald Brown, and Fred Goodwin, made a strong impression on me. If these people had found a link between reduced serotonin metabolites and aggression in depressed patients, alcoholic offenders, and members of the armed services, I thought there should be a similar relationship between serotonin abnormalities and the impulsive/aggressive behavior common in personality disorders. But because they are not classified among the major psychiatric diseases (Axis I in *DSM-IV*—see Chapter 6), personality disorders had received little attention from biological psychiatry. No one had yet evaluated a group of personality disorder patients with a serotonergic probe like the fenfluramine test. When I came to Mount Sinai in 1982, I brought the investigative tools I had learned at NIMH and began to apply them to the personality disorders.

Emil Coccaro, who joined me during his last year of training—the year I arrived at Mount Sinai—had read about our work at NIMH and was eager to start a similar research program at Mount Sinai. He developed a series of studies of fenfluramine effects in depressed and personality disorder patients. Emil found reduced average prolactin responses to fenfluramine, compared with a healthy control group, not only in the depressed patients but in the personality disorder patients as well. While not entirely unexpected, this was a substantial discovery, both exciting and confusing: *another* group of disorders with abnormal serotonin function!

But averages can be deceiving. What we really found was even more interesting. In both the depressed and personality disorder patients, the averages were skewed by a significant minority whose response was considerably depressed, while the rest of the group was about the same as the controls. What accounted for this difference? It did not correlate with severity of depression in the depressed group or with history or severity of depression in the personality disorder group, nor with time off antidepressant medication, plasma concentrations of fenfluramine, season of the year, age, weight, or any of a number of demographic characteristics. What it did correlate with was a history of suicide attempts. Suicide attempters had below-normal prolactin responses to fenfluramine; non–suicide attempters did not. These results were consistent with studies of the serotonin metabolite, 5-HIAA, in the cerebrospinal fluid of depressed patients: reduced serotonergic activity seems to be associated with suicidal behavior. But by demonstrating the same association in a previously untested population—personality disorder patients—we had subtly changed our own understanding. To us the link between serotonin and suicide was no longer about depression or any other disease. It was a direct correlation between a brain chemical and a specific behavior pattern.

Emil and I then took this correlation a step further. We looked at the relationship between the fenfluramine response and externally directed aggression, the fights and arguments that disrupt so many personality disorder patients' lives. Many psychological tests exist to measure aggression in various ways. The Buss-Durkee Hostility Inventory, for instance, evaluates a subject's readiness to engage in physical violence by asking the subject to endorse (or not) such statements as "Once in a while I cannot control my urge to harm others"; "If somebody hits me, I let them have it"; "When I really lose my temper, I am capable of slapping someone"; "I often feel like a powder keg ready to explode"; or "It makes my blood boil to have somebody make fun of me." The Barrett Impulsivity Scale rates impulsive motor behaviors such as restlessness, carelessness, hastiness, and sloppiness. The Brown-Goodwin Life History of Aggression quantifies a subject's aggressive and violent behavior throughout life in terms of number and severity of arguments, fights, and other violent incidents. The reduced-prolactin response group scored higher on all of these tests, supporting our idea that the serotonin system is less sensitive in patients with a predisposition to aggression. The effect of this insensitivity appears to be highly specific. Emil found a strong correlation between reduced prolactin response to fenfluramine and increased irritable aggression, but none with anxiety, suspiciousness, or other pathologic symptoms.

Moreover, the effect is strongly dimensional: there seemed to be a *continuous* relationship between an index of serotonin function and irritable aggression.

Studies like this must be replicated several times to be believed. Emil followed up by evaluating prolactin responses to other medications acting on specific receptors in the serotonin system. Later, after he moved to the Medical College of Pennsylvania and began working with a new population of personality disorder patients, he began a similar series of studies using a form of fenfluramine that is more selective for the serotonin system. He is continuing to find the same relationship between reduced prolactin response and impulsive aggression. A group in Ireland has also reported reduced prolactin responses associated with antisocial disorder. And we are seeing the same association consistently in my own laboratory, with a particularly strong correlation between prolactin response and self-injury such as cutting or stabbing. We are also starting to find, as the number of people we've studied continues to grow, that these relationships may vary significantly between men and women—an indication of the importance of sex differences in the expression of biochemical abnormalities.

The relationship between serotonin, suicide, and impulsive aggression is one of the most robust and consistent in biological psychiatry, and it illustrates the power of the dimensional approach in explaining the relationship between the variability of brain systems and alterations in behavior. Instead of thinking of serotonin as implicated in one category of mental disorder, we can envision a range of serotonergic activity associated with a range of aggressive behaviors. But is this relationship uniform across every population?

§

One group of patients didn't fit the pattern. In remitted depressed patients—those who have suffered an episode of depression and recovered and who do not have a major personality disorder—the same measures of impulsivity and aggression did not correlate at all with prolactin responses to serotonergic challenges. Yet the prolactin response did correlate with history and intended severity of suicide attempts.

Why should this group be different? Let's take another look at the noradrenergic system. This system, as we saw in Chapter 2, mediates a person's emotional reactivity to his or her surroundings. Its main nucleus, the locus ceruleus, is particularly responsive to novel, threatening, or provocative stimuli. One of the characteristic features of depression is disengagement from the environment: severely depressed patients show little response to the people or events around them. Whether they are "slowed down" or agitated and pacing, severely depressed people often seem strangely detached, giving their depression an autonomous quality. Underlying this unreactivity may be a noradrenergic system that does not adjust itself sensitively or accurately enough to enable the brain to detect and respond to important environmental changes.

People with personality disorders, by contrast, are often excessively involved with their surroundings. They may be exquisitely sensitive, growing furious at a slight provocation or exhilarated at a minor compliment, and quick to act on momentary impulses as well. In fact, their responses are disordered in precisely the opposite way from those of depressed patients. Could their noradrenergic systems be *hyperreactive?* In a study of pathological gamblers, whom they chose as a good example of a nonviolent group with poor impulse control, Alec Roy and Markku Linnoila found evidence to suggest precisely this. Not only did these people have higher-than-normal norepinephrine levels, but many measures of norepinephrine activity showed a strong correlation with psychological measures of arousal and impulsivity. Arousal plays an important role in gambling: gamblers often report that excitement is a strong reason why they do it. Looking at this and other evidence, we wondered if we could draw a more general conclusion about norepinephrine's roles in human behavior.

So we began to study the noradrenergic systems of personality disorder patients using the same biologic probes we used in depression—testing the growth hormone response to clonidine. Just about this time, Nancy entered our program and agreed to be tested. She presented a remarkable profile: very high noradrenergic activity coupled with the lowest measure of serotonergic response we had ever seen. But she was not atypical: in the entire group of personality disorder patients that we studied, the growth hormone response to clonidine ranged from normal to augmented. Moreover, the greater this response, the higher the patients tended to score on our tests of irritability and hostility.

This sequence led us to a very simple model of how two neurotransmitter systems may interact. While the serotonin system mediates impulsivity, irritability, and aggression, the norepinephrine system influences the direction of its expression by helping to determine the degree of reactivity to the environment. Here was a good, useful advance over the one neurotransmitter–one disease idea: rather than considering neuromodulator systems in isolation, we would look at their interactions and see how the expression of disorders in one system was affected by disorders in another. In animals, you need to maintain an intact noradrenergic system in order to see the increased violence associated with a serotonergic deficit—destroying the noradrenergic neurons abolishes the aggressive behavior. Increased noradrenergic activity brings increased aggression. We can put this relationship on a chart:

		SEROTONIN	
		Underreactive	Overreactive
NOREPINEPHRINE	Underreactive	Reduced responsiveness to environment; inward-directed aggression leading to suicide attempts	Withdrawn, ruminative, or obsessional symptoms
	Overreactive	External aggression, risk taking, novelty seeking, excessive reactivity to environment associated with impulsive activity	Heightened reactivity associated with anxiety symptoms; phobic, avoidant, anxiety-related personality trait

Note that we're comparing not the overall levels of these chemicals but the reactivity of the different systems—how quickly and strongly they adjust to changes in their environment. The first box, underreactive/ underreactive, is occupied by severely depressed people at high risk of suicide. Both serotonergic and noradrenergic function is impaired, and while aggressive impulses are not well controlled, neither can they be directed at the outside world. So they emerge as self-punishment, ranging from tortured rumination over past sins to self-directed violence. All of the people we tested who fit into this category—who had blunted responses to both the clonidine and fenfluramine challenges—were depressed patients with a history of suicide attempts; moreover, no depressed patients with a history of suicide attempts fell outside this category. Although the numbers are too small (seven patients out of fifty in this study) to permit any definitive conclusions, still we were struck by the perfect correspondence between clinical histories and neurochemical results. The box below that one (underreactive serotonin, overreactive norepinephrine) describes many of the dramatic cluster patients we tested: a high degree of engagement with the environment—whether expressed in the sociopath's manipulative charm, the histrionic's exaggerated seductiveness, or the narcissist's exquisite sensitivity to real or imagined criticism—coupled with loosely checked aggression.

The two boxes on the right have been less well studied. Excessive sensitivity to one's surroundings coupled with excessive inhibition of aggression may lead to the protective, avoidant, or dependent traits seen in the anxiety-related personality disorders, and in extreme cases to recurrent panic attacks. (I will discuss these in Chapter 6.) Disengagement from the environment with overly inhibited aggression may be associated with the more withdrawn obsessional symptoms, reminiscent of the rhythmic, self-directed activity that Barry Jacobs observed in his cats when their serotonergic systems were most active. People with obsessive-compulsive disorders marked by compulsive rituals like hand washing and "checking" (for example, being unable to leave their apartment without entering the kitchen fifteen or twenty times to be sure the stove is turned off) may be behaviorally hypersensitive to serotonergic probes yet may show a blunted response to clonidine.

In fact these two neurotransmitter systems may have broad implications for personality style. The distinctions I've drawn here roughly parallel more general factors characterized by psychologists as "externalization" and "internalization." The person who externalizes tends to focus on external circumstances and, when frustrated, to blame something or someone outside of the self. The person who internalizes tends to detach herself from her environment and to see problems as her own fault. These people are prone to depression and guilt; they ruminate over past mistakes, and when they express direct aggression, they turn it inward as self-punishment. It's possible that the same interaction between norepinephrine and serotonin, at more normal levels than those common to depression and personality disorders, contributes to these personality styles.

Intriguing as it is, this scheme of norepinephrine/serotonin interaction is still highly speculative and at best simplistic. The serotonin system alone is much more complex than a simple two-dimensional graph can ever suggest. For instance, one type of serotonin receptor, $5HT_{1a}$, is an inhibitory receptor, modulating serotonin release as well as acting post-synaptically on other neuronal systems. The $5HT_2$ receptor, on the other hand, plays an excitatory role throughout the cortex, which then serves to inhibit more primitive brain areas. We know of at least twelve other serotonin receptor subtypes, many of whose functional significance is entirely unknown. Depression and personality disorders, moreover, both involve far more than serotonin and norepinephrine. When we remember that the brain contains hundreds of neurotransmitter systems, we can see that the biology of neurotransmitters provides a very rich vocabulary of temperamental traits that are then combined, modified, and elaborated over a person's lifetime. Scientists are now beginning to glimpse the barest rudiments of this vocabulary.

Acetylcholine, for instance, is norepinephrine's direct opposite. Where norepinephrine outside the brain acts through the sympathetic nervous system to speed up heartbeat, shut down digestion, constrict blood vessels in the skin, and generally prepare the body for combat, acetylcholine, through the parasympathetic nervous system, does the reverse: slows the heart, increases blood flow to the gut, and enhances internal bodily functions. In the brain the acetylcholine system is called the cholinergic system. Stimulating the cholinergic system in animals causes lethargy and decreased exploration of new environments.

If you give people a drug, such as physostigmine, to inhibit the enzyme that breaks down acetylcholine—if you stimulate the cholinergic system, in other words—they become drowsy and lethargic, and some report feeling depressed. This reaction is more pronounced in people who are susceptible to depression. In these people, physostigmine produces a transient, depression-like syndrome that usually lasts less than an hour, and this effect occurs whether or not these people are presently in a depressed phase of their illness. It can even occur during a manic phase. The explanation, we think, is that unlike the norepinephrine receptors, the acetylcholine receptors are actually more sensitive in people who are subject to mood disorders. In fact, some preliminary studies done by myself and Craig Risch, then at NIMH, suggested the two systems may be linked—that an enhanced response to the cholinergic challenge in depressed patients correlates with a blunted response to clonidine. David Janowsky and John Davis have proposed a cholinergic–adrenergic balance theory to explain depression, suggesting that it arises from a combination of excessive cholinergic activity and diminished adrenergic activity, leading the brain away from an alert, active state to a more depressed one. Because the two systems work in opposition, this hypothesis has some appeal but has yet to be definitively tested with probes of both systems.

In personality disorders, the cholinergic system's contribution to affective instability has been studied even less, but there are still some intriguing clues. One of the things the cholinergic system does is bring on rapid-eye-movement (REM) sleep, and a drug that stimulates the cholinergic receptors reduces the REM latency period, the period between falling asleep and the start of the REM phase. This effect, too, is more pronounced in patients who are vulnerable to depression. It may also be magnified, though less predictably, in patients with borderline disorder. Borderline disorder patients also seem to be significantly more susceptible than normal volunteers to transient depression after administration of physostigmine compared to a placebo (when neither nursing staff nor patient knows which the patient is receiving).

Our study of this phenomenon, which is still in progress, seems to be showing that borderline patients with a great deal of emotional instability often develop brief but strong depressed moods that are gone an hour after the physostigmine infusion. Some have reported intense sadness, while others have expressed pessimism about the future. While short-lived and well tolerated in an experimental context, these feelings paralleled more significant moods that affected these patients' lives. One woman told us she felt exactly as she does just before her period—an especially vulnerable time for many women with emotional instability. While it's important to realize that these findings are much more tentative than what we've learned about the serotonin system, they suggest that the cholinergic system may contain a key to understanding sudden emotional shifts. It may be more sensitive or reactive in the emotionally labile person with borderline disorder. Still, it is not the only key: the serotonin system seems to be involved here as well. When we tested the same borderline patients with fenfluramine, they again differed from the normal volunteers in experiencing a dramatic mood change, but in the opposite direction—they became mildly euphoric.

This finding raises an intriguing possibility. Since these patients showed abnormal mood changes when we tried different probes, it's unlikely the explanation for their illness lies in just one neurotransmitter system. Could these people be suffering from a more basic defect—perhaps in the systems within their neurons that amplify the message coming from the synaptic receptors—that disrupts several neurotransmitter systems at once? This is the kind of speculation that we are now equipped to investigate as we begin to understand the cascade of chemical events that alter a neuron's activity and even the expression of its genes.

Another example of the complexity of the relation between brain chemicals and behavior can be seen in some new studies showing a genetic link between catecholamines and impulsivity. In this case the chemical involved is dopamine—specifically, the D_4 receptor, a particular variant of which has been associated with the personality trait of novelty seeking (a tendency to seek out novel, risky, or exciting experiences) in two of three separate studies. This finding is consistent with animal studies showing that, like norepinephrine, dopamine plays a role in mediating the degree of engagement with the environment. Again, this association does not mean the gene "caused" the behavior but that it is one of a number of genes that contribute to the personality trait. Indeed, these studies and another by Klaus-Peter Lesch, Dennis Murphy, and colleagues (which suggests that a variant of the gene controlling the amount of the serotonin transporter produced in the nerve cell is associated with increased anxiety) indicate that the effect of each such gene is modest, and something on the order of ten genes would better account for the variability in these traits.

෧

How do we use biological reasoning to sort out the complicated nexus of disorders in the dramatic cluster? The new thinking suggests that neurotransmitter systems are more closely associated with dimensions of behavior than with categories of illness, and the idea that a few basic dimensions of behavior cut across diagnostic categories has been under investigation for years. So, linking these ideas, we can envision a bridge from brain chemicals to character traits to psychiatric diseases.

The dramatic cluster in particular often makes me think of the blind men and the elephant. We still don't know whether the four disorders in this group represent distinct entities or variations on a limited set of biologically determined traits that get patterned into recognizable types in the course of development. But I incline toward the latter view. Varying combinations of a few distinct temperamental predispositions—impulsivity, affective instability, anxiety—may supply the foundations for the different diagnoses.

For example, some individuals, such as those with antisocial disorder, show marked impulsivity but lack the affective sensitivity seen in borderline, histrionic, and some narcissistic patients. In fact, the psychopath shows a peculiar indifference to emotional stimuli. Such an innate combination might make it more likely that a person will develop antisocial traits. Further, traits vary in severity. A less impulsive psychopath may be assertive and decisive without showing any dyscontrol of aggression, yet have an extreme emotional indifference that allows him glibly and charmingly to manipulate others. Rather than engaging in violence, such a person might be drawn to shady or deceptive business practices (or to any community whose unwritten rule is that the only crime is getting caught) and might even be quite successful. A still "healthier" individual, sharing the same grandiose traits and emotional insensitivity to a lesser degree, who never becomes impulsively aggressive, may function perfectly well at work, though her interpersonal relationships may lack depth.

Other people may have affective instability but without any remarkable degree of impulsive aggression or reactivity to their environment. They may go through frequent mood swings that bear little relation to life events, which they react to less impulsively than borderline or histrionic patients. Their symptoms resemble manic depressive disease but are less severe, and the cycles they go through are measured in days rather than weeks. Psychiatrists call this cyclothymia and classify it as a mood disorder—a variety of depression.

Borderline and histrionic patients, as well as some narcissists, may share the sociopath's impulsivity but may be at the other end of the scale in emotional reactivity. Their exquisite sensitivity to emotions allows them to empathize strongly with others. But their unstable moods bring inner turmoil as their emotions swing widely in response to minor events. This exaggerated emotional expression combines with impulsivity to make their changes in feelings very visible to others. Unlike the sociopath, people with borderline and histrionic traits feel emotional distress intensely even while they inflict it. This distress—their difficulty in stabilizing their self-esteem, their need to be protected, to avoid abandonment, to be the center of attention—drives borderline patients into desperate acts that appear controlling and manipulative. But people with borderline disorder experience these tactics as essential to their emotional survival. They know how to discharge their intense emotional storms only through self-destructive acts and angry outbursts. When they feel abandoned, they do not act cynically or callously but in the blind intensity of rage and humiliation. In fact, this physical acting out of inner pain so as to influence others' behavior is a more consistent feature of borderline disorder than any particular social quality such as stinginess, compassion, or self-centeredness.

This behavior makes perfect sense if we think of affective instability as partly an inborn biological trait. Such a trait would have a dominating influence in personality development. A person subject to extreme mood swings in response to external events may come to think of his internal state as something outside his personal control. So strongly and painfully does it depend on the actions of others that he may come to see it as entirely a function of changes in his interpersonal environment. Having never learned any techniques to calm himself down or cheer himself up when he needs to—in many cases having no real sense that such a feat is even possible—he is likely to resort to controlling his environment as a means of controlling his internal state. John Gunderson, who introduced me to the concept of borderline personality disorder at McLean Hospital, used to emphasize to us residents that the borderline is "purposively" behaving and organizing his world "to maintain communication with and control over" the people he must depend on. People who have ingrained this habit over many years as part of their personalities are often at a loss to understand why others find it objectionable that they create emergencies in order to draw attention to themselves, because they don't know there is any alternative. What did they expect me to do? they ask in wounded innocence.

While histrionic people, being likewise externally focused, may also engage others in dramatizations of their dilemmas, their apparent reactivity may sometimes disguise an indifference, an inability to experience emotions in depth, more characteristic of the psychopath. This range of affective sensitivity, from the hyperreactive on one end to the hyperstable on the other—in which emotional swings are so greatly dampened that they can hardly be said to exist at all—can be seen in a number of dramatic cluster disorders. Narcissists show a similar spectrum. At one end is the vulnerable narcissist, closely attuned to others, self-centered, and highly reactive to humiliation. At the other end are people who resemble the psychopath in callousness but who are less impulsive and less likely to violate social norms in their search for self-aggrandizement.

The concept of state-dependent memory, which plays an important role in the emotional cycles of affective disorders, also helps us understand some aspects of emotional instability in the dramatic cluster—in particular, the "splitting" often seen in borderline patients. The psychoanalyst Otto Kernberg considers the internal representations, or schemas, of our interpersonal world as units consisting broadly of three parts: images of the self in relation to an important person, colored by an emotional background. One unit, for instance, might consist of an abandoned, unloved, loathsome self relating to a cold, critical, angry parent, colored by feelings of shame and rage. Another schema might contain a submissive, eager-to-please self relating to a benevolent, nurturing parent, colored by feelings of security, gratitude, and love. But since important relationships are almost never one-dimensional, we are likely to use several schemas to represent our relations with any one person. (We also frequently apply the same schema, not always appropriately, across more than one relationship.)

These representations may be brought out by events that affect our self-perceptions. For example, if a therapist ends a session while the patient still wants more nurturance, the patient may experience this as an abandonment, with emerging feelings of inadequacy and rage at a therapist she suddenly sees as coldly persecuting and heartless—often an experience the patient has felt with a parent. People with borderline disorder, whose unusually intense and unstable emotions lead to strongly polarized images of themselves and others, may use a separation of their "good" and "bad" schemas to preserve islands of positive feeling from contamination by their disappointment and anger—a phenomenon called dissociation. In the extreme, this dissociation may take the form of splitting, where two images of the same person, occupying two different schemas, scarcely connect to each other at all. While experiencing the unit of worthless self–heartless therapist, the patient will have no emotional access to, and may even have difficulty remembering, the more positive perceptions she may have held but very recently. These splits may in fact reflect profoundly different neurochemical states that do not permit easy access from one to another.

Giving physostigmine to borderline patients to stimulate their cholinergic systems often brings on depressive feelings. But though transient and chemically induced, these feelings are in no way foreign: they replicate emotional states these patients find all too familiar. A typical example is the woman I mentioned above, who felt miserable and defective as a person and wary of others in almost exactly the same way she always did before her period. The shift in her perceptions and self-esteem brought on by the pharmacologic challenge paralleled the hormonally driven state change she undergoes every month. To me, stories like this demonstrate that schemas rooted in the environment—in a person's self-image and ways of relating to others—can be brought to the surface by biological changes. Like Jack's relapse into depression, they are examples of state-dependent memory.

How important is state-dependent memory in borderline disorder? As I write this, my colleagues and I are conducting a study with borderline patients to see if physostigmine-induced state changes affect their capacity to recall emotionally charged words. Will people with a depressive response to physostigmine have better recall of negatively charged words like "garbage" or "slime" when they try to memorize them in the depressed state? Our hypothesis is that they will recall them better than neutral words and that people who are given physostigmine but do not have a depressive response will show no such difference. Could state-dependent memory contribute to the clinical phenomenon of splitting?

In addition to helping us understand specific pathologic features such as splitting, the constant interaction of inborn and external influences on perceptions, moods, and memories raises many larger questions. If the dramatic cluster represents a small number of innate personality traits elaborated along different developmental pathways, what are the pathways and how do they work? What determines whether someone will become a psychopath rather than a narcissist? Why do the four diagnoses divide so disproportionately among men and women? And why this particular set of four—are there other personality styles, as yet unrecognized by psychiatrists (perhaps because we don't consider them pathological), that arise from the same underlying traits? Are there other traits or predispositions that we have not yet characterized? And are these traits the "atoms" of personality, or do they in turn have many components? These questions lie squarely on the interface between biology and environment. A clearer view of the biology of the dramatic cluster should lead us to a better understanding of how the different factors interact to create the adult personality.

One element of that clearer view will be a better idea of how serotonin works. So far in this chapter, I have treated the brain as a "black box"—if you insert certain chemical changes, you get as output certain behavioral changes, but what happens in between remains a mystery. (Of course, serotonin itself was once *inside* the box.) As we continue to pry at it from many directions, the black box is turning out to be no simple chamber but a complex labyrinth. Here are some of the more interesting items from its vestibule.

The hormonal changes we use in our pharmacological challenges—for instance, measuring prolactin levels in response to a dose of fenfluramine—don't mediate aggression themselves but only act as signals of serotonin activity in specific brain areas, such as the hypothalamus, that modulate hormonal output. The source of aggression lies elsewhere. One approach to understanding serotonin action is to use more finely tuned pharmacologic challenges that act primarily on specific receptor subtypes, and to correlate these results with brain imaging studies and molecular genetic approaches.

The cerebral cortex, in evolutionary terms a newer, advanced part of the brain, is closely involved in regulating aggression. The frontal cortex in particular plays a central role in planning, goal-directed behavior, the suppression of more primitive, impulsive behaviors, and the regulation of the more primitive brain regions from which those impulses presumably arise. A classic demonstration of the frontal cortex's role was provided by the case of Phineas Gage, recently recounted by neurologist Antonio Damasio in his book *Descartes' Error.*

In September of 1848, Phineas Gage, a twenty-five-year-old construction foreman for the Rutland & Burlington Railroad of Vermont, was severely injured when an accidental explosion sent a thirteen-pound stake rocketing through his head at high speed. The three-and-a-half-foot iron bar entered his left cheekbone and exited the top of his skull, leaving a gaping hole over an inch in diameter. Despite this massive injury, Gage remained conscious and lucid while a local doctor, John Harlow, treated his wounds; he survived the inevitable wound infection and made, apparently, a miraculous recovery. But he was not the same man. Although he suffered no paralysis or loss of sensory function except for blindness in his left eye, and lost none of his intellectual capacities or language ability, his personality was utterly changed.

Before the accident, Gage had been clearly marked for success: highly skilled, a perfectionist at his difficult work; a popular leader respected by his subordinates; admired as a shrewd, energetic, and persistent businessman; temperate in his personal habits and respectful in his speech. Afterward he was undisciplined, impulsive, erratic. His employers had to let him go a few months after he returned to work—not because he had lost any skill but because he had grown so irresponsible. His language became so foul that ladies were warned away. His health and behavior followed a relentless downhill course; he never again held a steady job for long, except as a circus attraction, and died in 1861 an occasional day laborer dependent on his mother and sister for support.

Antonio Damasio's wife and colleague at the University of Iowa, Hanna Damasio, has reconstructed on a computer the iron stake's path through Gage's head and confirmed that his injury was localized to a particular area, the inner (facing) parts of the right and left orbital frontal lobes, as well as some part of the back region of the frontal lobes. (*Orbit* means "eye socket"; the orbital frontal lobes are the lobes at the front of the cortex, just above and behind the eyes.) Impairment in this region is associated with impaired decision making, especially in personal and social areas; reduced capacity for emotion; and disinhibited aggression and fits of temper. The region is also full of $5HT_2$ receptors, the excitatory serotonin receptor.

The syndromes of orbital frontal lobe damage that the Damasios investigated—Gage's case and others—are not the same as the dramatic cluster, but the similarities are compelling. Could reduced or dysregulated serotonin activity disrupt the efficiency of the frontal lobe brain circuits crucial to appropriate social behavior and inhibition of aggression? Michael Raleigh has shown in monkeys that the density of serotonin receptors in the frontal lobes—as well as in two related areas, the amygdala and the temporal cortices—correlates with personality.

Aggressive, belligerent monkeys tended to have a lower receptor density than more sociable animals. These personality differences also correlate with the monkeys' responses to the fenfluramine challenge: just as in humans, a reduced prolactin response was strongly associated with antisocial behavior.

For the past few years we have been able to view metabolic activity in the living brain. PET, or positron emission tomography, is a computerized method of brain imaging. Unlike CAT—computed axial tomography, which uses standard X rays to measure the density of tissue (as radiologists have been doing for most of this century) and then by computer assembles different views into a reconstruction of specific slices of the brain—PET can actually measure brain metabolism in living tissue. The subject inhales or is injected with a radioactive compound, which then decays in the bloodstream, emitting a positron. The positron soon collides with an electron; the two particles annihilate each other and generate two photons that are detected by cameras installed outside the subject's head. The more such photons the cameras detect in any one area, the more blood flow must be present in that area and, by implication, the more energy that region must be using. Since the firing of neurons requires a great deal of energy (at 1 to 2 percent of the body's weight, the nervous system consumes 25 percent of its energy), more metabolic activity equals more brain activity, and you can analyze the PET images to quantify brain activity by region. PET literally makes the most active areas light up.

Pete Goyer, now at Case Western Reserve, used PET scans to study patients with borderline personality disorder and found reduced metabolic activity in parts of the prefrontal cortex. And a group at the University of Southern California led by Adrian Raine and Monte S. Buchsbaum found diminished frontal circulation in PET scans of violent felons. Issues of sample size, medication, and other methodological concerns prevent us from regarding any of these results as better than tentative. Still, they all point in the same direction: the orbital prefrontal cortex may be a particularly important part of the brain circuitry for modulating aggression and creating socially appropriate behavior.

We are trying to strengthen this inference by combining investigative techniques. How does the fenfluramine challenge affect PET results? If it stimulates the serotonin system and the serotonin system is really an important part of prefrontal circuitry, then fenfluramine will light up the orbital prefrontal cortex on a PET scan (as preliminary studies in fact suggest). In my laboratory we are now beginning a program to test whether the blunted response we see in borderline disorder patients also shows up as a smaller change in PET scans before and after a dose of fenfluramine. Other approaches include direct visualization of serotonin receptors by positron-emitting chemicals that bind to these receptors, to see whether there are consistent differences in the patterns of receptor binding between impulsive patients and normal controls.

Yet another approach is to correlate neurochemical results with genetic ones. Studies of patients with borderline personality disorder suggest that the disorder itself is not heritable but that certain dimensions, especially impulsive aggression and affective instability, are. Relatives of borderline patients are more likely to be either impulsive or affectively unstable than relatives of patients with other personality disorders. Emil Coccaro has demonstrated a much higher concordance of aggression in identical twins than in fraternal twins—suggesting not only a genetic basis but multiple genetic factors, since the difference in concordance rates was far higher than the 2:1 ratio we might expect a single dominant gene to produce. In other words, if two or more interactive genes are necessary to produce a behavior such as aggression, the ratio of concordance in identical versus fraternal twins may be considerably higher, because fraternal twins are much less likely to inherit both (or all) genes.

That the behavioral tendency, rather than the disease, should be heritable fits well with the notion that neurochemical differences are linked to dimensions of behavior. But I would urge extreme caution: what is inherited is not a behavior but only a tendency, modulated in part by the serotonin system. Indeed, reduced activity in a patient's serotonin system, as shown by a blunted protein response in fenfluramine, is a better predictor of impulsivity in the patient's relatives than is the trait of impulsivity itself. This suggests that the serotonergic abnormality, *not* the behavior, is inheritable. The net activity of the serotonin system may be affected by modest differences in the activity of key enzymes or receptors in the serotonergic system, based on differences in the bits of DNA that code for the amino acid sequences of these proteins. One of these genetic differences—a polymorphism, or site of variability in the DNA sequence—occurs in the gene for tryptophan hydroxylase, a key enzyme in serotonin synthesis. Two variants (alleles) of this gene have been identified: an L allele, found in about 60 percent of the Caucasian population, and a U allele, found in less than 40 percent. Since each person has two sets of chromosomes, these alleles can appear in three different combinations, or genotypes: LL, found in approximately 30 to 35 percent of the population; UL (50 to 55 percent); or, the rarest, UU (15 percent). In one study of Finnish violent felons later replicated in a second series, the U allele was associated with higher concentrations of the serotonin metabolite, 5-HIAA, in the cerebrospinal fluid; the L allele was associated with a history of suicide attempts but not with impulsivity.

In a pilot study in my lab, we are finding that the LL genotype—the more common of the two homozygous varieties—seems to be associated with higher self-ratings on the Irritability and Assault subscales of the Buss-Durkee Hostility Inventory, the same subscales associated with a reduced prolactin response to fenfluramine. While it must be replicated in other populations (to avoid statistical complications from gender and ethnic differences, these data reflect only white males, our largest subsample), this work raises the possibility that this gene makes some contribution to a tendency toward aggression, presumably by affecting serotonergic activity. Now other genes related to the serotonergic system are being investigated, with promising initial results.

It is important not to overinterpret findings like this. Behaviors like impulsive aggression represent a potential that we all possess, and it would be a mistake to think of the tryptophan hydroxylase gene as "the gene for aggression." It is only one of many genes that affect the serotonin system. A less active synthetic enzyme, if coupled, for example, with a less responsive serotonin receptor, could produce a less effective inhibitory serotonergic system. Whether this system's setpoint ultimately results in a greater frequency of violent behavior in any one person depends on many other factors—including genetic ones, any number of prenatal events, developmental influences, and social and cultural factors. A gene does not dictate its own expression. Indeed, in our family studies of personality disorder patients, a blunted prolactin response to fenfluramine is a better predictor of impulsive aggression in relatives than is the patient's own degree of impulsivity—consistent with the idea that what's truly inherited is only a neurochemical trait, whose behavioral effects may be very different in different people.

℘

Of all the personality disorders, antisocial disorder is probably the most difficult to understand and treat. People with this condition seldom visit a psychiatrist unless they are mandated by the courts. We can best understand antisocial disorder in terms of two dimensions: first, impulsive aggression, and second, a "psychopathic" dimension characterized by glib, manipulative, callous deceptiveness—what Cleckley called "the mask of sanity." I have already discussed the role of biology in mediating aggression; the second dimension as well has biological links.

As I mentioned in discussing a particular cortical region, the orbital prefrontal lobes, the cortex is the part of the brain involved in higher-order processing of information: sensation, voluntary movement, language, rational thought, and most other aspects of our conscious experience. As part of this processing function, the cortex inhibits action while it evaluates a situation and reflects on what to do. Personality theorists have suggested that people with psychopathic traits have reduced cortical arousal, while anxious, inhibited people have excessive cortical arousal. Electroencephalograms, or EEGs, which measure electrical arousal directly via electrodes, offer good evidence to support this idea. Antisocial patients show reduced cortical activity on evoked potentials (measurement of cortical activity in response to a specific stimulus) compared to both normal controls and anxiety-disorder patients. Pharmacologic studies show the same thing. When anxious and sociopathic patients are given a sedative, the sociopathic patients show a lower threshold for sedation—they require a smaller dose to achieve the same effect—suggesting a less aroused central nervous system. This may explain why psychopathic individuals seek stimulation from their environment. Anxious people, with higher levels of internal arousal, are more inhibited about engaging their surroundings.

But the most remarkable difference shown by evoked potential studies is in the response to emotional stimuli. When given a series of words, most people will respond to emotionally laden ones very differently from the way they respond to neutral words. This difference shows up clearly in characteristic EEG signatures, suggesting that the brain processes emotional stimuli one way and neutral stimuli another. But people with antisocial personality disorder do not make this distinction: their EEG signatures for emotion-laden words are similar to those for neutral words and different from those of a normal comparison group. In an imaging study, my colleague Joanne Intrator found that the temporal cortex was not processing emotional words as efficiently in sociopaths as in comparison groups. Psychopaths respond to emotions much as you or I might react to the weather report for a foreign city. If empathy is an important source of moral sensibility, then the lack of it may explain why these people seem immune to moral considerations. Their ability to perceive emotions in others, and their shamelessness in both manipulating and disregarding others' feelings, may both stem from their relative insensitivity to emotions' effects.

They may also be relatively insensitive to the threat of punishment. The serotonin-deficient rats I mentioned earlier took a long time to unlearn unwanted behavior despite repeated punishment. There is probably no behavioral test—certainly no ethical one—that could demonstrate the same effect so neatly in humans. But physiologic tests suggest a similar principle may be at work in psychopaths. You can use electrodes to measure the electrical potential of the skin ("skin conductance") under resting conditions and in response to sounds and lights, and these measures of skin conductance can give clues to the state of the autonomic nervous system. When presented with an aversive stimulus, psychopathic patients showed the same changes in skin conductance as normal control subjects, but their electrodermal response in *anticipation* of the stimulus was considerably less in some studies. This finding, which is over a generation old, has been generally interpreted to mean that fear conditioning in psychopaths is deficient. But the most cursory look at many psychopaths' life histories should make it obvious that this deficiency is not the result of an abnormally safe environment that did not expose them to threats. More likely it has a biological component: as with the serotonin-deficient rats, the system that mediates their behavioral inhibition may be less effective than normal. The threat of punishment may be less of a deterrent to antisocial acts in the psychopathic individual.

Violent aggression, rule breaking, thrill seeking, and deception are, of course, hallmarks of crime. Antisocial individuals, almost by definition, engage in criminal acts, and a high proportion of criminals have antisocial personality disorder. It may be tempting, therefore, to jump from a discussion of the genetics of impulsive aggression and psychopathy to unwarranted speculation about the causes and solutions of criminality. While biological information may indeed help us understand the roots of criminality, it is important to remember that crime is socially defined. It has multiple determinants, including very powerful social and cultural roots. An undue emphasis on the biology of impulsivity can have destructive consequences: it may turn attention away from potentially beneficial social interventions or may cause violent aggression to be seen less as a legal and social problem than a medical one.

The first concern is that the search for biological factors in criminal behavior can easily become an exercise in blaming the victims of social injustice. Like race-based theories of intelligence or the faddish "murderous" XYY chromosome abnormality, the attempt to link antisocial behavior to brain differences and thence to genetic differences may obscure important environmental causes of violence. Dorothy Nelkin and Susan Lindee summarize this view in their book *The DNA Mystique:*

> *The appeal of biological explanations of crime, addiction, and anti-social behavior grows with the intransigence of many contemporary social problems, combined with disillusionment about the efficacy of political and social*

reforms. In fact, whatever the influence of genetics, bio-logical "predispositions" are hardly necessary to explain why an inner city African American, growing up in a cli-mate of racism, drug abuse, and violence and without much hope of escaping that culture, might become indif-ferent to human life. Between 1980 and 1990 the Federal Government withdrew $260 billion from direct support of inner city communities. Loss of jobs and a declining tax base weakened the community's infrastructure. Yet it is expedient to believe that problems rest less with society than with inherent predispositions; for claims about "pre-disposition" are unfalsifiable and irrefutable. Any behav-ior can be explained in terms of an individual's genetic tendencies to respond either poorly or well to a particular environment. Some have "built-in resistance"; others have "evil in the genes," and the outcome—the way they even-tually function as adults—will appear as evidence of their genetic constitution.

Genetic studies can certainly be misused to buttress a Calvinist view that the more fortunate and prosperous members of society are the "elect," while the rest of us are tainted by our bad predispositions. The same studies could be used to argue that the perpetrators of vio-lent crime couldn't help what they were doing: violence is somehow hardwired into their brains. Both views seriously underestimate the complexity of gene-environment interactions in determining behavior and make light of individual responsibility, both for one's own actions and for one's community.

Neither environmental nor genetic factors provide the entire expla-nation of criminal behavior. Genetic explanations do not, for instance, account for behavioral differences found even in identical twins. If there is a genetics of impulsivity, it is unlikely to account for recent increases in urban crime despite a relatively constant gene pool. In some communities joining a gang or organized crime may represent the most available road to affluence, rendering considerations of tempera-ment largely irrelevant (although deviant individuals with a propensity to aggression will thrive better in some environments than in others). And while many genetic diseases, such as sickle-cell anemia and Tay-Sachs disease, overwhelmingly affect one ethnic group more than others, antisocial disorder is not one of them. Blacks and Hispanics are no more subject to it than whites—in fact, slightly less. You cannot use the epidemiology of antisocial disorder as a genetic argument to explain why the ethnic makeup of prison populations differs so markedly from that of the population as a whole.

Environmental views alone, on the other hand, don't easily account for the extremely varied fates of people who come from very similar circumstances. The majority of people who grow up in a climate of racism, drug abuse, violence, and hopelessness do not, in fact, become indifferent to human life. Many lead exemplary lives. Some earn positions of great honor. On the other hand, criminality is no respecter of social class: violent criminals also come from comfortable, even wealthy backgrounds.

A detailed discussion of these issues is beyond the scope of this book and largely outside the province of psychiatry. I have raised them only to point out the danger of extrapolating genetic and behavioral findings to reach facile conclusions about social policy. Neither the genes nor the environment operates in a vacuum, and their impact can be observed only in the context of a uniquely developing individual interacting with a unique set of life circumstances.

§

The boundary between the genetics of normal personality variation and the more severe personality disorders is not clear. It seems likely that many genes influence normal personality and contribute in minor ways to personality disorders, while other, less common genes predispose some people to major behavioral and mood disturbances. These two sets of genes might interact in the same way as those that affect heart disease. Some of these genes have a small impact: their effects on baseline cholesterol levels or the structure of the arterial lining may together confer a risk of heart disease that also depends strongly on diet and stress. But a few people carry a gene that all but disables their ability to remove cholesterol from their system. They suffer from a rare form of heart disease with very high cholesterol that is essentially independent of any lifestyle changes they could make.

The genetics of diabetes shows a similar pattern. Many factors, including the capacity of the body's cells to use insulin and the efficiency of the insulin-producing cells in the pancreas, contribute in a small way to one's susceptibility to diabetes. They may mean the difference between being mildly diabetic or not at all, or they may help determine the severity of the disease. Adult-onset diabetes can be entirely a product of these milder factors working in combination with diet and stress. Other genes can cripple the production of insulin. They don't render either the milder factors or the environment irrelevant, but they can move the disease into a whole different spectrum of severity. Because there are not one but many genes involved, the inheritance of diabetes is not straightforward: it skips unpredictably across generations and may even appear to come from nowhere, when a child inherits some of the necessary genes from each of his unaffected parents.

A team in England led by John Todd of Oxford University recently completed a long search for these genes, involving nearly three hundred families in Great Britain and the United States and three hundred different genetic markers. One of the first important fruits of the Human Genome Project, the study used a new technique that allows researchers to scan the entire genome. They found five different sites on the genome that are clearly implicated in diabetes, including two previously confirmed sites—one near the complex that encodes the immune system and one on the insulin gene itself—plus three new ones. They also found thirteen additional sites that may make a contribution. But even the most important of these genes—the one near the immune-system complex, which probably accounts for 40 percent of a person's susceptibility to diabetes—is not sufficient by itself to bring on the disease. The environment and other genes must contribute as well.

The riddle of multigenic inheritance is the same one that puzzled Robert Burton when he wrote in *The Anatomy of Melancholy* that "it skips in some families the father, and goes to the son, or takes every other, and sometimes every third in a lineal descent." And this observation did not originate with Burton: he was quoting a still older source. The Human Genome Project is helping us resolve some truly ancient mysteries.

If antisocial behavior follows a genetic pattern similar to diabetes', then we can expect that some people will commit violent crimes no matter what anybody around them does; others will be difficult to help; and there will be a large group for whom the correct environmental changes will make a huge difference. This analogy suggests that we may eventually be able to identify developmental factors that bear the same relation to antisocial disorder that a high-cholesterol diet bears to heart disease. If so, then we can improve both the case for selective intervention and the rate of success. And given the high social costs of violence, a truly successful intervention program would be worth a very large investment.

Like any other knowledge, a better understanding of the genetic bases of psychiatric diseases carries a risk of being misused. Just as genetics could be used to deny insurance coverage to healthy people because they carry a susceptibility to a disease, so the identification of biological risk factors for antisocial disorder could be used to deny people's civil rights—to withhold housing, education, or the presumption of innocence in the courts. The more we know about the way genes actually work, the less likely such misuses appear.

The eugenic programs that were so fashionable in early twentieth-century America, and that reached their horrifying peak in Germany under the Nazis, were based on a misunderstanding of the complexity of inheritance. Eugenicists thought they could separate out "desirable" and "undesirable" human genetic features as easily as they bred strains of smooth and wrinkled peas. But the genetics of mental disorders tells us that genes do not rigidly determine a particular pattern of behavior. They set the limits of an individual's strengths and susceptibilities— whether to depression, disordered thought, or impulsivity—but within these boundaries, temperament can be expressed in ways ranging from severe schizophrenia to creative eccentricity. The biases in our genes often give rise to coping strategies, such as creating artworks or devoting oneself to business or science, that produce great social benefits. Moreover, the genes themselves are diverse, and their interactions are complex. The inheritance of a major mental disorder probably includes major genes that are uncommon in the general population, as well as many common modifying genes that also have important implications for personality. Even the major genes are unlikely to be uniform across the entire population of disease sufferers; more likely, they vary from one family to another. As for the modifying genes, who knows how many sites on the genome are important in personality, and how many varieties exist at those sites? We probably won't be equipped to approach these questions for another generation.

For now, the task is to identify the major genes in some families of people with severe mental disorders, because they would help us understand the underlying causes of the illness. They would not necessarily tell us who in the general population is or is not susceptible to a particular disorder, although they would help us determine susceptibility in individual families. This knowledge will present hard choices, as it does in families with Huntington's disease, a neurological disorder with gradual onset in middle age marked by memory loss, personality change, and involuntary movements leading to dementia and early death. The genetics of this disease are simple: a single defective gene is passed on directly from one parent. It is a dominant disorder, meaning that only one copy of the defective gene, rather than two, is needed to produce the illness, and "penetrance" is 100 percent by age eighty, meaning that a carrier of the gene is virtually certain to have the disease by that age. Now that the section of the genome where this gene resides has been identified (it is on the short arm of chromosome 4), geneticists can determine with a high degree of confidence whether someone with an affected parent has the gene. The option to take this test presents a host of psychological and ethical dilemmas that each person must sort out for himself. But for many potential carriers of the gene, simply having the choice of knowing or not knowing has been very important.

To me, the most compelling argument for studying the biological bases of violence rests on the individual's opportunity for self-knowledge. As well as being a social problem, impulsive aggression is one of many disturbing personality traits that interfere with people's lives and relationships. Most of the patients we evaluate are not criminals in trouble with the law but people whose lives have been torn apart by conflicts with their families and coworkers. These people can benefit from an understanding of why they act the way they do and how they can get their lives under control. If we can give them that understanding, we should.

⑤

Just as important, this knowledge can provide the basis for better-informed treatment. Many of the drugs developed for depression may also turn out to help personality disorder patients. Lithium, which increases the responsiveness of serotonin receptors, has been shown to reduce aggressiveness in criminals. Pilot studies suggest that SSRIs such as Prozac may reduce impulsive aggression, as can serotonin agonists, which directly stimulate serotonin receptors. More definitive studies are now under way, propelled by the research associating serotonin with aggression. A variety of drugs, most of them blood-pressure medications, dampen the effects of the norepinephrine system and so may lessen the thrill of novelty seeking—a helpful change for people who need to control their impulses. Drugs that control seizure disorders, such as carbamezepine (Tegretol) or valproate (Depakote), have been used to dampen mood swings in patients with affective instability. Monoamine oxidase inhibitors increase the responsiveness of the noradrenergic system and may help stabilize its functioning; they have been shown to improve both depressive symptoms and rejection sensitivity in histrionic and borderline patients. Some people suggest that anticholinergic agents may help with these patients' affective instability, but this idea will have to await more study. There is only limited evidence that these drugs are even helpful in depression.

Although the usefulness of drugs in treating personality disorders is still largely unproven, many personality disorder patients have recently begun receiving treatment. This fact alone makes me think the drugs are probably beneficial. Ten years ago, when setting up a biological study using personality disorder patients, we seldom had to allow for medication withdrawal as part of the protocol, since most subjects were not receiving any. Now we often get inquiries from people who are already on medications.

The biological roots of personality disorders are relevant to talking therapies as well. They provide a foundation for a truly empathetic understanding of the patient. If therapists appreciate the predispositions underlying their patients' inner vulnerabilities, they can be less judgmental and more realistic in their expectations. A tendency in someone like Nancy to act out her conflicts and act precipitously to solve her dilemmas has strong temperamental underpinnings: it is a learned habit, but not only that. Her therapist must understand how Nancy is driven by her intense emotionality before there can be any useful investigation of the types of events that trigger her powerful reactions.

Medication can help. By offering respite from extreme emotional swings and reducing the tendency to impulsive action, drugs may allow a patient to step back and reflect on his mood. Because these patients' emotional states are so powerful and their ability to reflect has been so regularly short-circuited by impulsive actions, they often have never learned to think about the connection between their feelings and their actions. Both drug and talk therapies must be focused on helping the patient acquire this difficult skill. The therapist offers as a model her own tolerance of intense feelings. She aids the patient in the struggle to contain feelings without generating action and to comprehend the timing and meaning of emotional shifts.

The failure of introspection is not an accident. It is a deeply ingrained defensive strategy that serves to protect people with personality disorders from the most painful aspects of their lives. The histrionic woman we saw in the last chapter, who complained of migraines rather than her husband's abusiveness, is one example. By short-circuiting any awareness of what was troubling her, she temporarily avoided its impact, only to have the feelings connected with the hurt resurface in unexpected ways. For borderline patients these feelings often have to do with separation. A female patient may not respond to her therapist's announcement of a vacation, for instance, but later in the hour, when discussing a casual acquaintance in her office who is leaving for another job, she may find herself weeping uncontrollably. This upwelling of profound sadness, far out of proportion to her feelings about her coworker, makes sense only if she connected her coworker's leaving with her therapist's impending vacation, which was truly a source of concern for her. It may later come out, over the course of treatment, that many of her reactions to loss come from a time in her childhood when her father left the house for several months after a period of bitter fighting with her mother; the patient has always been very sensitive to separation but did not even remember her parents' estrangement until after an intensive discussion of her reaction to her therapist's vacation. Her attempts at numbing herself, to her therapist's absence and, more importantly, to her childhood separation from her father, both fail. The feelings emerge in disguise, removed from the trauma she does not want to confront. Psychodynamic therapy helps her understand connections and patterns that are outside her awareness but that powerfully affect her life nonetheless.

Some people with intense underlying emotional sensitivities try to dampen deeply upsetting experiences because they fear that thinking about them will be unbearably painful or will lead to impulsive behavior outside their control. For others, impulsive acts themselves deflect emotional pain. Still others manage their oscillating emotions by manipulating the people around them to prevent them from acting in a way that will touch off painful feelings. A therapist who recognizes these tactics for what they are can help the patient gain a realistic mastery of his or her feelings that does not depend on outrageous behavior or the control of others. Sometimes the therapist must set strict guidelines to emphasize that certain behaviors will not be tolerated while the patient is in therapy: wrist cutting, suicide attempts, drug use, and so on. Only after such measures are no longer an option can patients begin to concentrate on dealing constructively with their intensely hurt feelings.

Cognitive behavioral therapy relies on individual sessions as well as group "skills" training to help patients recognize the onset of upsetting feelings and find alternative strategies to cope with them. Patients are rewarded for taking responsibility for themselves, not for self-destructive behavior. Pioneering studies by Marcia Linehan suggest that DBT, dialectic behavioral therapy, a specific form of cognitive behavior therapy, may be a more effective treatment for the affectively unstable, impulsive borderline patient than standard psychotherapy.

Antisocial individuals are very difficult to treat, especially if they are very impulsive. They may be so used to taking aggressive action in response to frustration that they cannot learn to reflect on their behavior. When this trait is combined with affective insensitivity, the person's capacity to empathize with others' feelings and suppress behavior that may hurt them becomes severely limited. Emotional connectedness, trust, and identification, the therapist's best tools for promoting change, are so blunted that people with pronounced psychopathic traits seldom repond well to psychotherapy. But they may respond to structured settings, including groups or institutional treatment, where their behavior is confronted by others who have gone through the same experiences. These communities, with clearly enforced privileges and punishments, may help the sociopathic person begin to internalize the sense of rules that we consider the germ of conscience. Groups like Alcoholics Anonymous may use confrontational techniques to reach people whose profound denial makes them impervious to individual psychotherapy. For people who have never experienced real compassion from others or even had significant limits put on them, such groups may provide an opening to feelings they have never before explored. Still, some with the combination of severe emotional insensitivity and impulsivity may be unreachable—for all our best efforts, incurable.

For narcissistic personalities, the therapist needs both to appreciate their underlying vulnerabilities and to confront and set limits on their sense of entitlement. Some therapists advocate "mirroring"—reflecting empathetically both the narcissist's feelings of grandiosity and the underlying humiliation that drives it. Certainly one of the keys to helping the narcissist shed his arrogant facade is to understand and bring to light the multifaceted emotions beneath it. Because they share the tendency to impulsivity, many narcissistic patients need first to learn the capacity to reflect before they act on their feelings. Group psychotherapy, self-help, or task-oriented groups provide an environment where dramatic cluster patients can learn from each other where their demands are excessive, their behavior too controlling, or their bland

denial of feelings too infuriating. In fact, because of its effectiveness and economy, group therapy is becoming the treatment of choice for many personality disorder patients.

All of us have known people with slight or severe dramatic cluster disorders. We have found them difficult, stormy, impenetrable, or irrational; they often did things that upset those around them. We need not indulge these people or tolerate intolerable behavior in order to understand the vulnerabilities they struggle with or to respect the fact that everyone does not confront life with the same strengths. While this understanding may translate into a firm insistence that such people take responsibility for their own lives, including their vulnerabilities, this insistence will be more effective if it is grounded in a realistic assessment of what those vulnerabilities entail. Just as a person with a genetic predisposition to high cholesterol needs to be reminded of the need for a prudent diet and generous exercise—and may, because of the weakness, be all the more tempted to cheat—so a person who is prone to angry outbursts and tantrums must be given limits that are defined and enforced. Neither approach—neither firmness nor empathy—needs to preclude the other.

CHAPTER FIVE

CROSSING REALITY AT AN ANGLE

I. ALBERT

> *Phenomenal nature shadows him wherever he goes. Clouds in the staring sky transmit to one another, by means of slow signs, incredibly detailed information regarding him. His inmost thoughts are discussed at nightfall, in manual alphabet, by darkly gesticulating trees. Pebbles or stains or sun flecks form patterns representing in some awful way messages which he must intercept. Everything is a cipher and of everything he is the theme. . . The very air he exhales is indexed and filed away.*
>
> — VLADIMIR NABOKOV

ALBERT WAS A QUIET BOY. His grades were good, and because he was tall and reasonably athletic, his high school gym teacher encouraged him to join the basketball team. This gave him the appearance of fitting in: girls liked him, he had a crowd to travel in, and even his parents did not notice that he had no close friends. He was certainly seen in others' company often enough. Nothing he said or did gave any hint of a disturbance. He was accepted by a large university in New England.

Once there, he had trouble concentrating on his studies. He dated a girl for a few weeks but she then began seeing somebody else. His normal despondency over this rejection took an unusual turn: as he continued to think about her, he grew certain she had *done* something to affect his thought processes. A month or so into the semester, it became apparent to Albert's dormitory mates that he was not just another freshman having difficulty adjusting to the demands of college life: he was starting to act peculiar.

Albert later described to me how he became convinced that this girl had not acted alone but was part of a college-wide conspiracy. One morning he walked into the bathroom down the hall from his room. Three boys were combing their hair at the mirror. Watching them, Albert realized they were conducting an elaborate performance for his benefit: the casual yet precise coordination of their gestures, the perfect flow of conversation from one boy to another, the way they pocketed their combs in a smoothly syncopated rhythm, could not be accidental. "It was," he said, "like watching Michael Jordan lead the Bulls on a fast break." As the three left the bathroom, one boy gave Albert a significant look through the mirror, as if to say, Did you catch that? Do you understand its meaning? The same day, a veiled reference in a student newspaper editorial to "the true situation on campus" confirmed his suspicions.

It became impossible to study or even listen to class lectures. Every chance remark, every gesture glistened with a meaning he could not fathom. What had he stumbled on? Perhaps the girl had slipped him a drug being developed under top-secret government supervision in one of the university's faceless laboratory buildings? With increasing vigilance, he detected further signs of collaboration. Other students would behave secretively when he approached, lowering their voices, turning away, or refusing to meet his direct gaze. On the other hand, he would occasionally turn suddenly to catch strangers staring at him—sometimes with sympathy, or else with coolly detached interest. Whatever the nature of the network, it became plain to him that some people on campus (mostly faculty and administrators) were running it; some students were active collaborators; most had no idea what was going on; and a few, whose ranks Albert had unwillingly joined, knew what was happening but were afraid to speak out. He must not mention the network to anyone. The penalties for doing so were communicated to Albert when he overheard the boy who had looked at him in the bathroom mirror tell a classmate that he had not slept for three days because he was in danger of flunking an upcoming mechanical engineering exam. To be punished with sleep deprivation for a mere glance! The network's omniscience and ruthlessness were terrifying.

Certain buildings had to be avoided, by elaborate detours if necessary. They were not real buildings, he later told me, but "roach motels." He began avoiding bathrooms as well, not only out of fear of receiving another illicit communication but also because personal hygiene was strongly connected with the social control that somehow lay at the root of the conspiracy. He could safely shower, change his clothes, or brush his teeth only once or twice a week, when he felt the pressure of the forces on his mind ease up slightly.

For while some drug may have been necessary to "initialize" his brain, as he put it, he perceived that the network was now trying to gain direct access to his thoughts. The stares of passersby and their avoidance of him had become unmistakable. To ward off attempts at hypnotism, he bought a pair of wraparound sunglasses and began wearing them night and day, indoors and out.

Albert was desperately homesick. Except for one week of basketball camp when he was fifteen, he had never left home for any extended period. He longed to tell his parents of his struggles and the dangerous information he had acquired, but that would only make him a more obvious target for the network. He felt his only chance was to lie low and hope they underestimated his resistance. So he restricted himself to one perfunctory phone call a week, in which he revealed nothing of his inner turmoil. He would act as normal as possible, "just as if I had no idea what they were up to."

For a while this strategy, aided by the sunglasses, seemed to work. In November he managed to complete a few homework assignments for the first time since early in the semester. He sat with some people at meals and even went to a fraternity party, though once there he spoke to no one. His visit home over Thanksgiving break passed uneventfully. His parents noticed that he seemed preoccupied, but they thought he was probably just concerned about his course work.

He returned to school, however, to find that the network had not forgotten him, only changed tactics. On his first night back, "they achieved the long-sought breakthrough" and transmitted the voices of the most dangerous conspirators directly into his mind. They were threatening voices, and evil: they told him, "We know all about you," and advised him to kill himself. On succeeding nights they spoke to him at length, preventing him from sleeping. In his anger and fear, Albert began answering them out loud, using special words of his own making, which he directed specifically against the power of the network. At this point his roommates and others in the dormitory became sufficiently concerned that they notified his student adviser, who contacted Albert's parents. He was brought back home for psychiatric evaluation.

Albert spent the next two weeks in the acute psychiatric inpatient unit of his hometown hospital, being treated with antipsychotic medications. The voices receded somewhat, and he began to relate more appropriately to the patients and staff. But his thinking remained disorganized: while he accepted the staff psychiatrists' assurances that they were trying to help him, he could never quite let go of the belief that the purpose of their help was to free him from the network's clutches. High school classmates who saw him over that Christmas break were struck by his extreme lack of emotional expression and by the far-off, preoccupied look in his eyes.

After his release from the hospital, Albert was clearly not ready to go back to school. He found a job at a local fast-food restaurant instead. But his continuing worries about the network, which he now detected extending far beyond his college, made him unreliable and error prone at work, and he was soon fired. He received this failure with equanimity, telling his parents, "I have bigger fish to fry," and punctuating this remark with an ironic, joyless little laugh that they would hear from him often as time went by. For the next few months he remained at home, almost a recluse in his bedroom. Irony became a chief mode of communication: when he would refuse to leave the house "because I'm an invalid," it was hard to tell whether he was mocking himself or those around him.

His symptoms slowly increased. By summer, his shouting matches with the voices of the network had become a nightly occurrence, and he was committed to a state hospital. Thus began the pattern of his adult life. Despite occasional lucid periods when he could relate normally to others, his disease followed a chronic downhill course. Several times the hospital released him, either to live at home again or, in later years, into a halfway house. Each time his psychotic ideas worsened, forcing his return to the institution. During one trial release, he vanished onto the streets of Manhattan, and the last thread of contact with the world of his youth was broken.

§

It is the alienness of schizophrenia that draws our attention. The sheer strangeness of the schizophrenic person's ideas and experiences fascinates and repels us; when he acts on those ideas, he becomes a pathetic and frightening figure. The manifestations of the disease are bewildering in their almost endless variety. Almost all people with schizophrenia hallucinate voices, and many also experience unreal visions, smells, tastes, or feelings on their skin or inside their bodies. Their sense of space and time may change radically. They have the sense that their thoughts and actions are no longer under their direct control: they may think others are broadcasting instructions and information directly into their brains or, conversely, that their inner thoughts can be perceived by others either distant or nearby. They often have "ideas of reference," the conviction that all conversations they overhear and all events, including accidental and natural ones, are intimately related to their own situation. They may weave unrelated events into a complex, massively detailed world view that they believe in wholeheartedly despite acknowledging its outrageous implausibility.

These psychotic manifestations—hallucinations, broadcasting of thoughts, delusional thinking, paranoia, and a general preoccupation with an unreal world—are the "positive symptoms" of schizophrenia. They constitute the madness that dominates most people's impressions of this illness. But there is another group of symptoms, the "negative" or "deficit" symptoms, without which one cannot make sense of what is happening to the schizophrenic person. The deficit traits provide the core of the symptomatology of the disease. Well before the sudden bloom of psychotic symptoms that led to his hospitalization, Albert suffered from a difficulty in attention, an inability to form deep relationships, and flattened emotional responses that grew dramatically more restricted as his illness progressed. The emotional reactivity that underlies successful relations with others was severely curtailed in

Albert. It was this deficit, more than his hallucinations and delusions, that prevented him from holding a job, maintaining friendships, or leading any sort of normal life.

A profound cognitive disorganization may accompany schizophrenia's negative symptoms. In addition to their difficulty in organizing their thoughts, schizophrenic patients have trouble monitoring their motor behavior. They may speak in a disjointed, stilted way, making up words or using existing words in strange contexts whose full meaning only they understand. Sometimes schizophrenic speech is sparse and almost telegraphic; other times its flowery abundance masks an impoverishment of ideas. The stream of their associations from one topic to another may be unconventional and impossible to follow because it is based on an idiosyncratic system of understanding the world rather than a frame of reference shared with the listener. On standard psychological tests such as the Rorschach test, their responses may range from inappropriately concrete to incomprehensibly abstract. As schizophrenic patients age, their psychotic symptoms often fade, leaving the deficit symptoms as the disease's most prominent features.

Psychosis can be seen in a variety of psychiatric diseases, notably mania and some severe forms of depression. As I mentioned in Chapter 3, it sometimes appears in attenuated form in the personality disorders. There are also some psychotic disorders, such as delusional disorder, that are distinct from schizophrenia. In schizophrenia, however, the positive and negative symptoms reinforce each other. Delusional systems often start out with a grain of truth—Albert's fellow students could well have been remarking on his strange appearance and avoiding his company—but it is the absence of that shared frame of reference, continually renewed by social contact, that permits them to grow out of control.

When he was growing up and living at home, Albert could mask his cognitive deficits with extreme passivity. He simply did what others told him to do, and for children there is no lack of authority figures willing to tell them in detail how to act. Since his cognitive deficits did not extend to rule-bound activities like writing and mathematics, he was able to satisfy the two main requirements for survival as a modern suburban child: he did as he was told and he got good grades. His classmates and to a great extent his teachers accepted him because he was good-looking and athletic; his taciturnity was attributed to shyness, and his lack of emotional response—his failure to share their enthusiasms, laugh when they laughed or get angry when they did—struck them as mellow, "laid back." His parents, also reasonably intelligent and socially awkward, though not nearly to the same degree as Albert, thought he would simply come out of his shell at some point.

Going away to college presented, as it does for many young people, a new and terrifying prospect. It was not the academic work that worried him, however—in fact he hardly seemed to think about it at all—but the social challenge. Albert had to adapt himself to a new community, learn its rules and traditions, and establish a place within it as an independent person. Well aware of his own handicaps, he found this task extremely threatening, especially since he knew he could never go back—college marked the end of his childhood dependency—but felt he had no resources or supports with which to go forward. He had always done what people expected of him, but now they expected the impossible. The sense of being trapped in a hopeless situation undoubtedly lent his delusions their sinister overtones. The idea of a vast hierarchical network, trying to influence Albert's mind in order to adapt him to some large, vaguely defined purpose, is a distorted representation of the actual reason kids are sent to college. But the stress he felt led him to see this purpose as entirely malignant.

At the same time, Albert's attentional deficits made him prone to misread, exaggerate, or ignore the wordless messages—the inflection of a voice, the nod of a head, or the timing of a smile—that provide the guideposts for normal communication. Unable to read this language appropriately or to synchronize his nonverbal cues with others, he could neither sustain relationships with his classmates nor correctly monitor their reactions to him, and so he became increasingly alienated and eccentric in his behavior. The same cognitive disorganization that interfered with his interpersonal relationships also led to oddities of thought. When he tried to understand why people acted as they did and what their words and gestures meant, he could not distinguish plausible reasons from wildly implausible ones. His inability to relate to the world around him left him no defense against the unreal world of his delusions. Albert's psychosis sustained his isolation; his isolation sustained his psychosis.

ଗ

Before the recent dominance of biological psychiatry, theorists offered a number of psychodynamic models to explain the causes of schizo-phrenia. (The splitting denoted by the prefix *schizo,* by the way, doesn't refer to split personality—which is now called dissociative iden-tity disorder—but to a more basic fragmentation of the patient's thoughts, emotions, and behavior. "Shattered personality" might be a more accurate description.) Most of these psychodynamic theories pos-tulated some trauma in infancy: an "anxious mother" transmitted intol-erable levels of anxiety to her baby; or a failure of maternal empathy caused the baby to be exposed to realities in a way that was out of phase with its developmental needs; or a failure of maternal protection caused, in a susceptible infant, the development of a dormant, psy-chotic, hallucinatory personality that under later stress emerged and began to dominate. After World War II, therapists began to observe that schizophrenic patients often were not the only members of their families who showed signs of irrationality, and the "schizophrenogenic family" came into vogue, in which one individual was "designated" to express symptoms for an entire family's illness. Schizophrenia was seen to grow out of pathological family interactions, such as Gregory Bateson and Donald Jackson's famous "double-bind," in which one parent habitually placed the child in a damned-if-you-do-damned-if-you-don't situation. Other pathological interactions included reversal of the parent-child relationship, "emotional divorce" among family members, and an eroticized parent-child relationship. It would be hard to consider many of these theories scientific, in the sense that one could point to specific parental behavior patterns that either did or did not correlate with development of the disease in the children. In any case, even if one could define these behavior patterns with sufficient clarity, such a correlation is unlikely. Many families that contain eroticized parent-child relationships, for instance, do not produce schizophrenia.

Despite this lack of scientific rigor, all of these theories came from original and often brilliant therapists who spent years working with schizophrenic patients, gaining profound insights into their thoughts and experiences. Much of this work describes interactions that, while perhaps not causative, may certainly influence the disease's course and outcome. And since, as I will shortly explain, we are sure that schizophrenia has *some* environmental triggers, it would be unwise to dismiss these theories out of hand. Still, when the patient's childhood environment was advanced as the sole cause of the disease, the effect was to place an immense burden of guilt on parents who were already suffering terrible anguish from seeing what was happening to their children and being helpless to stop it. When all the nuances of differing theories were washed away, what was left in many people's minds—-and what causes bitter anger at the psychiatric community even today—was a sense that parents, especially mothers, were somehow to blame for raising their children schizophrenic. This message, even though unintentional, is one of the cruelest hoaxes ever wrought by modern medicine.

Parents are almost certainly not to blame. Although we cannot yet point to exact mechanisms, there is clearly a biological substrate underlying schizophrenia. Our certainty of this rests on three kinds of evidence: first, genetic factors seem to operate in the transmission of the disease; second, schizophrenic patients respond reliably to a particular class of antipsychotic medications, the neuroleptics; and third, researchers have found numerous brain abnormalities specific to schizophrenia. No single chain of events is likely to be found to cause the disease. It probably arises out of a combination of genetic susceptibilities and environmental events, which together constitute the cause of the final illness. Nor are the environmental factors necessarily psychological. Some evidence suggests that a viral disease or prenatal undernourishment may play a role. Other theories posit nongenetic biological factors, present as early as conception, that may affect the development of the brain. Still others focus on psychological events but emphasize stresses that start around the time of onset and continue through adult life, perhaps contributing to the illness's downward course.

A "natural experiment" that has been carefully studied is the Dutch Hunger Winter of 1944–45, when a Nazi blockade in the last months of World War II caused a sudden, severe, but relatively brief famine in a population that maintained good birth and health records. At the height of the famine, from February to April 1945, many adults' food intake was less than 1,000 calories per day, but food supplies were restored quickly after the blockade was broken in May. Children conceived during or shortly before these months were approximately twice as likely to be hospitalized for schizophrenia during their twenties as their compatriots conceived at other times from 1944 to 1946. There was no similar disparity for neurological disorders or mental retardation. This study shows clearly that early environmental influences can have an impact on later mental health; it suggests that poverty and malnutrition may be putting people at risk for schizophrenia today as well.

ᕓ

Schizophrenia is a complex disease of the brain that affects its structure and neuropsychological function as well as neurochemistry. But we may be getting close to a time when anatomical, functional, and chemical abnormalities can be woven together into a coherent, unified picture.

ABNORMALITIES IN BRAIN STRUCTURE. At first glance, one might think that any structural brain abnormalities associated with schizophrenia would have to be very subtle. This disease emerges only after many years of normal functioning, and in any case the idea of associating such a complex mental disturbance with large, visible brain differences smacks of phrenology—trying to correlate personality types with bumps on the skull. Surprisingly, this prejudice turns out to be incorrect. If you put a radiologic image of the brain of a schizophrenic individual side by side with that of a normal brain, you can often see clear differences between them. The most striking difference, and the first one consistently observed, is that the ventricular system, a network of chambers within the brain containing the cerebrospinal fluid that bathes the central nervous system, is visibly enlarged in many schizophrenic patients. The lateral ventricles particularly—located about two-thirds of the way back on either side within the cerebrum—have been shown to be enlarged in patients with social withdrawal, blunted affect, and certain neuropsychological impairments. Some studies have shown the same association for the third ventricle, which is farther forward and more centrally located.

If the ventricles, which are essentially fluid-filled caverns, are larger, did something else shrink, or perhaps fail to grow to normal size? If so, when did this happen? We don't know. All brains atrophy somewhat with age, but in schizophrenia the ventricular enlargement may arise from a developmental abnormality early in life. Or the enlargement may progress abnormally over time. Perhaps both processes occur in varying combinations that in some unknown way affect the onset and course of the disease.

As for what structures are shrunken, magnetic resonance studies of schizophrenic patients have shown reductions in the temporal and sometimes the frontal cortex—differences also found on postmortem examination—as well as in the thalamus, a key sensory relay station in the more primitive subcortical part of the brain. More important than a simple reduction in size, however, is that these structures seem to suffer from "faulty wiring." As the fetal and infant brain grows, it organizes itself by the migration of neurons to appointed spots, a process that may go awry in babies who later develop schizophrenia. Neurons may go past the correct location or not reach it, resulting in faulty synaptic connections or abnormal packing and orientation of nerve cells. Although this process remains poorly understood, a number of studies in deceased schizophrenic patients suggest a disorganization at the level of neuronal connections that may result in inefficient or inconsistent patterns of neural transmission.

Ventricular size varies somewhat in everyone and is partly genetically based, but it also seems to be affected by environmental factors. Daniel Weinberger and his colleagues at NIMH compared ventricular size in pairs of identical twins, of whom one had been diagnosed with schizophrenia and the other had not, and found that in most cases the ventricles were larger in the schizophrenic twin. They suggested that there is a genetically determined equilibrium to the growth of brain structures that is somehow disturbed in schizophrenia. This finding strongly implies multiple factors: the genetic predisposition toward this disease is activated by some environmental event or condition. We now think that the genetic factors that contribute to faulty development of neuronal organization and brain structure may also make a person more susceptible to early adverse circumstances. Complications of childbirth, trauma, or fever—any of which can temporarily alter the brain's supply of oxygen—or viral illness or poor nutrition during pregnancy may cause no lasting effects in most infants but in a susceptible few may lead to early brain damage. Abnormalities in the size and structure of the ventricles, volume of various brain regions, and neuronal organization may be the result of this interaction between genetic susceptibility and environmental insult.

Disorganized neural connections contribute to disordered thinking and perceptions. The brain areas where these abnormalities occur—the temporal and frontal cortex, the hippocampus, and the limbic system—are all important in the regulation of thinking and emotion. The brain's frontal areas serve an executive function, integrating complex sensory information into a working model of the environment to compare with past experiences and other memories so as to plan appropriate actions. In monkeys, frontal lobe lesions impair performance on tasks that require them to remember an object that is no longer visible. For instance, if the experimenter shows a normal monkey a piece of food and then places it under one of three cups, the monkey will turn over the correct cup and grab the food without hesitation. A monkey with an experimental lesion in one part of its frontal lobe has much more difficulty. Frontal lobe defects in humans may lead to a lack of motivation, planning, and initiative, as well as poorly modulated emotion. The temporal areas and the hippocampal system seem to be implicated in verbal learning and short-term memory. The limbic system, a cluster of interrelated organs surrounding the brainstem that includes the hippocampus, the olfactory organs, and other structures, is thought to play a role in relating visceral functions and senses to emotion—the relation of smell to memory, for instance, or the emotional content of pain and hunger. If these systems are disrupted, they could produce many of the bizarre symptoms we see in schizophrenia: the wildly inappropriate emotional responses as well as the delusional thinking.

DISORDERS OF BRAIN FUNCTION. Over the years, psychologists have developed a number of tests that are sensitive to dysfunction in specific brain regions, and most schizophrenic patients show characteristic deficits in tests of frontal or temporal lobe function. For example, in the Wisconsin Card Sort Task, the examiner presents the subject with cards showing designs in various shapes and colors. One card might show three yellow triangles, while the next has one blue square. By relying on the examiner to tell her whether she's done it correctly, the subject must decide whether to sort the cards by shape, color, or the number of designs on the card. At regular intervals the sorting criteria change, but the subject must figure this out from the response she gets from the examiner. Schizophrenic patients have difficulty changing their sorting strategy when this is called for; once they've settled on a criterion, they persist with it too long. They also invent unusual criteria, which may be as inappropriately concrete as the presence or absence of dust specks on a card or as abstract as an interpretation of meaning in the designs.

Daniel Weinberger, Karen Berman, and their colleagues have used PET to evaluate cerebral blood flow in subjects taking the Wisconsin Card Sort test. (As I mentioned on page 110, PET uses an injection of radio-labeled compounds to light up the brain areas having the highest blood flow, indicating the most energy use and therefore the greatest neural activity.) They found that schizophrenic patients, as a group, not only performed less well on the Wisconsin Card Sort than normal subjects but also showed less brain activation in their frontal regions while taking the test. Other tests have revealed no such difference. When Weinberger and Berman tested schizophrenics' spatial skills, for instance, their blood flow patterns were no different from the controls'. This finding complemented previous work—such as that done by Monte Buchsbaum, then at NIMH—suggesting reduced frontal lobe activity ("hypofrontality") compared to posterior brain activity.

Weinberger and Berman interpreted these results as showing a selective brain dysfunction in schizophrenia having to do with the frontal lobe's role in organizing information and planning appropriate behavior. The Wisconsin Card Sort demands a high level of integration. Subjects must not only recognize patterns and interpret social cues but also coordinate these efforts in order to continue receiving "desirable" cues from the examiner. These tasks require them to organize their sensory impressions, place them in categories, and decide which ones to focus on. If they cannot organize perceptual information into useful patterns, they cannot use it as a guide to future behavior. People with schizophrenia have a hard time forming realistic, coherent models of their environment, especially the most complex and subtle aspect of all, the workings of interpersonal relationships. Someone who has difficulty tuning in to social cues may ignore a friendly comment or smile—perhaps instead becoming preoccupied with the shape of an eyebrow—and so never find out whether the person is interested in a social interaction. Further, in attempting to make sense of an inchoate flood of impressions, he may piece together unrelated facts to come up with theories that bear little relation to reality but are driven by some underlying distress, as Albert's network theory was driven by his fear of independence and having to make a life for himself in a new community.

Weinberger and Berman have recently taken these results a step further and linked frontal lobe dysfunction to abnormalities in the temporal and hippocampal regions, with which the frontal lobes are densely connected. (Other researchers, such as Raquel and Ruben Grur of the University of Pennsylvania and McCarley and Shenton of Harvard, have identified structural and functional abnormalities in the temporal lobe as key to the pathology of schizophrenia.) Their findings here parallel animal studies that show that lesions in the temporal and hippocampal organs of infant rats will result in behavioral changes in adult rats that mimic frontal lobe dysfunction. It may be that this early impairment in the hippocampal areas actually brings about changes in frontal lobe activity and secondary limbic hyperactivity. These three areas—the frontal and temporal lobes, limbic system, and the hippocampus—are involved in the key brain circuits that process and organize sensory information, evaluate it in relation to past experience, and plan and direct future actions. It's not hard to imagine that alterations in these circuits would profoundly affect the way a person perceives and responds to the world. Interestingly, individual genetic differences in lesioned animals, for example in dopamine system responsiveness, may influence whether these lesions are relatively "silent" or whether they result in behavioral disturbances perhaps analogous to psychosis. Among people with a susceptibility to schizophrenia, similar differences in the regulation of modulating systems such as the dopamine system could help determine whether they become psychotic, as Albert did, or merely eccentric and isolated. A factor like this might offer a key to treating or preventing full-blown psychosis.

NEUROCHEMICAL DEFECTS AND THE DOPAMINE HYPOTHESIS. Of the same vintage as the catecholamine and indoleamine hypotheses of depression, the dopamine hypothesis of schizophrenia was stimulated by the observation that the neuroleptic (antipsychotic) medications available in the 1960s all share a common property: they block dopamine receptors. The first neuroleptics, the phenothiazines, of which Thorazine was probably the most widely used, were originally developed as surgical anesthetics. In 1952, John Delay and Pierre Deniker tried using Thorazine to placate agitated psychotic patients and found that it restored a remarkable degree of normal functioning. So quickly did its use become almost universal that today few people remember how completely this drug changed the atmosphere of mental hospitals. In an era when many patients could be controlled only by physical restraints—straitjackets and padded rooms—by heavy sedation with barbiturates, or by lobotomy, the phenothiazines' arrival did away with the feeling of medieval Bedlam that had possessed these places; profoundly psychotic patients became able to talk with their doctors for the first time. The astonishing decrease in the number of permanent residents of American mental hospitals, from over 500,000 in the early 1950s to a fraction of that number today, dates from the introduction of Thorazine.

Other phenothiazines were introduced throughout the 1950s and '60s, and soon new types of neuroleptic medications, distinct from the phenothiazine family, were developed as well. In 1963, Solomon Snyder of Johns Hopkins and Philip Seamans of Toronto demonstrated that the single common feature of all these drugs was the ability to reduce the activity of dopamine at post-synaptic receptors. They showed that the effective dose of any neuroleptic medication was inversely proportional to its potency as a dopamine receptor antagonist. The more effectively the drug blocked the dopamine receptor, the less was needed to restore lucidity in a psychotic patient. This convincing demonstration of a direct relationship between clinical efficacy and dopamine antagonism spurred a rush of research on dopamine activity in the brains of schizophrenic patients.

Much as they had theorized that depression might be a disease of too little norepinephrine, many researchers asked whether schizophrenia was a disease of too much dopamine. As they did with norepinephrine and serotonin, they assessed dopamine levels indirectly, by measuring its metabolic products. Dopamine is broken down to homovanillic acid (HVA) in both the peripheral and central nervous systems. In an effort to measure how much dopamine was being metabolized in the brain, a number of investigators in the 1970s and 1980s measured HVA levels in the cerebrospinal fluid of schizophrenic patients and normal controls, hoping to find a consistent difference that would dovetail nicely with Snyder and Seamans's findings. No such difference was found.

Some studies, however, raised the possibility that the more acute, paranoid schizophrenic patients show increased cerebrospinal fluid levels of HVA, while these concentrations are below normal in the forms of schizophrenia that are characterized mainly by negative or deficit symptoms. More recently investigators have begun measuring HVA levels in blood plasma, a more accessible source. There is a problem in doing this, however, since most of the HVA you can measure in this way comes from the peripheral nerves rather than the brain; still, it's likely that variations in plasma HVA levels at least partly reflect variations in brain dopamine levels. Ken Davis and Michael Davidson at Mount Sinai, as well as Dave Pickar at NIMH, have found that higher quantities of plasma HVA correlate with the more psychotic symptoms. Their findings have not been entirely consistent, but they point to a relationship between dopamine and the altered behavior of schizophrenia. Moreover, patients with this profile—high plasma HVA, strong psychotic symptoms—show the most improvement on neuroleptic drugs, which bring HVA levels down over the course of treatment. Patients with lower plasma HVA and fewer psychotic symptoms are less likely to show improvement with neuroleptic treatment.

This finding puts us on familiar ground. Once again we find ourselves building a bridge from brain chemicals to personality traits to psychiatric diseases. This time, however, the personality trait has to do not with regulation of emotions, as in the mood disorders, nor with the capacity to contain aggressive impulses, as in the dramatic cluster personality disorders, but with the quality of one's thinking about the world. Patients with the greatest dopamine activity and the most psychotic symptoms appear to be the most responsive to the neuroleptic medications. Increased dopamine activity, therefore, is associated with the psychotic symptoms of schizophrenia, and reductions in dopamine activity may lead to their improvement. But there is a complication.

Schizophrenia has another side: the social withdrawal, emotional constriction, and difficulty in experiencing pleasure that make up the deficit symptoms. Although these may attenuate as part of a general improvement with medication, they are not necessarily helped by treatment with neuroleptics. In fact they may be made worse. Neuroleptic medication may, for example, mimic the "blunt affect," or flatness of emotional expression, which is one of the most persistent features of the schizophrenic syndrome. Some evidence suggests a correlation between decreased concentrations of dopamine and emotional flattening and social withdrawal. It would be tempting, then, simply to place all these symptoms on a spectrum, as we did with norepinephrine and engagement with the environment: high dopamine activity yields positive symptoms, and low dopamine activity yields negative symptoms. But we can't, because the positive and negative symptoms often coexist in the same patient. And unlike the coexistence of depression and mania, which give way to each other over time, schizophrenia's positive and negative symptoms are simultaneous. How can one person show symptoms of both high and low dopamine activity at the same time?

The answer may have to do with the interaction between dopamine and the structural abnormalities common to schizophrenia. If you damage the frontal lobes of rats, especially the dopaminergic neurons there, dopaminergic neurons in other areas of the brain become more active. The frontal brain systems in general exert an inhibitory influence on more primitive, subcortical areas. Dopaminergic neurons in the frontal areas appear to be responsible for maintaining working memory and information processing. If these are damaged by a progressive developmental defect (stemming from a genetic predisposition activated by an environmental stress), the result may be greater activation of dopaminergic neurons in the limbic areas, which promote more ritualized ways of coping with the environment. Inadequate function in the frontal areas coupled with overactivity in the subcortical areas might explain why complex, realistic models of the world are replaced by emotionally charged, stereotypic representations of reality. These primitive modes of thinking may easily merge into psychosis.

We sometimes see something similar happening in chronic amphetamine users. Amphetamines broadly stimulate the nervous system, increasing dopamine and norepinephrine activity as well as that of other neurotransmitter systems. When amphetamine users become suspicious, paranoid, or even actively delusional, it is probably due to chronic overstimulation of the limbic system. Dopamine antagonists—antipsychotic medications—may relieve these symptoms in amphetamine abusers just as they do in schizophrenics. But dopamine antagonists can do nothing for a *deficit* in dopamine activity, except perhaps make it worse. (Conversely, amphetamine may actually improve some of the cognitive deficits, such as errors on the Wisconsin Card Sort Test, that we see in schizotypal patients.) We are beginning experiments with drugs called dopamine agonists that specifically activate the D_1 receptor, the most abundant dopamine receptor in the cortex, in the hope that they will improve working memory, motivation, and other aspects of frontal lobe function in the schizophrenic-related personality disorders. It's not clear how far a chemical treatment can go in overcoming a structural deficiency, but any progress at all will be better than nothing.

Another way to think about the relation of the two sets of dopaminergic neurons, one in the cortex and the other in the limbic system, is to envision an old-fashioned phonograph record played on a cheap record player. The record is scratchy and the sound is tinny, but you can still make out a melody and the words to a song. We can view this situation as analogous to a low-stress life for a person susceptible to schizophrenia: cortical and limbic system activity are both low, and the person gets by with poor social functioning but few apparent psychotic symptoms. But if something happens to stimulate the dopamine system—some long-term stress that calls upon its activating functions—it is like putting the scratchy old record onto an expensive stereo system and turning up the volume. With the full range of frequencies booming out at you, the dust, scratches, and other imperfections in the record become overwhelming: you can no longer hear the music over the noise.

§

Despite tremendous advances in understanding the biology of schizophrenia, we still have little other than the neuroleptics for its treatment. These drugs have well-known effects on the neuromuscular system: restlessness and fidgeting, an inability to sit still, muscle stiffening similar to that seen in Parkinson's disease, or spasmodic muscle movements. These side effects appear to be caused by a disruption of the balance between the cholinergic and dopaminergic systems when the latter is blocked by neuroleptic drugs. Anticholinergic drugs can restore the balance and reduce the symptoms.

Unfortunately, anticholinergic drugs do not prevent a more serious disorder of involuntary movements, called tardive dyskinesia, that develops with long-term treatment with neuroleptics. It commonly involves lip smacking, chewing, and sucking motions but may also include breathing disturbances and abnormal trunk and limb movements. Some of the newer neuroleptic drugs, such as clozapine (Clozaril), have a different structure from the older ones and seem to antagonize both dopamine and serotonin receptors. The serotonin receptors that clozapine blocks, the $5HT_2$ receptors, appear to be involved in LSD's psychotogenic effects, and clozapine's antipsychotic action may be related to its effect on these receptors. Risperidone (Risperdal), another drug in this class, also blocks $5HT_2$ receptors. Olanzepine (Zyprexo) and sertindole (Serlect) are the newest additions to the atypical neuroleptics. These new agents cause fewer Parkinsonian reactions, such as stiffness or shuffling gait, and seem to pose less risk of tardive dyskinesia. (Clozapine can, however, depress the number of white blood cells, a very rare but still potentially serious side effect.)

Sometimes psychiatrists prescribe ECT, electroconvulsive shock therapy, for severely psychotic schizophrenic patients who do not respond to drugs. ECT is much more commonly used to treat severe depression, but it may actually be as effective in schizophrenia.

While the serotonin-dopamine blockers improve deficit symptoms somewhat, this side of schizophrenia is still hard to budge. It's not hard, however, to envision a drug that would improve these symptoms. Researchers would need to identify the specific dopamine receptor subtypes that predominate in the brain regions involved in the deficit symptoms and then design a drug that activates those particular receptors. In fact the research on dopamine agonists that I mentioned above represents the beginning of just such an effort. Still, it's clear that dopamine is not solely responsible for these symptoms, just as neither norepinephrine nor serotonin is solely responsible for depression, and newer theories emphasize excitatory neurotransmitters such as glutamate or inhibitory systems such as GABA. Moreover, schizophrenia's anatomical defects, which are well established by the time the disease is diagnosed, make it impossible to restore anything approaching normal frontal lobe function. But the dopamine system is a logical place to begin.

II. JERRY

> They all immediately rushed out into the hall to have a look at Akaky's new overcoat. Congratulations and good wishes were showered upon him. At first Akaky just smiled, then he felt rather embarrassed. But when all surrounded him and began telling him that he ought to celebrate his acquisition of a new overcoat and that the least he could do was invite them all to a party, Akaky Akakyevich was thrown into utter confusion and did not know what to do, what to say to them all, or how to extricate himself from that very awkward situation.
>
> — NIKOLAI GOGOL

THE DIVISION OF SCHIZOPHRENIA into positive and negative symptoms immediately suggests a cluster of related disorders. What if a person had only the positive symptoms or only the negative ones? What if these symptoms occurred with varying severity in different people? The diagnosis of schizophrenia might then mark a region in an imaginary coordinate space determined by psychosis along one axis, deficit symptoms along another, and cognitive disorganization on a third. Some people may be reasonably sociable but have psychotic-like symptoms and cognitive disorganization; others may have poor social function without psychotic symptoms. These variants may correspond to different biological syndromes: some people may have dysregulated dopamine systems without any structural alterations, and others may have the structural alterations without the dysregulation.

These different combinations of symptoms, falling short of full schizophrenia, comprise the "odd cluster" personality disorders. Many features of schizophrenia—anatomical defects, neurochemical abnormalities, cognitive and neuropsychological deficiencies, attentional and information processing deficits, and behavioral and emotional symptoms—appear in the odd cluster disorders, sometimes in mild form. People with these disorders often are reasonably self-sufficient and neither seek nor perhaps need the help of a mental health professional. In still milder cases these syndromes are not disorders at all but simply personality variants.

Many schizophrenic patients' family members have no discernible psychological problems other than those stemming from caring for a loved one who is chronically ill; other relatives, however, may be vulnerable to difficulty in organizing their thinking, yet show no signs of psychosis. While remaining functional members of their community, they still may seem significantly out of step with others. Rather than give this fact a psychosocial interpretation, as a previous generation did, modern psychiatrists look at it biologically, as evidence of shared genetic traits. Albert's family was not untypical, and while he was in my care I learned about his older cousin, Jerry.

Jerry was the son of Albert's father's older sister; he and Albert shared a grandmother, Irene, and a grandfather, Frank, who grew up on the same street and married while still in their teens. Irene was a dour, suspicious woman who seems to have been disliked by almost everyone who knew her. The brief glimpses she allowed of her inner landscape were dominated by a virulent racism that blamed almost everything wrong in the world on the presence of certain ethnic groups. Frank, who held one position at a large accounting firm for forty years without ever being promoted, was punctilious in his work and flawlessly informed in the minutiae of the tax codes. But he continually talked under his breath and sometimes chuckled incongruously; his speech was marked by oddly jumbled clichés (he once commented that an investigation of a bankrupt firm had "hardly tipped the scale of the iceberg"); and he was considered incapable of supervising others. He tended to fall apart under pressure, taking offense at routine questions from his superiors and becoming angry and abusive over the slightest mistake. It was also common knowledge around his office that he attributed mystical significance to certain combinations of numerals and that he believed he had once predicted a man's accidental death from the frequent appearance of the number 88 in his tax return.

Tax time—the weeks leading up to the deadline for filing income taxes—was especially difficult for him, and it was a family tradition that his every whim be humored during this season. This pampering did not prevent several psychotic episodes over the years, in which Frank would hear the voices of the "demon spirits" that were controlling his coworkers' behavior and would sometimes see grotesque faces in the shadows on his bedroom wall at night. These episodes never caused him to miss any days of work and in any case always cleared up in early May, when he would take a two-week vacation. He never sought psychiatric treatment. In the early 1970s, when Frank's company merged with another accounting firm, he found the change to new offices and procedures so upsetting that he asked for early retirement. But once retired, he never found anything to do with himself and within a year was dead of pneumonia. A few family members and one former supervisor attended the funeral.

Jerry, Frank's grandson, was only a few years younger than Albert's parents and went to many of the same schools. They remarked that he always, even from early childhood, seemed unaware of how different he was from others. He could be startled by the sound of a distant bus no one else could hear, yet be too preoccupied to notice people talking loudly in the same room. In high school in the late sixties, when tight blue jeans and a T-shirt were practically a uniform, Jerry persisted in wearing baggy slacks whose cuffs were always tattered in the back because they dragged on the floor. He favored fountain pens but seldom remembered to replace the cap when he put them in his pocket; ink stains on his shirt became almost a trademark.

When his classmates laughed, he often seemed to miss the joke. When he occasionally did get it, he would continue to repeat it long after others had stopped finding it funny. Chance encounters with people he knew never failed to unnerve him; afterward he would wonder whether he had said the right thing. He once confided to Albert's father that after these brief meetings he would repeat to himself every word that was spoken, over and over perhaps hundreds of times, until they had lost all meaning to him. He never knew if other kids were being genuinely friendly or were making fun of him, and so he was sometimes the victim of cruel pranks.

Jerry sometimes wondered aloud why it was so hard for him to relate to other people. He wistfully speculated about what it must be like to be able to make friends effortlessly, but he had little idea how to go about this. His overtures toward others were often bizarrely inappropriate—as a senior in high school, he once asked a classmate whether he'd like to go to a local pond after school to catch frogs—and often met with ridicule. Yet he seemed strangely unaware of, and incurious about, the oddities in his behavior that set him apart. After school, when the other boys played touch football, visited each others' houses, or worked at part-time jobs, Jerry went home and daydreamed. He felt comfortable only when playing with his ham radio equipment or reading science fiction. As his classmates began dating, he found himself even more isolated than before. The prospect of having a girlfriend seemed unimaginable.

He continued to live with his parents after high school, earning a degree in electrical engineering from a nearby college and then finding a job designing circuits for a local electronic instrument manufacturer. His facility with computers and electronics, which he found far more satisfying than people, not only helped him find jobs but gave him a measure of stability and self-confidence. In this inanimate world, where he could be competent and creative, he found an escape from the intimidating demands of others. Still, he grew increasingly wary, limiting his conversations with coworkers to perfunctory greetings and quick, superficial observations. In crowds, on trains and buses, in restaurants or any unfamiliar place, he often had the sense that strangers were pointing him out to make fun of him. While he knew his suspicions were largely baseless, his discomfort in interacting with others never eased, and as fax transmission, electronic mail, and other modern conveniences became more widespread, he began arranging more and more to work out of his home. He became increasingly sequestered and attached to a fixed routine.

Jerry never became overtly delusional, but he did sometimes worry that his thoughts would come true. In times of great stress or concern, he would hear his mother's voice whispering his name. While he was sure this sound did not come from her, it seemed to emanate from outside himself. Some nights, lying in bed half awake, he would hear the ordinary sounds from outside his window turn into something strange and frightening: he would become convinced aliens had landed in a spaceship and were rounding up people from nearby streets or that a terrible fire was making its way across town toward him. Sometimes he could assure himself that he was only imagining it, but often he would go repeatedly to the window and be surprised to find only a calm night outside. His ideas about society, involving a cult of interlocking political conspiracies, grew more and more unusual. Jerry never confessed these feelings to Albert's father; I found out about them only after I met him.

೧

People may be eccentric for any number of reasons that have nothing to do with mental illness: they may have been raised in unusual surroundings or have an unconventional approach to life or a set of strongly held beliefs that differ from most other people's—or they may belong to a culture, like the English, that admires and encourages slightly odd behavior as part of its national identity. But there are other people whose eccentricity is grounded in incapacity. They have a hard time relating to others or organizing their thoughts and perceptions in a realistic, effective manner. The remarkable prevalence in schizophrenic patients' families of people like Jerry—eccentric, isolated, yet without overt psychotic symptoms, hallucinations, or delusions—has led many psychiatrists to believe in a genetic connection. We feel there are common underlying causes that in some cases result in the chronic psychosis of schizophrenia but in others lead to the milder eccentricities of the odd cluster: schizotypal, paranoid, and schizoid personality disorders. In fact, since these personality disorders are more common in families of schizophrenic patients than schizophrenia itself, they may be the more likely manifestation of the same underlying genotype.

SCHIZOTYPAL PERSONALITY DISORDER. It is hard for many people to imagine how demanding and complicated maintaining a relationship can seem to someone like Jerry. Most of us rely on subtle nonverbal cues that we use continuously and often unconsciously to guide our interpretation of how others are reacting to us and what they expect from us. We also send these signals to others. But Jerry, like Albert, could not easily decipher the social cues that others presented him and so found it almost impossible to interact fluently with the people around him. What he could not easily grasp he came to view as ominous and threatening. As he grew older, he became suspicious and withdrawn, finally existing in chronic, profound isolation.

This life course is typical of schizotypal personalities: solitary and reclusive, growing more so as time goes on. The schizotypal person experiences any unstructured interaction, even so superficial as chatting with a neighbor, as fraught with problems and intensely uncomfortable. Even the most continuous, uncomplicated opportunities to strike up an acquaintance, such as sharing an office with a coworker, are often shunned. Schizotypal individuals differ in this respect from the merely shy. The latter feel conflict; they often wish to make contact, may even yearn to do so, but are inhibited by fear. And shy people "warm up" once you "break the ice" (there is a reason why these phrases are clichés)—once they get past their inhibitions, they are perfectly capable of maintaining long, satisfying relationships. With schizotypal personality disorder there is no breaking the ice. These people feel as awkward the twentieth time you talk to them as the first, and they keep to themselves as a matter of preference. Whereas a shy person's inhibitions tend to be rooted in feelings of inadequacy, the schizotypal person's social anxieties come from suspiciousness regarding the motives of the new people they encounter. Coming to a party at which he knows only the host, a shy person may gradually relax and find compatible people to talk with; the schizotypal person is more likely to brood that he was only invited to serve as an object of ridicule.

It is possible that, like stroke patients who lose not only the use of the left sides of their bodies but the very *idea* of leftness, people with schizotypal personality are missing some essential representation in their brains that most of us take for granted. They are not simply bad at handling the elements of social interaction—image and status, anticipating how others will react, casual conversation, courtesy or the well-timed compliment—they seem curiously insensitive to the idea that such things exist at all. While they may wish in an abstract way to "be more normal," this wish does not translate into any impulse to do the things that would make them "more normal": to pursue closeness with others. They usually have no close friends and rarely share personal feelings with others, except perhaps a close relative or spouse. The occasional successful marriages between people with schizotypal traits often lack the close sharing of thoughts and feelings most people associate with marriage; they are more like intimate but strangely inert coexistences highly constrained by mutual habit. These people lack not only the tools for intimacy but, more profoundly, the urge for it as well. Only when blindsided, so to speak, by a world that contains elements wholly missing from their internal representation of it are they made aware something is wrong.

Imagine growing up in a world where everybody has some sixth sense that you lack. They employ it all the time, habitually refer to it in myriad ways, use it as an essential ingredient of art and business (as well as sex, cuisine, police work, and everything else they do), and assume everybody, without exception, has it. Yet you, lacking the neural circuitry to process the relevant information, remain only dimly aware that it even exists, and then only because you sense that the reason you don't fit in is that others possess some unfathomable, unimaginable advantage. At crucial times you simply have no clue to what they're talking about or why they do what they do. This is the situation in which, to varying degrees, schizotypal personality disorder confines its victims.

Thus we have the paradox that schizotypal people's suspiciousness is rooted in fact: they *do* look and act different, and it *is* noticed—just as we would notice that a congenitally deaf person acted differently even if we had no concept of deafness. People with schizotypal traits often dress oddly because the idea that clothing presents an image is entirely lost on them: their clothes may be inappropriate, unfashionable, unkempt, and apparently chosen at random. They are frequently oblivious to social conventions. They may carry themselves oddly or display strange mannerisms. In conversation they may be stiff, awkward, gratuitously silly or aloof, or sometimes extremely nervous for no apparent reason, and their emotional expression is unusually limited. This does not change as one gets to know them. Their speech is also odd: sometimes desultory, digressing from one topic to another without control or focus, or else extremely terse. In either case it may be vague and hard to follow, featuring idiosyncratic or unusual words and phrases.

At the same time, however, the cognitive deficits that give rise to this behavior make the schizotypal person unable to take the true measure of others' response to it. So they often exaggerate to a wildly implausible degree the amount of attention they draw. Jerry's feeling that everyone on a train or bus had their eyes on him for some reason he didn't understand clearly could not be justified. Suspicions like this are part of a general pattern of distorted perceptions that may even include mild auditory hallucinations. A schizotypal person may on occasion hear his thoughts out loud, like a distinct voice, but unlike the schizophrenic, he will not be strongly convinced that it comes from outside his own head. He will recognize the content as part of his own thoughts—it just *sounds* like an external voice. (Many people have such experiences in times of extreme stress or altered emotions. A schizotypal person requires a much lower level of stress—sometimes none—to generate these distortions.)

Distortions often occur at night or during half-waking states. Clothes draped over a chair, for instance, may become a gnomelike, ominous figure in dim light. Unlike the short-lived illusions many people have at these times, which they never really believe, the distortions of the schizotypal individual are more vivid and carry a greater conviction of reality—but not as great or as long-lasting as those of schizophrenia, where the line between real and unreal may be completely erased. People with schizotypal personality ultimately recognize that these illusions come from inside rather than outside.

PARANOID PERSONALITY DISORDER. Individuals with paranoid personality disorder routinely assume that people mean them harm. While they lack the thinking and perceptual distortions of schizotypal disorder, they have an all-encompassing distrust of the motives of others that bears little relation to objective evidence or past behavior. Everyone they encounter is malicious or threatening, planning to take advantage of them. Friends, relatives, and associates must constantly be scrutinized for hints of untrustworthiness, and even the most ambiguous remark or unexplained action is seen as sure evidence of betrayal. A paranoid husband may constantly question his wife's faithfulness; a paranoid manager may see her subordinates, colleagues, and superiors largely as actual or potential enemies in an ongoing conspiracy to undermine her position. No doubt these concerns are sometimes valid. But it is the pervasiveness of suspicion, far beyond the support of any evidence, that distinguishes this disorder from plain wariness. The crux of paranoia is the tendency to construe the behavior of others in light of a fixed presumption that they mean to do harm or take advantage. Because the disorder involves the interpretation of a reality in which they are usually well grounded, paranoid individuals are not generally considered psychotic and seldom become so.

These people read malign meanings into the most mundane actions. They often cannot recognize that a cab driver may have chosen an unexpected route to save time or that a teasing jibe from a coworker does not represent an organized campaign of disinformation. It is hard for them to confide in other people because they fear that any intimate revelation will be used against them. Quick to perceive threats, they are also quick to counterattack. Paranoid individuals are guarded, secretive, evasive, tense, and often argumentative. In addition to belligerence, their hostility may be more indirectly expressed through complaints, sarcasm, or aloofness. They are difficult to get along with.

When they come to focus on broader issues, they gravitate toward religious and political ideologies that reinforce their mistrust. The same suspicion they feel for individuals may be directed at whole nations and races in the form of negative and sometimes vicious stereotypes, which support a black-and-white world view populated by many sworn enemies and a few friends. The friends tend to be those who share this absolutist belief system, sometimes in the context of extremist or cult groups. In these circumstances, listening and talking only to each other and willfully closing themselves off from the outside world, they may fail to realize how fanatical they appear to others.

Highly sensitive to issues of power and rank, people with this disorder may resent those in positions of authority over them at the same time that they question the loyalty of their own subordinates. They are tremendously fearful of slipping down in the hierarchy of power in which they perceive themselves. This intense self-protectiveness sometimes leads them to present a nearly impenetrable facade of objectivity and rationality. They avoid the complexities of intimacy, choosing excessive self-reliance instead, and are attracted by work and personal situations that offer simplicity and order. Any hint of ambiguity, paradox, or even ordinary flexibility makes them feel threatened.

Paranoia may be brought on or exaggerated by a physical handicap, especially a hearing impairment. Someone with a suspicious nature, faced with a permanent loss of information about the world, may become even more wary of others and interpret harmless situations as threatening. By attributing threat to others, they achieve a sense that the threat can be averted. They thus compensate for their feelings of loss of control over their own bodies and perceptions due to age, illness, or the many other misfortunes we can do nothing about.

SCHIZOID PERSONALITY DISORDER. Like the still-unvalidated depressive personality disorder among the mood disorders, schizoid personality disorder occupies the far edge of the penumbra of diseases related to schizophrenia. While it is better defined than depressive personality disorder and thus is accepted as a *DSM-IV* diagnosis, it remains in many ways a mystery. People with this syndrome seldom seek treatment, and we have little sense of its prevalence or long-term outcome.

Schizoid personality disorder is marked by an absence of close relationships, a limited range of emotional expression, and a detached, inner-oriented quality. Schizoid individuals are loners: they prefer solitary pursuits, avoid situations that bring them close to other people, and have few or no close friends or confidants. There may be one important relationship with a parent or sibling; now and then they marry. Generally speaking, they do not seem to feel an urge for closeness. A certain dullness pervades the schizoid person's interactions with others—the same dullness that is termed blunt affect in schizophrenic patients. They appear out of tune with, or wholly oblivious to, the nuances and intricacies of social relationships. Others find them aloof and blandly indifferent to praise or ridicule. Even direct provocation often fails to ignite their temper, leading some people to think they actually lack emotion.

It's true that what many of us find enjoyable, people with schizoid traits do not: in addition to social pleasures, they often appear to disdain sensual ones such as gourmet food, music, natural scenery, or sex. They do well at technological, mechanical or intellectual tasks that remove them from interpersonal situations, and they sometimes take up strange, obsessive hobbies. To all appearances, they are happiest when preoccupied and alone. Still, is this sufficient ground to give this condition a diagnostic classification? Isn't it the height of arrogance, even a little frightening, to label people who simply want to be left alone as having a "disorder"?

In some people, appearances do not tell the whole story. The schizoid person's indifferent facade sometimes conceals a great deal of pain and despair over their difficulties with social interactions. Without quite knowing what they're missing, many of these people suffer a deep sense of unfulfillment, which they acknowledge in the rare situations when they are willing to confide in others. While they spurn romantic opportunities, especially those that might lead to emotional involvement, they sometimes maintain a rich and highly developed sexual fantasy life—an indication that, on some level at least, they desire a sensuality they cannot pursue. Many schizoid individuals are profoundly discontent with the directionless quality of their lives—their inability to set clearly defined goals for themselves, to take initiative, or to respond appropriately to crises.

It's impossible to know how widespread this syndrome is. Even in severe form, it is not the kind of disease that leads to crises. Paranoia or schizotypal traits usually lead up to some outbreak of depression, a failure of reality testing, or some other life crisis that, sooner or later, brings people with these disorders into contact with mental-health professionals. Because schizoid personality disorder does not usually bring on such crises, psychiatrists have little sense of how many people the disease affects and how severely, what degree of unhappiness it typically causes, or even whether the sufferers we do see are in any way typical.

Having a better grasp of schizotypal disorder would undoubtedly help clarify a genetic picture that is in many ways confused. We know that schizophrenia-related personality disorders tend to run in families. We also know, most notably from an important study of Irish families done by Ken Kendler of the Medical College of Virginia, that schizotypal, paranoid, schizoid, and perhaps even avoidant personality disorders (see Chapter 6) are more common in relatives of schizophrenic patients than in those of affective disorder patients or controls. (The broader definition of schizophrenia to include schizophrenia-related disorders also increases the significance of a linkage that Kendler and his colleagues have found on chromosome 6.) Such features as eccentricity, isolation, and cognitive and perceptual distortions are more likely to show up in relatives of people diagnosed with schizotypal or paranoid disorder than among relatives of normal controls. Twin studies have shown that identical twins have a significantly greater concordance for schizotypal personality disorder than fraternal twins, supporting the argument for a genetic basis. And in studies of schizophrenic adoptees, researchers found a greater-than-normal prevalence of schizophrenia-related personality disorders among the adoptees' biological relatives, but not among their adoptive relatives or among either the adoptive or biological relatives of adoptees who are not schizophrenic. This work is important not only for the odd cluster disorders; the recognition of these disorders is what permitted researchers to establish the genetic basis of schizophrenia.

But since the criteria for schizophrenia-related personality disorders were originally derived from studies of relatives of schizophrenic patients, all of these results are to some extent based on circular reasoning. If you use a genetic link as part of your definition of *schizophrenia-related*, then any diseases you define this way will inevitably show a genetic link. This circularity doesn't invalidate these studies— the genetic link really exists—but it warns us that things may be less clear-cut than we would like. It is still not clear to what extent schizophrenia and its related syndromes are different expressions of the same genotype, or perhaps similar expressions of different genotypes that share some characteristics. If we can understand the parallels and differences between schizophrenia and the odd cluster disorders, we may begin to approach an understanding of the core pathophysiology of these diseases. This understanding, in turn, could help us learn what places people at greater or lesser risk for chronic schizophrenia.

Some evidence suggests that the same personality traits—isolation, eccentricity, and cognitive/perceptual distortions—are also increased in relatives of affective disorder patients. Does a genetic predisposition to affective disorder also bring a susceptibility to schizotypal traits? Apparently, yes and no. People with affective disorders or affective-related personality traits may have altered perceptions and disorganized thinking and may even speak digressively under strong emotional stress. And just as both schizophrenic and severely depressed or manic patients may suffer from psychosis, so both schizophrenia-related and affective-related personality disorder patients may have psychotic-like symptoms. But the latter don't show the ongoing perceptual disturbances or the stable eccentricity seen in people with true schizotypal traits. Long-term detachment and poor rapport, the hallmarks of the schizophrenia-related disorders, seem to be specific to relatives of schizophrenic patients. But these differences need to be clarified.

In clinical settings we seldom see people with paranoid personality disorder who don't also have many schizotypal features; the two disorders overlap. It is not surprising, therefore, that individuals with paranoid features are also found among the relatives of schizophrenic patients. It may be that paranoid personality disorder has a particularly strong link to paranoid or delusional disorder, in which delusions of being persecuted reach psychotic proportions but other psychotic symptoms are absent. This question has yet to be resolved.

If defined broadly, as indecisiveness, inability to make commitments, and inadequate strength of personality, schizoid personality disorder does not seem to be related to chronic schizophrenia. But a more restrictive interpretation of the disease, as presented in *DSM-IV,* may be related: relatives of schizophrenic patients may have a pervasive social isolation that lacks the psychotic-like symptoms seen in schizotypal disorder. There have been few studies, however, that could clarify either the definition of schizoid disorder or its association with other diseases.

Those are a few of the many things we don't know, but would like to know, about the genetics of schizophrenia and its related personality disorders. It seems that the positive and negative symptoms are inherited independently, and we think the positive symptoms are less specific to this group of diseases than the negative symptoms. Social withdrawal, inability to relate to others, suspicion, and lack of emotional expression appear to occupy a central place genetically as well as clinically. It may be that the odd cluster disorders are something like the "default" option for expression of these traits. When these genes coexist with a susceptibility to positive symptoms, and the environment pulls the trigger, then the result is full schizophrenia.

☙

Between family studies and clinical disease comes biology. A genetic link implies a biological process: the expression of a gene is the production of a particular protein that leads to certain physical effects in the nervous system. What kind of biological process could account for peculiarity, suspiciousness, and chronic isolation?

My colleagues and I are trying to approach this question by studying odd cluster patients in the laboratory. One line of evidence suggests that these people, like schizophrenic patients, may suffer an impairment in their capacity to organize information from their environment and respond appropriately. While this difficulty may never grow severe enough to cause a break in their appreciation of reality, decoding ordinary human communication may become hard enough that their interactions become stilted and awkward. We have been looking for simple ways to measure attention capacity and information processing so that we can see whether they really are less efficient in eccentric and socially isolated people.

One simple perceptual task that relies on these abilities is eye tracking. Humans use two kinds of eye movements to direct our eyes to the part of our visual environment that we find of greatest interest. One is the saccade, a quick, darting movement that flicks the gaze rapidly from one point to another. The other is the smooth-pursuit movement, by which we follow a moving object such as a running animal. Smooth pursuit permits the eye to keep the image of a moving target in the central part of the retina, where acuity is greatest. (If you've never noticed these two types of eye movement, you can get a sense of the difference between them by trying to move your eyes smoothly and slowly across your visual field, as if you were following the flight of a bird, when nothing in sight is moving. Most people can't do it; their eyes make a series of staccato jumps instead. These are saccades.)

Since eye movement is under voluntary control, a researcher can activate the smooth-pursuit system simply by asking an experimental subject to follow a moving target, such as a pendulum or a dot moving across a computer screen. If eye tracking is accurate, the eye's movement should follow the movement of the target. This can be measured: you can use an electrooculograph to record the electrical potential derived from the movement of the muscles controlling the eye's position, or you can measure the eyes' movements directly by bouncing an infrared light off the eye to record changes in the position of the iris's border. The accuracy of smooth-pursuit eye tracking can be assessed by comparing the change in eye position to the change in position of the target.

Targets can be presented in different ways. A pendulum, for instance, traces out a sine wave if you record its position through time. It reaches its maximum velocity in the middle of its swing, gradually slows to a stop as it reaches its outer limits, and then reverses itself. Other targets maintain a constant velocity. If you inspect recordings of eye tracking of many people, you can see wide variation. Some subjects show great accuracy: when asked to follow a pendulum, their tracking patterns exhibit an almost perfect sine wave. But in others, the pattern is choppy, interrupted by numerous saccades. Sometimes their eyes fall behind the target and use saccades to catch up; at other times their eyes jump ahead. Some people's eye movement is so badly impaired that no sine wave pattern is even visible.

Schizophrenic patients are more likely than normal volunteers to show impaired smooth-pursuit eye movements. Philip Holzman at Harvard found this. This impairment is found in no other psychiatric patients except acutely ill affective disorder patients, particularly if they are psychotic. But it also shows up in people with schizophrenia-related personality traits. Do these findings point to a subtle defect in information processing, even in the absence of overt psychosis, that inhibits effective social communication?

Some years ago I teamed up with Bob Coursey, Monte Buchsbaum, and Dennis Murphy to study a simple eye-tracking task using volunteers from a community college in Maryland. The students were asked to watch a pendulum while an electrooculograph measured their eye movements and were told that they might be asked to undergo more extensive testing on the basis of this initial screening. Of close to three hundred original subjects, we chose the twenty most accurate tracking records and the thirty-one least accurate and brought these people to NIMH for extensive biological and clinical evaluations. The tracking records were coded and sealed, to be opened only at the end of the study, and the fifty-one volunteers were evaluated by scientists who did not know the results of the tracking tests. The students participated in detailed clinical interviews covering all aspects of their social, interpersonal, and occupational lives, as well as a battery of psychological, neurologic, psychophysiologic, and biochemical tests. Their eye tracking was also re-evaluated, this time with an infrared detecting device.

At the end of the study, when we unsealed the initial eye-tracking data, the results were astonishingly consistent. Individuals with poor eye tracking were more likely to be isolated, have few friends, date infrequently, and have difficulty establishing rapport with others. Not only were these findings consistent between the two groups, but within the groups the *degree* of eye-tracking impairment correlated with the *degree* of social impairment: how frequently the person dated, how satisfied he was with his sex life, how many friends he had, and so on. (We also found a correlation between eye tracking and the experience of cognitive and perceptual distortions, but because these are not that common in a volunteer population, this association was less robust.) Eye-tracking results, moreover, correlated only with social function: the people with poor performance did not have psychological or behavioral problems across the board. They were no more likely to have symptoms of anxiety, depression, phobias, or other psychiatric disorders—and in fact were less likely to have problems with drug abuse, alcohol abuse, or violations of the law. Generally, they were quiet people who often lived with their parents, kept up their studies, and had little desire for a social life.

I talked with a number of the study participants before the blind was broken and made notes of my impressions. Many seemed difficult to engage, to be in a kind of bubble that insulated them from others. They often had difficulty maintaining eye contact and might spend much of the interview staring at the ground. Some subjects blandly denied any social difficulties but showed markedly poor rapport and seemed to have few real friends. At the end of the study I compared my notes against the eye-tracking data. Almost every participant who fit this description fell in the poor-tracking group.

Members of this group had other abnormalities as well. While generally lacking any gross neurological impairment, they often had difficulty with motor coordination, such as repeating alternating movements rapidly. Many of their psychophysiologic and psychological responses were poor, for instance, on tests involving reaction time or sustained attention. It appears that eye-tracking accuracy, which can be quantified by specific indices of the number and type of saccades, is a good measure of a broad group of neuropsychological functions, and that these functions in turn correlate strongly with the ability to negotiate social situations.

This study is an example of the "biologic high-risk strategy" that Monte Buchsbaum developed with some colleagues while he was at

NIMH. Monte suggested that if a biologic measure is strongly correlated with a particular illness, then by selecting from a group of volunteers those with an abnormality in that biologic measure, you should also select out those likely to have symptoms related to the disorder. This approach reverses biological psychiatrists' usual strategy, which is to choose patients by their clinical characteristics and then measure their biological variables. Monte used this strategy to screen students for performance on a psychological test called the Continuous Performance Task (CPT); those with poor performance tended to have evidence of learning dysfunction and hyperactivity, and within that group, eye-tracking impairment was correlated with social isolation as well as perceptual difficulties.

Among families of schizophrenic patients, abnormalities in eye tracking not only are more prevalent than normal but are strongly associated with thought disturbances and schizotypal characteristics. When schizotypal personality disorder patients have been tested for eye-tracking function, their performances have correlated closely with measures of social isolation and decreased desire for contact. Other tests lead us to similar conclusions. Poor results on the CPT and other attentional tests in the offspring of schizophrenic patients have been correlated with social detachment and a lack of sensitivity to the inner experiences of others. College students selected for schizotypal features have shown impairment on the CPT. Barbara Cornblatt has shown that CPT abnormalities are more common in children of schizophrenic patients than in children of affective disorder patients. These abnormalities are associated with isolation in schizophrenic patients' children and predict the development of schizotypal traits.

The type of information processing involved in CPT is different from conventional IQ—in which both schizotypal and schizophrenic patients score about the same as the general population. (This difference explains why some people get labeled "book smart but not street smart" or vice versa.) What the eye-tracking and other tests measure has to do with selecting appropriate stimuli from the environment and responding to them in a fluid way. In this way, it parallels the complexity of social interaction, which may, at any moment, involve rea-

soning, emotion, motor control, vision, hearing, or the tactile senses—
or all at once—in coordination with one or several other people who
are all doing the same thing. A finely tuned rhythm develops in social
communication. If the integrative mechanisms that organize a person's
responses to social cues are impaired, this rhythm is thrown off, meanings are misconstrued, and emotional connections are not made or are
turned negative. The same timing that comedy is famously dependent
on permeates our daily life: think what you would infer if, for instance,
a friend of yours hesitated before expressing congratulations on some
accomplishment or accepting a dinner invitation. How much impairment is necessary before what should be a smooth, easy flow becomes
constantly stiff, awkward, humiliating, an experience to be dreaded and
avoided?

Intuitively, it seems an easy step from this condition to paranoia,
and so it may be. Information processing has not been studied so
extensively in paranoid individuals, but experimental situations have
been constructed in which the subject believes she is being evaluated
but does not know whether the experimenter's opinion is positive or
negative. Increasing the subject's difficulty in understanding what the
experimenter is saying increases the likelihood that the subject infers a
negative opinion. The less clear the information being presented, the
more likely a person may suspect a potential threat. This observation
may explain why people with other kinds of information-processing
difficulties, such as the hard-of-hearing, are also more likely to suspect
mischief or malign intent.

From this kind of impairment to the isolation we see in schizotypal individuals is an even easier step. A vast number of sometimes
ambiguous cues must be interpreted and conditional judgments made
in even the most casual encounter. Interactions that carry a possibility
of romantic involvement and courtship call for accurate reading and
immediate response to the minutest of signals. They may be the most
subtle and demanding thing many people ever attempt, and most of us
have a very high failure rate. As relationships deepen, these judgments
only grow more complex and the stakes higher. People whose cognitive
impairments shut them out from the rewards of these encounters, who
can experience them only as all effort and no pleasure, may easily

decide—like an untalented child who is made to try violin lessons—that they would rather do without. They gravitate into an isolation and rigid routine most of us could not tolerate.

Jerry was in his mid-forties when he came to my office, but he looked more than ten years older. He was a frail man with sparse brown hair and a weak, clammy handshake, and so stoop-shouldered that at first I thought he was walking with a cane. His shirt, a faded yellow-orange flannel, was half tucked into green trousers that ended some inches above his ankles and were held up by a half-buckled belt. He looked inexpressibly forlorn and out of place.

In a flat, emotionless voice he described his life—the difficult childhood, problems in dealing with people, and perceptual distortions I mentioned earlier. He had steady work writing software for a consultant who specialized in reprogramming mainframe computers. These were generally old machines using outdated programming languages, and they had to be adapted to interact with the smaller, more versatile machines that sit on everybody's desktop. It was undemanding work, but he could do it at home and he didn't have to talk to anyone but his immediate supervisor, perhaps twice a month. Otherwise, he watched TV, did crossword puzzles, and bought groceries for himself and his mother, whom he visited for dinner every day. He could not tell me the last time he had gone to a movie, for a drive in the country, to a museum, or anywhere for enjoyment. His visit to my office was the first that had taken him outside his regular paths in several years.

"Are you happy?" I asked.

He was, in fact, profoundly miserable. "When Frankie [Albert's father, Jerry's uncle] told me you wanted me for some research project, I thought why do I want some asshole shrink using me as a guinea pig? But I've been so damn depressed lately I thought I should give it a shot. I feel like life is passing me by. Other people *do* stuff: they go out to dinner, go golfing with their buddies, or get married and stuff like that. I never do anything. I'm just watching the parade." Jerry said this while staring at the floor. Except for a brief glance when he came in, he never made eye contact with me during the entire interview.

He was not going through a clinical depression—there was no weight loss, loss of appetite, sleep disturbance, agitation, psychomotor retardation, or any of depression's other biological symptoms. But his life utterly lacked enjoyment. As most people would understand the term, he was certainly depressed. I felt, however, that he was not so much depressed as unhappy, and that the source of his unhappiness was an odd cluster personality disorder.

Jerry made numerous errors on the Wisconsin Card Sort Test of a kind common to both schizophrenic and schizotypal patients: he repeatedly failed to change sorting strategies when needed. He scored better after a dose of amphetamine than after a placebo. Otherwise he tested normal in IQ and visual spatial perception. X rays of his brain showed a reduced ratio of brain size to ventricle size, and the concentration of the dopamine metabolite, homovanillic acid, in his bloodstream was slightly on the low side. In schizotypal patients with prominent psychotic-like symptoms, HVA concentration is often elevated; in a schizotypal patient with primarily deficit symptoms, a low HVA is not surprising. On the backward masking test, he started off quite well, but after two consecutive errors he became visibly flustered and then angry at the tester, and his performance fell off sharply. In talking it over with me later, Jerry acknowledged that this was a familiar pattern in his life—whenever he got nervous, he felt "all tangled up, like I'm trying to run but my shoelaces are tied together." I explained that his ability to organize information seemed to decline rapidly under pressure and asked whether he had ever before lashed out at sources of distress.

That question prompted the following recollection. When he was about twelve, several of the boys in his school got into the habit of playing "keep-away" with items of Jerry's clothing—his hat, his gym shorts, sometimes one of his shoes. (Keep-away is a form of bullying in which a group of children toss something belonging to the victim from one to another, continually teasing the victim with it but not letting him get it.) For Jerry these incidents were nightmarish; as he grew enraged, he became increasingly clumsy, until he could barely run without falling down, and increasingly unable to talk coherently. The games ended with him stumbling away, blubbering in humiliation. The boys always found these performances highly amusing. During one such episode, Jerry suddenly jumped onto the back of one of his larger assailants, sank his teeth into the back of the boy's neck, and bit him so hard that he needed several stitches. This put an end to the keep-away games but not to the taunting—now the boys called him Dracula. The incident marked a turning point in Jerry's life: "From then on, I knew I was an outcast."

At the end of the testing, I described to Jerry what we now think about the relation of schizotypal personality disorder to schizophrenia—that his problems in selecting relevant information from his environment and acting on it might be due to deficits in frontal lobe function, and that these deficits might be mediated by reduced activity in the dopaminergic system. Feeling that at last he had been understood, Jerry seized on this explanation as the key to solving his problems—it was all simply a chemical imbalance, and once we got the chemicals straightened out, his life would improve dramatically. I had to tell him that this research is still preliminary and that we could not pinpoint the source of his cognitive problems with certainty. In any case, the therapies now available promise a small improvement at best. The deficit symptoms common to schizophrenia and the odd cluster are among the most intractable of all psychiatric disorders.

Only a small proportion of schizotypal individuals go on to develop schizophrenia; once established, whatever factors lead people into the path of schizotypal disorder rather than schizophrenia seem to confer relative stability. But their overall level of functioning does not improve with time. The course of this disease more closely resembles schizophrenia than it does the affective disorders or other personality disorders.

Also as in schizophrenia, the positive, psychotic-related symptoms seem to be more amenable to treatment. People who have ideas of reference, cognitive perceptual distortions, or obsessional symptoms appear to respond to neuroleptic medications—a finding consistent with the idea that these symptoms come from excessive dopaminergic activity in the subcortical areas of the brain. People with paranoid traits who feel a need for constant vigilance against an unnamed threat may find that neuroleptics permit them to relax. But for someone like Jerry, whose mild perceptual distortions are far from the biggest concern, neuroleptics offer little help. The new drugs that stimulate the D_1 receptor in order to improve attention and working memory may help in the odd cluster disorders as well as in schizophrenia.

In psychotherapy and other psychosocial treatments, a grasp of the biology of odd cluster disorders compels us to respect these patients' limited capacity for intimacy and their vulnerability to stress. Changes that tax their cognitive capacities—such as a new task at work that involves evaluating ambiguous information or weighing costs and benefits in a number of conflicting areas—may provoke extreme anxiety, demoralization, and even somatic symptoms. Life changes that most people take in stride, such as having to move to a new neighborhood or even something as small as the closing of a familiar store, may be unusually upsetting. Occasionally a withdrawn schizotypal or schizoid person becomes involved in a relationship that stirs up more feelings than can be easily dealt with, and so may come in for treatment. Pressure from the therapist to develop more and closer relationships may only make such patients anxious, drive them away, or perhaps even bring on psychotic-like symptoms. Psychotherapy groups are also problematic for many such patients; they exacerbate these people's social anxieties.

I saw Jerry into psychotherapy coupled with pharmocologic treatment with low-dose neuroleptic medication and later referred him for behaviorally oriented social skills training. No amount of training can ever make him into a vivacious person, but by helping him practice handling specific situations, she has given him the tools to function better in work and other everyday settings. The psychotherapy has helped him to understand and accept the kind of person he is. Rather than brood about what he is missing, he is learning to think about what kinds of activities he is likely to find enjoyment in. Recently, after two years in therapy, he summoned up the courage to enroll in a drawing class. He finds drawing very relaxing. It is a solitary pursuit; he does it faithfully for two hours each day, and the physical act of putting pencil to paper soothes him. His life is not joyful, but it is stable and not without satisfactions.

CHAPTER SIX

THE PRUDENT ATOM

. . .The prudent atom
Simply insists upon its safety now,
Security at all costs. . . .

— W. H. AUDEN

L ENA WAS A FORTY-THREE-YEAR-OLD HOUSEWIFE whose two sons, Lloyd and Bill, had both left home for college within the past two years. A shy, plump, nervous woman, she had devoted her life since marriage to taking care of her husband, Fred, and the two boys. Lena and Fred had stopped having a sexual relationship years ago; she had never found it very satisfying anyway, and she was secretly relieved when Fred seemed finally to lose interest. She had not held a job since her early twenties and had never lived on her own. She moved straight from her parents' home into the house she and Fred bought when they were married and where they still lived.

Fred was an auto mechanic who had recently leveraged some of their retirement savings to buy a partnership in a successful gas station and repair garage. Anticipating a higher income from his new business, he had lately begun talking about buying a new home or perhaps a summer house—talk that greatly unnerved Lena. Thinking she was worried about the added expense when they had two children in college, Fred carefully showed her how they could afford it. This only made Lena feel worse. She had been heartbroken when her second son, Bill, left for college, but was ashamed to admit the true depth of her feelings. Every morning when Fred left for work (which he'd lately been doing six or even seven days a week), she felt terribly lonely, as if some tide were carrying away all the familiar elements of her life and now threatened to sweep her up as well.

Through the fall and winter after Bill left home, she became increasingly anxious and fearful. It became more and more difficult to leave the house. At first she was bothered by vague imaginings—robberies in the stores she visited, accidents, carjackings, assaults in a parking lot—and then by scenes and places she had known all her life. The teenagers hanging out at the shopping mall seemed increasingly hostile and threatening; in the dimly lit hardware store, with its narrow aisles stuffed with strange implements giving off oily, masculine smells, she found it hard to breathe and had to get out quickly without buying anything. She ventured out less and less. One spring day, leaving the house and seeing the way to her car blocked by a large patch of half-melted ice, she felt a sudden, overwhelming terror and a conviction that if she didn't get inside the house immediately she would die. She found herself sweating, flushed; her rapid heartbeat pounded in her ears; and between her panting and trembling she was barely able to get the front-door key into the lock.

This happened on a Tuesday. Because she had done her grocery shopping on Monday, Lena was able to get through the rest of the week without going outside the house or telling Fred about her problem. A package from her mother languishing at the post office, a couple of unbought garden tools, some sweaters left at the dry cleaners, and a lunch date with friends were all allowed to slide. Every time she tried stepping out the door, she felt the same panic. The attacks would last anywhere from five to fifteen minutes and leave her exhausted and demoralized as she retreated to her living room sofa. As long as she stayed indoors, she was bored and lonely, but at least she did not feel this overwhelming fear. But as soon as she tried to think about leaving the house again, she grew anxious and could feel her heart beat faster. She could make the anxiety subside only by deciding that she would not go out; it was too frightening.

She dreaded the inevitable moment when Fred would find out about her condition—but not, in the end, as much as she dreaded the outdoors. On Saturday night he came home early from the garage, showered loudly, and got dressed for their regular dinner and card game with a couple across town. Lena dutifully got herself ready and even put her coat on, but when it was time to leave, she could not bring herself to set foot across the threshold. Her tearful agitation and the strength of her refusal soon convinced Fred that something was seriously wrong.

Fred thought the attacks were caused by some problem with her "glands"—that they were related to menopause—and he tried to get Lena to visit an endocrinologist recommended by a physician whose car he worked on. Lena wouldn't leave the house to see her. On learning of this, the endocrinologist gave Fred the name of a psychiatrist, who came to their house and talked to Lena at some length. He diagnosed her as having agoraphobia, a fear of open places (the *agora* was the ancient Greek town square, a market and gathering place), and prescribed an antidepressant for her panic attacks. Even though these drugs were originally developed to help with depression, they have been shown to relieve the symptoms of panic disorder as well.

The antidepressant allowed Lena to resume her daily routine, but it didn't solve all her problems. It removed the immediate crisis of the panic attacks, so she could address those problems in a less pressured atmosphere. The psychiatrist emphasized to her, "It's no coincidence that this happened now"—at a time when all of the people she had devoted herself to caring for were making major changes that made their dependence on her less immediate and significantly less certain. As the psychiatrist later said to me when we discussed the case, "She wasn't panicking about getting in her car; she was panicking about having to reinvent her life." Lena and Fred decided to enter counseling together. Six months after starting the antidepressants, she was less demoralized and was able to stop taking the medication. A year later Lena had found a part-time job, was doing volunteer work at a local thrift shop, and reported that her relationship with Fred was much improved. Fred left counseling at this time, but Lena joined a weekly group for anxiety disorder patients.

§

Few diseases erase the distinction between "mind" and "body" as thoroughly as panic disorder. Lena's attacks were severely physiological:

they involved an intense activation of the autonomic nervous system, with sweating, dilation of the blood vessels in the skin, a strong, rapid heartbeat, panting, and the uncontrollable trembling that comes with the voluntary muscles being put on hair-trigger alert. This is the physiological state in which the body fights (or runs) for its life. Yet what she felt was none of these things. What she felt was terror. It's a natural impulse to say that the terror is the cause of the bodily response, but the antidepressant drug Lena took had a physiological effect, smoothing out the regulation of norepinephrine function much as it does in depressed patients. When the physiological symptoms went away, why did the terror go away too? Did Lena's physiology cause her emotional state? This isn't correct either: the attacks were all of a piece, a single phenomenon whose manifestations we choose to put into different categories, some physical and some mental.

Under most circumstances and in most people, panic and its more moderate counterpart, fear, serve a useful purpose. Both the emotions and their physiological accompaniments provide us a signal that the behavior we are engaging in or contemplating may be dangerous to us. If we choose to proceed anyway, we can do so only with extreme vigilance—the body compels it. But although anxiety and fear closely resemble each other, it is important to distinguish them. Fear is rational. If you are walking alone in a dangerous neighborhood at night, you are right to be afraid, and the anticipation of danger may be sufficient to make you change your route or take a cab. If for some reason you can't, then your fear will be translated into a heightened watchfulness and readiness to escape. Pathological anxiety, on the other hand, is an excessive sensitivity to the prospect of future punishment. The anxious person reacts to innocuous situations as if they were dangerous and may foresee bad consequences in so many instances that she is immobilized.

Children often express anxiety through fear of new situations. They may be afraid to change schools, for instance, because they worry about unknowingly breaking a rule and being punished; or they may resist taking up new sports because they are afraid of being hit by a baseball or drowning in a swimming pool. An adult about to go to a dinner party with new people may be excessively anxious about possible rejection. Yet he may not understand why he feels this way: his anxiety may come out of unconscious assumptions. For instance, an anxious man who fears success may inadvertently arrange situations so that he is bound to fail. It may emerge in therapy that, as a child, he came to associate doing well with being mercilessly teased by his jealous older sister and that he now avoids success because of the anxiety it arouses about being noticed and vilified by others. He may also be afraid to stir up the rage he feels toward his sister. People who are overly anxious often fear the consequences of their aggression—they are afraid of hurting someone they love or of losing control of their anger.

As the extreme expression of anxiety, panic attacks are usually brought on by exposure (or the threat of exposure) to situations that an anxiety sufferer experiences as fearful. Because the triggers of these attacks are irrational—because they embody fear of things or situations that are not life-threatening and in many cases not threatening at all—these fears are called phobias. Panic attacks may occur without specific phobias, and phobias may exist without panic attacks, but often the two are linked. The fear may be of a specific type of animal, such as snakes or dogs; of a specific circumstance, such as being in an enclosed space or going outside; or of a situation, such as public speaking. Most people who have phobias deal with them by avoiding whatever triggers them, and in many cases—for instance with fear of snakes—this avoidance does not seriously interfere with their daily activities. Even a fear of public speaking need not be a problem for, say, a longshoreman or a grocery store clerk, though it might threaten a teacher's livelihood. More than one performing career has been cut short by stage fright. Lena's problem, a fear of going outside, would clearly affect almost anyone's functioning. It is precisely when the precipitants of phobic anxiety cannot be avoided that panic attacks tend to occur.

The attacks themselves become occasions for enormous dread. Like depression, a panic attack is painful not only because of what it is "about"—not only because of fear of the phobic object—but for the experience of panic itself. The stimulus or situation that brings on the phobic reaction becomes associated with the experience of anxiety and the anticipation of its recurrence, and this apprehension increases the likelihood that an episode will occur. Thus the irrational phobia becomes reinforced by a rational fear of its effects, and the resulting vicious cycle leaves its victims less and less room to function. What begins as the autonomic nervous system's useful response to emergency, a series of physical and mental adjustments to prepare the body for intense activity, takes on a life of its own. Whereas an authentic threat can be dealt with by fighting or escaping, panic disorder leaves no way to resolve the situation, since the panic is part of its own cause. It is like a fire alarm that cannot be shut off or ignored.

While it sometimes occurs on its own, as it did with Lena, agoraphobia may also arise as a secondary result of panic disorder. People who have had panic attacks, from whatever cause, may start to fear any place they cannot escape easily should an attack begin. They often avoid public transportation, department stores, elevators—sometimes any crowded place at all. In these cases the agoraphobia may range from mild to debilitating.

A number of phobias seem to echo our evolutionary past and could well be the result of inborn tendencies. Fear of open places could be an exaggerated expression of a long-buried, instinctive urge to stay hidden from predators on the savanna. Snakes may provoke phobias not by the action of their phallic appearance on the unconscious but because in many environments they are natural enemies of primates. In their recent book, *Why We Get Sick,* psychiatrist Randolph Nesse and evolutionary biologist George Williams point out that most of the common phobias, such as agoraphobia, fear of the dark, or fear of heights, are associated with situations our ancestors would have considered dangerous. Phobias involving modern dangers, such as high-fat foods, guns, or drugs, are much rarer. Moreover, Nesse and Williams write that certain fears are "prepared." You can create a lifelong terror of snakes in monkeys by a single showing of a video in which a monkey is alarmed by a snake, but it is impossible to create a fear of flowers this way. Similarly, some phobias seem to be much more easily induced in humans than others. To a certain extent, then, panic disorder may be an environmental disease with roots in the disparity between what humans feared for most of our evolutionary history and what threatens, or doesn't threaten, us now.

Anxiety occupies a central place in twentieth-century psychological theories. Most schemes that classify normal personality variations have included anxiety as one of their core dimensions, and psychoanalytic and behavioral theories both assign anxiety a key role in personality development. In his later writings, Freud described many personality disorder traits as coping strategies aimed at preventing the emergence of anxiety in response to unconscious conflicts. Learning theorists have emphasized anxiety's role in mediating inhibition of behaviors that have been punished in the past.

Psychoanalytic theory has traditionally focused on the meaning of the object that generates anxiety. In his classic case study of "Little Hans," Freud described a five-year-old boy who developed a phobia of horses after he became afraid one would bite him. This fear, in Freud's interpretation, represented Little Hans's worry that his father would harm him in retaliation for the boy's love for his mother and his wish to have his father out of the way. Thus the anxiety stimulus is always displaced from the real object of fear. Moreover, the fear expresses a projection of the person's own wishes: it was Little Hans who originally wanted to harm his father. But these connections between original wishes, which the person regards as forbidden and dangerous, and the feared object always lie outside the person's awareness—they are unconscious. In this view, Lena's agoraphobia might have grown out of a fear of a repressed desire to free herself of her family responsibilities, perhaps to become a prostitute: to abandon her husband and family and take up a life of sex with strangers. She may have unconsciously coveted the independence the other family members were asserting even while she consciously dreaded it.

Other psychiatrists are less sure of the association between phobic stimuli and unconscious fantasies, a proposition that is difficult to validate or disprove empirically, but they agree that, whatever their origin, these fears become deeply ingrained and are difficult to reverse. A variety of approaches—ranging from pharmacologic treatment to behavioral desensitization techniques to psychodynamic treatment of the underlying unconscious conflicts—have been used to bring anxiety under control.

᷃

Panic disorder is the most extravagant of the anxiety disorders, a traditional grouping whose justification is becoming less clear as we learn

175

more about the biology of the individual diseases. The others evolve over a longer term and are not punctuated by crises to the same extent. Generalized anxiety disorder, for example, is characterized by longer-lasting but less dramatic feelings of anxiety, including nervousness, a sense of tension, sometimes a rapid heartbeat and other physical signs, but without the emergencies of dread that denote a panic attack. A similar chronic anxiety may accompany several psychiatric disorders, including depression and schizophrenia, but in generalized anxiety disorder it is the primary problem, not secondary to some larger problem.

Although it is classed with the anxiety disorders, obsessive-compulsive disorder is phenomenologically and, it seems, biologically different. An obsession, which bears some resemblance to a phobia, is a recurring, disturbing idea that the individual knows is irrational but cannot get out of his mind. He may worry obsessively that a loved one will have an accident or that he himself will stab a pet or a child; milder obsessions include a mother's fear of dropping her baby, an urge to take one's clothes off in public (and the fear that it will one day be uncontrollable), and a fear of leaving the stove on and setting the house on fire.

If obsessions are unbidden, uncontrollable thoughts that precipitate anxiety, compulsions are the conscious behavioral or mental responses—counting, checking, avoiding—that serve to reduce anxiety. As the obsessions are relentlessly persistent, so the resulting compulsions can be endlessly repetitive and time-consuming. A person who is worried about leaving the stove on may return to her apartment twenty or thirty times to make sure it is really turned off. Compulsions can take up so much time that they rule out any normal life and may even endanger one's health. A person obsessed with germs may refuse to touch doorknobs that could have been touched recently by someone else and may spend so many hours in the shower each day that his skin becomes raw and bleeding. Until very recently, this disorder often went unrecognized and was thought to be rare. We now know that it affects 2 to 3 percent of the population in at least mild form at some point in their lives, making it the fourth most common psychiatric disorder. (Phobias are the most common, followed by substance abuse and depression.)

Post-traumatic stress disorder (PTSD) develops after a specific severely traumatic event that afterward is recalled involuntarily and with fear. This disorder was reported among World War II and Korean War veterans but has received wider publicity since the Vietnam War. It may be that this conflict subjected American soldiers to unusually disturbing and stressful conditions—the customary rules of war did not apply, many of the enemy were concealed among the civilian population, and veterans felt unsupported at home—but the appearance of an increased incidence may be simply a result of our increased awareness of the disorder. Certainly other wars had their horrors.

Studies with animals have shown that repeated exposure to a sufficiently intense stressful stimulus will eventually bring about a heightened response. In the same way, when people are exposed to an ongoing, highly stressful experience such as combat, where they may at any moment come under deadly attack from any number of sources, they may become painfully sensitized to such things as loud noises or reminders of the war on film. A veteran may undergo such strikingly lifelike recollections of a major battle that he may momentarily feel he is back in the midst of the event; a Holocaust victim may relive the horrors of the concentration camp.

Post-traumatic stress disorder may also be brought on by natural disasters, automobile accidents, or being the victim of a violent crime. All of these events bring an overwhelming stimulation that floods the body's natural arousal systems, upsetting their regulation long after the trauma has ended. Stimuli that evoke memories of the experience trigger a physical and emotional response that may be overwhelming: the autonomic nervous system and related endocrine systems such as the adrenal glands react as if the emergency were once again real. And re-experiencing the hormonal and neurochemical state may help make the memory itself unbearably vivid. The trigger need not be so obvious as a movie about Vietnam; an idle thought or a chance stimulus can bring on a vivid flashback or intense nightmares in which the event is relived.

Between these crises, people with this disorder may suffer an emotional flatness resembling depression. They often complain of being unable to experience pleasure or of being emotionally numb, as if their experience placed a veil over everything that came after it. Many

Vietnam veterans whom I see as PTSD patients at the Bronx VA Hospital were popular and successful before entering the service but upon returning home became detached, alienated, and isolated. Others, who may have had susceptibilities to anxiety, depression, or major psychoses when they went to Vietnam, came back afflicted for life with chronic, serious psychiatric illnesses.

§

In addition to these four so-called Axis I disorders—panic disorder, generalized anxiety disorder, obsessive-compulsive disorder, and post-traumatic stress disorder, which are classified as Axis I disorders because they are "clinical," meaning they are likely to bring a person into therapy—anxiety also figures in a number of Axis II disorders, or personality disorders. These are less episodic, less acutely symptomatic, and more persistently maladaptive. As I discussed in Chapter 3, the personality disorders involve a person's deeply ingrained habits for coping with the world. Disorders on these two axes may coexist, and in fact an Axis II disorder may, under stress, help precipitate the kind of crisis that gets labeled an Axis I disorder, as well as influence its course. Thus, narcissistic personality disorder may make one prone to depression, or an anxious personality disorder may sometimes give way to panic disorder. A psychiatrist treating such patients might make both diagnoses, along different axes. (The current diagnostic system also contains three other axes: Axis III, general medical conditions; Axis IV, psychosocial and environmental problems, such as educational, occupational, housing, economic, legal, or family difficulties; and Axis V, a global assessment of functioning. The purpose of the axial system is to encourage psychiatrists to consider all five dimensions in evaluating their patients and to realize that, far from being mutually exclusive, these dimensions coexist and interact with each other.) Like the cluster surrounding schizophrenia, the anxiety-related personality disorders share common biological underpinnings with their Axis I counterparts.

Not all those biological underpinnings are the same, however, and like the Axis I anxiety disorders, the anxiety-related personality disorders may not all be closely related to each other. But all feature coping strategies meant to ward off anxiety, even though these efforts may be constricting or maladaptive. This group contains three disorders: avoidant, dependent, and obsessive-compulsive.

AVOIDANT PERSONALITY DISORDER. This disorder is defined by a pattern of uneasiness in social situations and avoidance of close attachments that carry a risk of rejection or disappointment. People with avoidant personalities fear disapproval to an extreme degree; they are terrified of others' judgments, wounded by the mildest criticism, and often shaken by innocuous remarks that they interpret as reflecting badly on them. When a coworker breaks off a casual conversation with them to answer the telephone, they see it as a rejection, a confirmation of their lesser importance. Because they persistently read negative evaluations into the reactions of others, they are constantly destroying their own confidence; a poor self-image becomes ingrained. They establish a pattern of tentativeness and insecurity and can seldom assert themselves with assurance, and they find in others' reactions to this behavior a steady validation of their low self-esteem.

New relationships carry a strong expectation of disappointment. Unless they receive persistent reassurance and evidence of uncritical support, they are very reluctant to develop a friendship or romance. So their social relationships often remain limited to family and a few old friends. These people crave familiarity and repetition and avoid any situation that might expose them to rejection, ridicule, or danger. At work, they may refuse advancements that threaten to bring them into greater contact with strangers.

Unlike schizoid or schizotypal individuals, who do not feel a great yearning for social contact, avoidant people fantasize about relationships and long for the acceptance of others. With people they know well, they can be charming and steadfast companions. But in other situations they are paralyzed by fear, and the more they worry about showing their fear by stammering and blushing, the more anxious they become. Their anxiety, like that of panic disorder, has a self-sustaining element. As a result, they are often forced into an unwanted, even tortured loneliness.

Part of the torture is the result of modern social pressure. Before the Industrial Revolution, when few people ever traveled more than a hundred miles from their birthplace and most lived in small communities where they knew the same people all their lives, such excruciating shyness might have been untroubling to many and could even have gone unnoticed for long periods. As the world has grown increasingly urban and mobile, however, it has become nearly impossible to escape the interactions with strangers and authority figures that avoidant persons fear so desperately. They cannot help being continually disappointed and angry with themselves for their inability to meet society's expectations for such encounters; the result is anxiety and depression.

DEPENDENT PERSONALITY DISORDER. The dependent person wards off anxiety by relying on other people to manage his life. Unable to make even the most ordinary or tentative decisions with confidence, he feels most comfortable when surrounded by others whom he can imitate and use for direction. Dependent people find it difficult to initiate projects or work by themselves, but they accept supervision well and can make good followers and team members. Their worst fear is isolation. Not surprisingly, this disorder most often appears in the context of a marriage, family, or close friendship. A husband or wife may take on the dependent role in a marriage by encouraging or even subtly forcing the partner to make all the decisions. A dependent child will take no initiative in even such minor choices as which friends to see, what courses to take, or how to spend her time after school. She may never go through the rebellious phase that marks an adolescent's transition to independence.

The end of a relationship, for such people, may be an overwhelming prospect. A temporary separation in a marriage or the departure of a friend who moves out of town is terribly frightening. Hypersensitive to the risk of abandonment, dependent people fear any disagreement that may lead to rejection. So they stay in bad situations—refusing to leave failed marriages, staying in their parents' house long after they should have moved out, or tolerating an exploitative roommate—and behave in an unreasonably agreeable manner. Even the worst relationship is preferable to being alone. Because their compliance makes them a target for people who need to be dominant, dependent people often find themselves in relationships with aggressive, controlling, even sadistic partners. They often must perform more and more demeaning tasks simply to maintain the relationship.

The assumption is that if they asserted themselves, they would have to forfeit desperately needed affection and support. Unlike the avoidant person, who fears rejection in any situation (except, sometimes, close relationships), the dependent person feels safe so long as he takes the submissive role. In both disorders, however, there is an undue fear of the consequences of aggression.

OBSESSIVE-COMPULSIVE PERSONALITY DISORDER. The crux of this disorder is the effort to stave off anxiety by controlling one's environment and the people in it. While lacking the uncontrollable thoughts and debilitating compulsions of the related Axis I disease, obsessive-compulsive disorder, the person with obsessive-compulsive personality still feels a craving for order and an overwhelming need for strictly defined rules. At work these people are apt to do quite well, up to a point. Abhorring disorder, mess, and being out of control, they scrupulously document the smallest details and adhere to every nuance of regulations. They have a natural affinity for bureaucratic positions where they have to administer intricate rules without flexibility or perspective. Others see them as perfectionist, authoritarian, strictly and sometimes obsequiously hierarchical, and often harshly judgmental. They may be preoccupied with maximizing efficiency and preventing waste.

But since the obsessive-compulsive person's need for order ultimately serves nothing larger than himself, it may easily become counterproductive. An assistant who has misplaced a file may spend hours looking for it rather then take a few minutes to retrieve the missing documents from a coworker. It is not the missing folder that disturbs him, but the fact that something is not in its proper place. An executive who feels compelled to study and act upon every single piece of paper that crosses her desk, without choosing among competing demands on her time, may find that she's working past midnight every night while her subordinates have little to do, and may miss crucial deadlines despite her absurdly late hours. Someone who, as a middle manager with a small staff, fared perfectly well by meticulously supervising every detail, making every decision personally, and allowing her staff only rote chores, may find upon being promoted and having managers now reporting to her that these habits lead to chaos and rebellion. It is not her subordinates' competence that worries her but an irrational fear that if she lets the smallest detail pass out of her control, that will be the detail that leads to catastrophe.

The order and regularity obsessive-compulsive people maintain at work often prove more elusive in their private lives. They are uncomfortable with spontaneous play and its implied loss of control and with the complexities of interpersonal relationships. Feelings, especially tender ones, are seen as "messy" and distressing—something to be isolated and denied lest they interfere with rational thought. People with compulsive features rely on convention and form; their stiff, pompous manner does not permit them to give easily of their emotions. Their need for control also makes them hold on to possessions because they may someday "come in handy." Old clothes and magazines stuff their closets, along with parts of broken appliances, used sandpaper, years' worth of unneeded receipts, and other odds and ends. Not wanting to let things go, compulsive individuals are usually parsimonious. Friends and acquaintances often see them as stingy in their capacity to give gifts, praise, or sympathy or even to pay for lunch.

Control is a means of warding off anxiety, and when compulsive people fear they will be unable to control a situation, they usually avoid it. When this proves impossible and they are forced into surroundings they cannot control, they may become angry or depressed. Like people with other disorders in this cluster, obsessive-compulsive individuals especially fear losing control of their aggression, although unlike avoidant and dependent personalities, they do find outlets for it. They often appear disgruntled at others' inability or unwillingness to meet their standards of organization and rule compliance, but they can express this anger only in response to very specific failures. Then they may subject their targets to treatment ranging from a long, insulting lecture to bemused but unmistakable contempt.

Psychoanalysts have suggested that obsessive-compulsives' need for order and their conflicts around the control of aggression may have important links to early trauma surrounding toilet training and their efforts to control their bowels. While this idea has not been confirmed scientifically—there is little evidence to correlate specific toilet-training practices with specific outcomes—still it resonates strongly with compulsive patients' use of language. Their fear of aggression, sexual excitement, or even ordinary positive feelings is often expressed metaphorically in images of mess and waste, versus the cleanliness and order of well-managed rationality. These polarities mask an ambivalence that pervades their lives and relationships with others.

§

The clinical disorders and related personality disorders described in this chapter all involve high levels of anxiety and exact a high price in the behavioral strategies used to deal with it. This anxiety is, of course, an exaggeration or distorted expression of fears we all have: of the unknown, of threatening situations, or of violating social expectations. As I discussed in Chapters 3 and 4, one feature of the dramatic cluster disorders is often an unusually low level of precisely these anxieties. Instead of a fear of the unknown, we see a hunger for novelty; instead of avoidance of threatening situations, we get thrill seeking; instead of an inhibition against violating social norms we find, in the extreme instance of the psychopath, a conscienceless flouting of every sort of rule of conduct and decency. (Since nothing in psychiatry is as simple as one might like, however, I must point out that this opposition is not perfectly consistent. Borderline personality disorder can easily coexist with anxiety.) If these aspects of the dramatic cluster disorders have underpinnings in inborn temperamental qualities, it makes sense to ask whether the anxiety-related personality disorders do too.

Jerome Kagan and his colleagues at Harvard University have demonstrated in a series of classic studies that extreme shyness and inhibition may be lifelong traits. Certain infants will stiffen and cry shrilly at the approach of a stranger or even at a loud or novel sound. When they are a bit older, the same babies secrete higher-than-normal levels of the stress hormone, cortisol, in their saliva and are more easily frightened by sudden changes in their environment. In play groups and day care centers, inhibited toddlers are often found sitting alone, outside the larger cluster of children. They approach other children tentatively and seem to be more comfortable playing by themselves or with familiar playmates. In the Harvard study, these children were found to have higher, more stable heart rates, indicating a more or less permanent arousal of the autonomic nervous system, the system that prepares the body to confront threat. Unlike other children, whose hearts speed up and slow down in response to environmental changes, the shyest children maintained a high heart rate even during sleep. They seemed to be on perpetual alert.

When Kagan followed these children for several years from early childhood, he found these traits to be quite stable. Often the children learned to cope with their levels of arousal, so that they did not act obviously shy among their peers, but their tendency to inhibition might resurface in novel situations. Their pattern of autonomic activity remained relatively constant. It is likely that they have a permanent lower threshold for subjective and physiologic arousal.

Kagan's work meshes well with the strong evidence in favor of a genetic contribution to fearful, inhibited behavior. Twin studies suggest that particular levels of "harm avoidance"—readiness to avoid harm or punishment as well as reactivity to stress—are largely heritable. People who respond more intensely to painful or punitive experiences may be more likely to try to avoid similar experiences, and depending on what strategies they develop, their personalities may be marked by inhibited, avoidant, dependent, or controlling traits.

Stephen Suomi and his colleagues, first at the University of Wisconsin and later at the National Institute for Child Health and Development, have selectively bred monkeys that are fearful or inhibited and that respond to stress with excessive arousal. Suomi got started on this project while working with the eminent animal behaviorist Harry Harlow, studying the effects of maternal separation on primate behavior. Suomi noticed that the amount of apparent distress caused by this separation varied widely. Many years later, monkeys that had seemed more upset by separation as infants also showed increased hormonal responses and behavioral arousal as adults when subjected to an experimental stress such as insertion of a feeding tube. This suggested that reactivity to stress was a stable trait in monkeys. Further, Suomi was able to show from breeding records that most of the monkeys with this trait were descended from the same few fathers. By selectively breeding these fathers' descendants, he developed a cohort of excessively fearful monkeys. When not exposed to stress, these monkeys seemed little different from normal. But separation from their mothers had long-lasting effects that impaired their ability to raise their own offspring.

Other monkeys in the original group proved relatively invulnerable to maternal separation. They showed few signs of anxiety at separation and, when grown, had among them a higher proportion of "good mothers" than a random group of monkeys. Their ability to recover from stressful circumstances was greater on average than that of randomly chosen monkeys who had not been separated from their mothers as infants.

Suomi went further. He took some offspring of fearful parents and gave them to normal, nonfearful monkeys to raise; others were left to be reared by their fearful parents. He also made the opposite exchange, giving some offspring of nonfearful monkeys to be raised by fearful parents while other nonfearful offspring remained with their natural parents. He found that whether or not they were raised by fearful parents, biological offspring of fearful monkeys were more responsive to the stress of maternal separation. But fearful infant monkeys raised by fearful mothers had more difficulty in reattaching after a separation than fearful monkeys raised by nonfearful mothers and, when grown, had a more difficult time raising their own offspring. Though it had lifelong consequences, this vulnerability was highly specific, appearing only in the context of separation and later parenting. These studies strongly suggest not only that at least one aspect of fearfulness is inherited but that the expression of this trait is strongly dependent on early experiences. There is an interaction between the inborn, apparently genetic vulnerability to maternal separation and a set of environmental conditions that "activate" the vulnerability, with long-lasting and perhaps multigenerational consequences.

Jerome Kagan also found a genetic element in the temperamental shyness he studied in children. The pattern of behavioral inhibition and chronic autonomic arousal was more common in children of panic-disordered/agoraphobic parents than in children whose parents had either no psychiatric history or a history of major depression. Thus, a lowered threshold for anxiety as a continuous behavioral trait has a link with at least one Axis I anxiety disorder. A fearful, inhibited personality style may be one way of coping with a lowered threshold of anxiety, even in people who never go on to develop an Axis I anxiety disorder. This evidence is consistent with a direct genetic link between avoidant personality disorder and panic disorder. Though it is less clear, there is also evidence supporting a relation between obsessive-compulsive personality disorder and its Axis I counterpart, obsessive-compulsive disorder.

One way to assess biological vulnerability to anxiety is to try to induce it through pharmacologic challenges. Patients with anxiety disorders, especially panic disorder, should be more likely to show symptoms of anxiety when challenged with the right drug. And if we know the drug's mechanism of action, it should give us some insights into the physiology of the anxiety disorders.

One of the first challenges to be used in this way was the lactate infusion test. Lactate is a normal metabolite of cellular respiration that circulates in the bloodstream. If sodium lactate is given intravenously, patients with a history of panic attacks are likely to feel symptoms of panic very similar to those that occur naturally. A standard salt solution without lactate yields no such effect. Among healthy volunteers with no history of panic disorder, very few show such symptoms following lactate infusion. Donald Klein, Michael Liebowitz, and their colleagues at the New York Psychiatric Institute (NYPI), who did this study, feel it indicates that panic disorder patients have a biologically lower threshold for the emergence of panic attacks. If these patients are put on a course of antidepressants, which reduce the number of panic attacks, the effects of lactate infusion are greatly diminished.

We don't know why this challenge works as it does. It may involve the body's acid-base balance or carbon dioxide metabolism. High levels of carbon dioxide in the bloodstream have also been shown to produce panic attacks in susceptible patients. Some researchers, including Jack Gorman at NYPI, have suggested that the receptors regulating CO_2 metabolite levels or acid-base balance in the bloodstream may have a different threshold of responsiveness in anxiety disorder patients than in healthy people. But the connection between these receptors and anxiety is not certain.

One very interesting theory, put forward by Donald Klein in 1993, suggests that panic attacks result from an overly sensitive "suffocation alarm system." Starting from the premise that humans' only exposure to high levels of carbon dioxide in the wild would have been in situations of imminent suffocation (such as during a cave-in, when they would have been forced to rebreathe exhaled air), Klein argues that the brain monitors its blood CO_2 levels as a way of monitoring the danger of asphyxiation. The physiological and behavioral responses to asphyxiation—hyperventilation, rapid heartbeat, a sense of extreme danger, an intense need to struggle and get away—strongly resemble the symptoms of panic disorder. Klein suggests that there is a general "suffocation detector" in the brain that integrates various cues—not only from blood gas levels but also from the smell of stuffy, stale air; being in a tightly packed, immobile crowd; or the sight of someone smothering—to trigger a panic response. If the receptors that monitor CO_2 levels were overly sensitive, they could trigger false alarms in the form of spontaneous panic attacks, especially if other cues were present. This relationship immediately brings to mind claustrophobia, and there is a close overlap between claustrophobia and panic disorder. Many claustrophobes have panic attacks in unenclosed places. But it's possible that abnormal breathing patterns, which can raise blood CO_2 levels, could trigger a suffocation response by themselves.

There is some evidence that this alarm system may be serotonergic. In an article in *Archives of General Psychiatry*, Klein mentions that a rare genetic disorder called Ondine's curse (more technically, congenital central hypoventilation syndrome) provides direct evidence of the existence of a suffocation detector. Infants with Ondine's curse breathe normally while awake, but once asleep, they stop breathing, become severely hypoxic, and die unless supported by artificial ventilation. This clear failure of the brain system that monitors breathing is also notable for the lack of a suffocation response: these infants can die quite peacefully. Curiously, this disorder often coexists with another rare genetic disorder, Hirschsprung's disease, that is characterized by a deficiency of serotonergic neurons in the gut. If the absence of a suffocation response is related to a serotonergic deficit, then this response's hypersensitivity may be related to a serotonergic abnormality as well.

The noradrenergic system, the body's alarm-arousal system, clearly plays some role in anxiety disorders. In primates, stimulating the locus ceruleus, a major center of noradrenergic neurons in the brain, brings on many of the behavioral and physiological symptoms of anxiety. This system may become dysregulated after chronic stress and has been shown to be abnormal in the affective disorders. As I noted in Chapters 1 and 2, anxiety very often accompanies depression. It makes intuitive sense that the alarm system's overactivity should contribute to an excessive susceptibility to anxiety, and this idea has been extensively tested.

Yohimbine is an antagonist of the $alpha_2$-adrenergic receptors, the feedback receptors that regulate norepinephrine release into the synapse. An infusion of yohimbine disinhibits the noradrenergic system, and Dennis Charney and his colleagues at Yale have shown that panic disorder patients respond to this with increased symptoms of anxiety as well as increased concentrations of MHPG, a norepinephrine metabolite. Clonidine, on the other hand, which reduces noradrenergic activity (as measured by MHPG concentrations), also reduces symptoms of anxiety in panic disorder patients as well as depressed patients. The reduction in MHPG is considerably greater in panic disorder patients than in healthy volunteers. These findings suggest that the noradrenergic system may be hyperresponsive in these patients. (On the other hand, the blunted growth hormone response to a clonidine challenge that is present in depressed patients can be found here as well, suggesting that some post-synaptic adrenergic receptors may have decreased responsiveness.)

Panic disorder patients show other noradrenergic abnormalities. Altered $alpha_2$-adrenergic receptor sensitivity has been found in the platelets of panic disorder patients, but while these receptors have increased sensitivity in depressed patients—perhaps reflecting an adjustment to chronically low norepinephrine levels—they are less sensitive in those with panic disorder. These findings give added weight to the idea that panic disorder entails noradrenergic dysregulation, but in a different pattern and with a different result from affective disorders. These same two abnormalities have been shown in generalized anxiety disorder, although this disease has in general been less thoroughly studied.

Autonomic dysfunction appears in post-traumatic stress disorder (PTSD) as well. Altered startle responses have been observed, as have changes in the adrenergic receptors on peripheral blood cells. In this disorder, however, the increased sensitivity to anxiety seems to have less to do with an innate susceptibility than with the sensitizing effect of some massive trauma. Some biological measures in PTSD patients, such as abnormalities in urinary excretion of cortisol and norepinephrine, differ from those seen in patients with anxiety disorders. Rachel Yehuda, a colleague of mine at Mount Sinai, has shown that instead of the high cortisol levels seen in other anxiety patients, these people actually show low baseline cortisol levels and increased sensitivity of the glucocorticoid receptors, the thermostat that provides feedback regulation of cortisol levels. This suggests a system tuned to be hyperresponsive.

PTSD patients also show above-normal suppression of cortisol after a dose of dexamethasone, precisely the opposite of the response we see in depressed patients. Again, it is as if the hypothalamic-pituitary axis—the main point of contact between the nervous and endocrine systems, which controls cortisol activity—were primed in PTSD to respond excessively to chemical and environmental challenges. When Yehuda and I compared the circadian rhythms of PTSD and depressed patients, we found contrasts here as well. Depressed patients' cortisol levels were high and relatively invariant, suggesting a chronically stressed system, while PTSD patients' rhythms showed exaggerated peaks and valleys. Although both depression and PTSD are considered stress-related disorders, they show quite different patterns of dysregulation. This difference seems to reflect a spectrum of receptor dysfunction, from underreactive to overreactive, like those in the noradrenergic and serotonergic neurotransmitter systems.

We saw in Chapter 4 that pathological gamblers appear to have hyperresponsive noradrenergic systems. By looking at what anxiety patients have in common with them—an abnormal sensitivity to environmental stimuli—and comparing it to depressed patients' *lack* of responsiveness, we can begin to see how disorders of a single neurochemical system, operating along a single dimension, can contribute to an astonishing range of personality styles. Some of this variation undoubtedly stems from interactions between various neurochemical systems. In the aggressive-impulsive disorders we typically saw a hyperreactive noradrenergic system alongside an underreactive serotonergic system, leading to an excessive engagement with the environment coupled with poorly controlled aggression. Some researchers believe that in the anxiety disorders we are seeing overreactivity of both the serotonergic and noradrenergic systems—the same excessive engagement with the environment, but this time coupled with an excessive inhibition of aggression and sensitivity to punishment. (When panic disorder patients have been challenged with the serotonergic receptor antagonist m-CPP, their heightened response has indicated an overactive serotonergic system.) The result is an alert, nervous, timid temperament prone to exaggerated and misplaced fears. Other researchers feel that both the norepinephrine and serotonin systems are secondary; the primary defect in anxiety, they suggest, involves some as-yet-undiscovered anxiogenic substance in the brain, which some people release in abnormally high amounts. This substance may be what is affected by changes in carbon dioxide or lactate levels. In any case, antidepressants, which serve to stabilize norepinephrine and/or serotonin, are currently the most effective treatment for panic disorder.

The most widely used drugs for generalized anxiety today are the benzodiazepines and related compounds, the class to which Valium belongs. The receptors to which benzodiazepines attach have been identified; they appear to modulate a system of neurons that use gamma-aminobutyric acid, or GABA, as their primary neurotransmitter. But GABA itself is something of a mystery. Although we know the GABAminergic system is one of the brain's major inhibitory systems, its physiological and behavioral effects are unclear. Researchers have associated GABAminergic abnormalities with such diseases as Huntington's disease, Parkinsonism, and schizophrenia, but not definitively in any case. Moreover, we don't really know how this system is affected by benzodiazepines. They appear to block receptors from "seeing" a naturally occurring substance that increases anxiety. It's very plausible that differences in the functioning of the GABA inhibitory system could be related to anxiety and inhibition, but nobody has found exactly what that relation is.

The biology of the anxiety-related personality disorders has not been investigated directly. Patients with "social phobias," a disorder largely overlapping avoidant personality disorder in which there is persistent fear of embarrassing oneself in public situations, appear to show heightened responses to serotonergic challenges such as fenfluramine or m-CPP but decreased responses to noradrenergic challenges such as clonidine. (These studies, however, have been inconsistent.) Could this represent a pattern opposite to what we saw in our borderline patients—increased serotonergic activity coupled with decreased noradrenergic activity?

Obsessive-compulsive disorder, which has been extensively studied, appears to be biologically different from the rest of the anxiety disorders and to involve mainly the serotonin system. The most effective medication for obsessive-compulsive disorder, clomipramine, acts by blocking the reuptake of serotonin at presynaptic terminals. Many studies have shown that clomipramine works better for this disorder than antidepressants that block norepinephrine or dopamine reuptake without affecting serotonin. Fluoxetine, the selective serotonin reuptake inhibitor, can also be effective in obsessive-compulsive disorder.

Yosi Zohar, with Dennis Murphy's group at NIMH, challenged obsessive-compulsive patients with m-CPP, which stimulates serotonin receptors, and found that it intensified their symptoms, but giving the patients a dose of clomipramine beforehand blocked this effect. Clomipramine and fluoxetine block serotonin's reuptake, increase the amount of serotonin in the synapse, and so stimulate the serotonergic system. If this reduces obsessive-compulsive symptoms, why should stimulating the serotonergic receptors with m-CPP increase those symptoms? The answer may be that when clomipramine increases serotonin levels in the synapse, these higher levels may desensitize the postsynaptic receptors, diminishing the response to m-CPP. Furthermore, there are many different serotonin systems in the brain, and while obsessive-compulsive patients show elevated responses to some sero-tonergic challenges, they show reduced responses to others. They show evidence of both heightened and lowered inhibitions as well. While their excessive fearfulness and anxiety when their rituals are not main-tained strongly resemble the other anxiety disorders, they also suffer a disinhibition resembling that of the impulse disorders—except that it occurs in the realm of uncontrollable thoughts rather than unsup-pressed actions. One of my colleagues at Mount Sinai, Eric Hollander, has suggested that there may be a continuum between impulsivity and compulsivity.

§

Anxiety forces adaptation. People with a high susceptibility to it, whether expressed as clinical anxiety disorders or as personality disor-ders, typically have learned to avoid situations that threaten to provoke their fears or raise them to uncomfortable levels. In fact their lives may be largely structured around strategies to avoid these confrontations. For this reason, reducing the overt symptoms of anxiety often has little immediate impact. Moreover, people develop a tolerance to many of the antianxiety medications. Drug treatment is mainly useful for reduc-ing anxiety's bodily symptoms—the signs of autonomic arousal—or for helping patients through new situations that they have previously avoided. Medications that stabilize serotonergic activity may be helpful here as well.

The more common forms of treatment, especially for the anxiety-related personality disorders, are psychological. Because anxiety is so often accompanied by a negative self-evaluation, cognitive psychothera-py is used to break the cycle of negative thoughts and help a person gen-erate a more positive outlook. Relaxation training, in which a person learns ways to reduce the racing heart, flushing and sweating, and other physical signs of acute nervousness, can greatly reduce the nervousness itself. People who are afraid of public situations often get so caught up in the fear of showing their anxiety to others that, once this is no longer a danger, they are better able to confront their own internal fears.

Desensitization techniques, in which the patient is trained to relax while visualizing the feared encounter, are used to modify the tendency to avoid threatening situations. Some therapists actually bring their patients into these situations—a cocktail party, for instance—as part of their training. These methods, which have been widely used for specific phobias, are now being applied more broadly to the anxiety-related disorders.

In psychodynamic treatments, the therapist emphasizes the role of unconscious conflict in maintaining the patient's symptoms—the maladaptive behaviors meant to ward off anxiety. Anxious children, for instance, may fear that overtly expressing their aggression toward parents and other authority figures will drive those figures away, leaving them alone and unprotected. The conflict between their very normal degrees of aggression and a strong fear of punishment or abandonment may result in marked, apparently unrelated inhibitions, such as a fear of the dark or of exercise. Inhibitions may be sexual as well if the child unconsciously fears that his or her parents will punish sexual excitement. Since these fantasies of withdrawal or punishment are not part of the child's conscious experience, the therapist must infer the child's underlying beliefs from dreams or from patterns of behavior that reflect compromises between the child's aggressive feelings and various feared outcomes.

These patterns may remain, unnoticed, long after their causes are forgotten, forming a template that determines many of the adult's ways of dealing with the world. In psychodynamically oriented treatments, patients are helped to explore these unconscious conflicts in an effort to unmask the anxiety they have been avoiding. By reawakening and reassessing these old fears, patients are able to separate the anxieties of the past from those of the present, develop more satisfying ways of dealing with present-day situations, and reduce their inhibitions. People with prominent anxiety-related personality traits or with specific inhibitions often have the capacity for introspection, which makes for good candidates for psychotherapy. At the same time, however, they have become so expert at repressing their emotions in an effort to control their anxieties that they may have great difficulty in relinquishing this control when this is needed. A compulsive patient may overintellectualize rather than confront her need to control her aggressive or sexual feelings; dependent or avoidant patients may resist attempts to change their defensive behaviors because they fear reawakening the childhood nightmares they are trying to avoid. The therapist's job is to convince an anxious patient that these nightmares and aggressions are not so bad—they are certainly less to be feared than the constricted, crippled life of untreated anxiety.

🌀 CHAPTER SEVEN

GOODNESS OF FIT

The brain is socially constructed.

— TERRENCE SEJNOWSKI

MARTIN AND SUSAN KEPT their aggressions under such tight control that they not only never fought but seldom even acknowledged angry or hateful feelings toward each other. To express annoyance, they would employ a freezing-cold formality— the tone of people not on speaking terms who must nonetheless speak—with which they might or might not mention the actual subject of their disagreement, depending on how sensitive it was. These "arguments" could continue for minutes or days; they usually ended, without resolution, when both sides more or less spontaneously began acting normally. Martin and Susan were considered to have an ideal marriage.

They had met in college and married shortly after Martin graduated. Susan dropped out after her sophomore year, and the couple went to live in the suburbs of New York, where Martin had landed a job as a trainee at the headquarters of a large multinational corporation. In his first few years there, he was required to travel occasionally on company business, an event the couple found very stressful. Each would worry that something dreadful had happened to the other. As soon as he could, Martin arranged to be transferred into a job that required no travel at all. From then on Martin and Susan lived as a unit, rarely permitting even brief separations from each other, except, of course, for Martin's daily trips to his office. They prided themselves on their moderate, well-regulated life.

At first they were not eager to have this comfortable routine disturbed by children, but in their thirties they began trying to have a baby. After two years, anxious and demoralized at being unable to conceive, they put themselves on the waiting list of an adoption agency. Three more years passed before they were finally notified that a baby was available for them. By this time they were in their late thirties, married for over fifteen years.

The child they adopted had been born out of wedlock to a rebellious and impulsive teenage girl who had become involved with a boy with a history of delinquency, who abandoned her on finding out she was pregnant. Unwilling to have an abortion but unable to care for the child, the girl had given her baby up for adoption. Martin and Susan named the baby Julia.

Julia was a lively and, it seemed to Susan, exceptionally loud baby. When happy, she could emit ear-piercing shrieks. Her frequent crying spells, which might arise for no apparent reason and seemed to go on interminably, left both parents feeling overwhelmed and desperate. Their first response was to feed her at any sign of distress. When this didn't work, they would pick her up and rock her, burp her, try to stick a pacifier in her mouth (which she often spat out), dangle toys in her face to try to distract her, take her for a long drive in the car, or put her next to a running vacuum cleaner or dishwasher, because Martin had heard being near a loud noise would calm babies down. Often their efforts only made her crying worse. Several dinner parties and many nights' sleep were ruined. Years later they admitted that on especially bad evenings they sometimes added small amounts of Susan's prescription tranquilizer to the baby's formula.

It made no difference that she was just an infant: Martin and Susan felt rejected and resentful of this willful, aggressive baby whom they could not easily manage. They looked forward to her growing out of this phase. Both of them nourished an unspoken assumption that as soon as she began talking and thus could be told what to do, Julia would become tractable and obedient.

She didn't.

If they had not felt such a strong need to present Julia to the outside world as a quiet, well-behaved little girl, they might have confessed some of their problems to friends, many of whom had considerably older children. They might have learned that toddlers regularly throw their food, drop it on the floor, and smear it in their hair, or that when you yell at a two-year-old, she will often respond by laughing, and this is not a sign of a malicious, contemptuous nature. Already, however, they had secretly begun to worry that their wild child was not just active but abnormal. Julia climbed bookcases, played jump rope with electrical cords, turned on the dishwasher a dozen times a day, took perishables from the refrigerator and hid them around the house, and generally plunged Martin and Susan's well-ordered life into chaos. She once managed to topple an étagère full of porcelain figurines. Sometimes her parents, feeling overwhelmed by an onslaught of large and small disasters, responded passively; other times they were excessively punitive, spanking her repeatedly and rationalizing that this was the only way to cure her "unacceptable" behavior. The spankings, which continued until Julia was seven, probably curbed her destructive tendencies but had no noticeable effect on her frequent temper tantrums, except perhaps to make them worse.

Some of these troubles died down when Julia entered school—she had learned by then how to avoid a spanking most of the time—but new troubles arose in their stead. Julia was not a very good student: she was slow in learning to read, her grasp of arithmetic was shaky, and she showed only occasional interest in study or homework. Still, she enjoyed school itself for the social scene. She did best in group activities and loved gym class, where she showed considerable athletic talent. Martin and Susan tolerated but did not encourage Julia's interest in sports, arguing that "it can't lead anywhere" (i.e., to a suitable career), and Susan disapproved of her many friends because, like Julia, they were too casual about their schoolwork.

A major blowup occurred when, at the end of second grade, the school tracked Julia into the slowest of three third-grade classes—a humiliating portent of college-admissions disaster for Martin and Susan, but a boon for Julia because the class happened to contain her two best friends. After her parents persuaded the principal to switch her into the middle-ranked class, she began playing hooky, partly out of anger and partly because it was the only way she could spend the day with her friends. They would skip school and hike for nearly an hour to a nearby shopping mall. Their journey took them through a poor neighborhood, along a commercial strip, and across a six-lane road with a speed limit of 50 miles per hour. One day one of the mall's store owners recognized the girls and called their school.

When Susan found out what Julia was doing, she lost her composure in public for the first time in decades, weeping uncontrollably in the principal's office. The thought of what could easily have happened to her daughter made her frantic with fear. Julia, when confronted by her parents, shouted, "You just want me to stay home and be in prison!" and ran to her bedroom in a tearful rage. Rather than tell Julia how worrisome her behavior was, Martin and Susan took an authoritarian approach: they threatened her with long groundings, no TV, and various other measures if she cut school again. She did it less frequently but never stopped entirely, and there were regular angry scenes about it, followed by regular punishments, throughout her elementary school years.

When Julia was eight, Susan unexpectedly found herself pregnant. At the age of forty-five, she gave birth to a healthy girl, whom they named Margaret. Margaret's arrival caused some setbacks in Julia's behavior: the frequency of her tantrums increased and she reverted to such infantile activities as crawling around the house and occasionally wetting her bed.

During these years Martin and Susan, for all their problems with Julia, would still have described their relationship with her as generally positive and loving. Her misbehavior, emotional outbursts, and mediocre grades were outweighed by her many good attributes and the good times the family had together. As she approached adolescence, however, this began to change. In junior high school she began skipping school more frequently. She spent time with students older than herself, many of them in high school, and got her first exposure to more mature forms of bad behavior. One new acquaintance introduced her to the combination of alcohol and sedatives, and she began spending Sunday afternoons drinking beer and taking "'ludes" (Quaaludes, a prescription tranquilizer used at that time as a sleeping aid) in a nearby park. When her parents realized why she was coming home so drowsy and silent, they began restricting her to the house and forbidding her to see her girlfriends, whom they saw as a bad influence. Julia would become furious at this, screaming at her parents that they were not allowing her to develop "a normal social life." Several times she ran away from home, only to return, tired and sheepish, a couple of days later. Martin and Susan found it increasingly difficult to welcome her back after these forays.

When they tried even more stringent restrictions—no visitors to the house, no after-school activities of any kind, no going out after dark under any circumstances—Julia became, if possible, still angrier and horrified her parents by becoming involved with a fifteen-year-old boy, Mark, who had dropped out of school. Mark terrified many parents in the community by dressing in leather with metal accessories and flaunting an intimate knowledge of handguns. On weekends he and his friends would drive by Martin and Susan's house late at night, whereupon Julia would climb out an upstairs window to join them, not returning until morning. Martin got to the point where he would break into a cold sweat at the sound of an unmuffled engine.

Barely halfway through her teens, Julia was staying out until all hours, partying with people up to twice her age in ways her parents didn't dare imagine. Martin and Susan felt she had gotten completely out of control. She would not obey them when they tried to set firm limits, and any attempt to discuss her behavior simply brought on a tantrum. It was a sign of how bad things had become that her performance in school, which had degenerated from lackluster to nonexistent, was barely even an issue. Midway through Julia's sophomore year in high school, when her report card arrived showing all D's and F's, her parents couldn't even bring themselves to discuss it with her. There was no point. At this they realized they had hit bottom. Their choices were to keep their daughter under lock and key, throw her out of the house, send her away to a private school for troubled youth, or seek counseling.

A psychologist who belonged to their country club suggested that Julia might have a conduct disorder and recommended a hospital in the next county that treated troubled adolescents. Martin and Susan were greatly relieved at the prospect of having a clear, authoritative explanation for Julia's unmanageable behavior and were therefore stunned when the hospital psychologist who interviewed Julia reported that she met some but not all the criteria for conduct disorder, and that the main source of the problem lay elsewhere. Julia was chronically dis-obedient, this psychologist said, but she was not physically violent, cruel, promiscuous, destructive, or deceitful; her defiance of authority seemed mainly limited to her parents—she seemed to like her teachers well enough and be liked in turn, even though she was failing most of her courses because of nonattendance—and she certainly had not suf-fered the kind of chaotic, negligent upbringing that is thought to put children at risk for this disorder. When Susan, utterly baffled by this analysis, blurted out, "But there's something wrong with her, isn't there?" the psychologist replied that rather than saddle Julia with a diagnosis of a milder disorder, disruptive behavior disorder, she thought it would be best if the whole family received counseling together. "I don't want you to start thinking," she said, "that all your difficulties arise because Julia has a problem. That would let you off the hook. You're all in this together, and you're going to have to start focus-ing on what you can do—together—to make things better."

In family meetings, it became clear that both Julia and her parents saw her as a "bad," spiteful girl. From a very early age, especially when she was frustrated or feeling very energetic, her image of herself crys-tallized around her parents' perception of her as malicious and out of control. Her temper tantrums and often destructive explorations stood as confirmation of these hateful qualities. While other parents might have been able to deal with her wildly spontaneous activity and low tol-erance for frustration by firmly but judiciously setting limits—by teaching her, for instance, that she was allowed to be angry and upset but not allowed to scream and throw things—Martin and Susan could not provide such limits because they did not have the experience of coping with their own angry, aggressive feelings. The only way they had developed to deal with their aggressions as adults was to pretend they didn't exist, something Julia was incapable of doing as a young child, and so they could offer her little guidance on what was an allowable expression of anger and what was not. When, in better moods, Julia would careen wildly around the house, shouting or singing loudly, her parents could not limit their concern to the chance that she might hurt herself or damage something. Such frenzied activity, with its implied loss of control, struck them as alarming in itself. Again, they could not train Julia to manage these impulses because they tried not to acknowledge them at all.

Martin and Susan had come to see Julia as their dark side: she embodied all the "negative" feelings they had worked so hard to expunge from their lives. These had now come back to haunt them in the person of their daughter. Julia adopted this view as well. When angry or excited, she experienced herself as full of hate and savagely unfit for adult society. When she became a teenager and began struggling with her budding sexuality and need for more independence, her view of herself as bad, barbaric, and out of control became romantically compelling. She began to build a lifestyle around it. Her group of like-minded friends dressed and acted in ways that flouted the conventions and values of their parents and school. Their cultural heroes were heavy metal bands and movie stars who projected a defiance of authority together with a self-pitying sense of victimization by ruling powers.

In the course of treatment, Martin and Susan acknowledged their difficulties in experiencing anger or tolerating even normal levels of aggression. Their abhorrence of separation, which they viewed as an aggressive, threatening act—a loved one going outside the family's direct observation and control—made it hard for them to give their children the autonomy they needed. Their other daughter, Maggie, who like Martin and Susan was forbidden to express anger directly, gained some independence by withdrawing into herself. She sometimes shut herself in her room and played alone for hours; when it was necessary to come out, she would speak only in terse, whispered replies to direct questions. Julia was less successful in finding ways to disengage from her parents. Instead she fought them, doing all the things she knew would infuriate them most. The three of them became locked in a vicious cycle: the more she misbehaved, the more they cracked down, the angrier she got, the more she misbehaved. Ultimately Julia was trapped in the very dependency she desperately wanted to avoid. Everything she did was in response (albeit opposition) to her parents' wishes. At one session she admitted to growing very tired of Mark and his friends—she often found their behavior pointless and scary—but felt if she stopped seeing them she would be giving in to her parents. Martin and Susan, for their part, wished fervently to be able to relax and have some relationship with Julia that did not revolve around their attempts to control her behavior, but they worried that any softening would be taken as a sign of approval of her friends and lifestyle.

When Martin and Susan began to understand that much of their image of Julia came from a projection of their own fears of aggressive behavior, they became able to learn to appreciate her outgoing nature. When Julia began to understand that she was not somehow incorrigible from birth, she became able to start building a positive image of herself that incorporated her impulsive, warm, sometimes raucous personality. Together they reached a number of practical compromises: Julia could pick her own friends but she promised to do nothing illegal and especially to stop drinking until she was eighteen, and to stop abusing drugs; she could go where she wanted after school, but she had to tell her parents where she was going and with whom; she could choose her own clothes but could no longer dye her hair strange colors; she had to observe a curfew; and her parents promised that if she maintained a c average in school, she could get a driver's license and have use of a car. These arrangements were not trivial. They were the tangible means by which Julia and her parents grew and tested their trust of each other from day to day. Julia felt she'd passed a milestone the first day she borrowed Susan's car to meet some friends at the shopping mall. Martin and Susan, however, felt the real milestone occurred one night when Julia came home half an hour late: when they asked her where she'd been, they were met not with anger but with an apology and an explanation of why she'd been unable to call. Then they all went to bed.

Gradually, with many setbacks, Julia acquired a taste for real self-sufficiency as opposed to childish rebellion. Martin and Susan, meanwhile, learned to prefer her ability to make her own choices over the false comfort of total control. Julia graduated from high school with mediocre but passing grades, didn't bother to apply to her parents' prestigious liberal arts college but got into a state college, and now teaches gym in a high school. She frequently acts as a confidante and adviser to girls with a variety of discipline and other problems. In summers she works as a guide on white-water rafting expeditions in the Pacific Northwest. At twenty-five, Julia is happy. She is able both to succeed as an adult and to live out her deep affection for the untamed.

᠑

The way parents, brothers, sisters, peers, and teachers relate to a growing child is strongly influenced by their own previous experiences and their feelings about various temperamental traits the child expresses. The tragedy of a child who disappoints his parents' expectations is that he often becomes the repository of his parents' self-doubt and self-hatred. When parents see what they consider their "bad sides" emerging in their children, they are tempted to feel they have somehow unintentionally taught their children these behaviors, and out of guilt, fright, or anger they may respond unusually harshly. Sometimes the story does not end as happily as Julia's.

While it is tempting to blame the parents in cases like this, we must remember that they are usually acting with the best of intentions, according to their own personality styles, however adaptive or maladaptive these may be. Sometimes, with children who are extremely sensitive, anxious, aggressive, or difficult to engage emotionally, only an unusually empathetic and devoted parent can successfully reach out and contain the growing child's vulnerabilities. Even these efforts may not be enough, in the end, to prevent significant psychological stress or emotional disturbance. But a better understanding of the biology of temperamental differences can help. Not only does it help parents to tolerate and accept their children's differing temperamental styles, but it aids professionals in guiding parents to tune in to their children and find ways to bolster their strengths and help compensate for their vulnerabilities.

Innate temperamental differences play a role in shaping a young child's experience of her environment and thus her strategies for coping with it. An impulsive child is likely to use action as a way of responding to external events or internal needs, but for an anxious, inhibited child, the increased engagement with the environment brought by action is itself a source of stress. Such a child is more likely to withdraw and say nothing; her stresses and their causes will be much more mysterious to adults. A child with affective instability will be particularly sensitive to the comings and goings of others and may use emotional outbursts to influence the responses of parents and other caretakers. A cognitively disorganized or detached child may react to a complex environment by restricting his attentional focus and avoiding ambiguous situations that make him uncomfortable, such as meeting new children. Individual differences like this are a central influence on the coping patterns and personality styles these children will later display as adults.

Such differences may come into play very early in a child's life. At ten months of age, babies are able to construct generalized prototypes of interactions between themselves and others; they quickly react to "mismatches," or deviations from anticipated matching behaviors by their mothers. By age two they can form representations of their environment, which they can retain in memory (most people's earliest memories date from about this age). These primitive representations appear to form the basis for the more complex and differentiated internal models that develop later—the schemas described in Chapter 2. These provide the vehicles by which our past experiences are encoded and through which we form our expectations of the future.

We do not know exactly how these early representations are retained in the brain. It is likely that they are stored as coherent units consisting of sensory and motor information—what the child sees, hears, and so on, and what his actions are—along with the emotional state associated with those circumstances. For example, an infant can learn very early on to detect facial patterns, and if shown a cartoon of a face, he will notice if a nose or eye is in the wrong place. One of the first objects an infant recognizes is his mother's face, which he associates with the release of pain and tension from hunger or loneliness. A representation of the mother develops that includes an encoding of her facial features, her smell, the texture and warmth of her skin, the sound of her voice, motor behavior such as cuddling, suckling, or play, and emotional associations that range from soothing calm to happy excitement.

Sometimes, however, life is not so ideal. An infant who experiences pain or frustration unusually strongly, whose feeding and sleep are troubled by colic, or whose mother's face and actions are deadened by depression may not develop such a comforting representation. While it's easy to understand that the mother's behavior and moods affect an infant's internal image of her, it's important to realize also that the infant plays an active role in this relationship as well. The intensity and stability of the infant's emotional regulation, the degree of organization of her motor movements, and her susceptibility to angry or impulsive outbursts all influence both the mother's responses and the way their interactions are represented in the infant's mind. Each temperament, then, strongly affects the other, and the way they interact, for better or worse, is what we term goodness of fit.

A mother struggling with her own cognitive vulnerabilities, who has trouble organizing her thoughts and behavior, may find it especially difficult to take care of a similarly impaired infant. The child's difficulty in coordinating his movements or managing his bodily states may seem incomprehensible and spiteful, especially if her attempts at care bring random, unsatisfying responses. An unusually nurturant and empathetic mother, by contrast, may help compensate for an infant's neuropsychological impairment. But an affectively unstable mother who requires intense interaction might overwhelm the same infant, who would be unable to organize his experience under such relentless stimulation. An anxious parent with a strong need to deny or control her own aggression may react badly with an extremely active, impulsive child; she might try to control his activity with excessive rules and punishments and ultimately come to see him as destructive and out of control. Their frequent struggles around aggression and control might result in a rebellious, alienated child. On the other hand, a more impulsive parent might indulge the child's impulsivity too much, to the extent that he does not internalize social norms appropriately.

We can extend this two-way process to cover the child's entire development. Just as environment influences how biological predispositions are expressed, a child's temperament will bias the reactions of parents, teachers, and other children. The ultimate adaptiveness of the adult personality depends a great deal on the goodness of fit between a child's predispositions and vulnerabilities and the resources and requirements of the caretaking environment, and on the way this interaction shapes the child's sense of self. For instance, extremely aggressive or hyperactive children may elicit a punitive response from adults who do not understand the biology underlying this behavior. Once these children get a reputation as troublemakers, they may be suspected of mischief they were not involved in, and their parents and teachers may punish them for behavior that a generally better-behaved child could get away with. These reactions, in turn, could lead to lowered self-esteem, increased anger, and more aggressive behavior.

Another possibility is that in learning to regulate her internal states and behavior in a way that will be acceptable to others, an impulsive child might learn to contain her aggression. In a strictly authoritarian environment, she might begin to identify with the values of her parents and impose restrictions on her own actions. This reaction might be healthy—she might develop firm discipline that still allows for a creatively aggressive impulsivity in sports, artistic pursuits, or simply a good sense of humor—or it might take the form of obsessional efforts at restriction and control or perhaps self-directed aggression. Much of Julia's remarkable transition to adulthood became possible when it dawned on her that she didn't have to suppress and deny her innate aggressiveness in order to become a good person: she could use it to create a positive role for herself. Once she stopped defining herself as a "bad person," she no longer needed to seek validation in the company and habits of other "bad people."

๖

Everyone brings to a marriage, and later to the birth of a child, his or her own background and emotional baggage. We may choose a partner who complements us—who has strengths we wish we had—even while our partner has chosen us for similar reasons. It is not uncommon, for instance, to see a straitlaced, emotionally constricted man, somewhat compulsive and quite successful in his work, married to a more histrionic, emotionally expressive woman. To him she is a free spirit who will help him overcome his rigidities; he is intrigued by her unpredictability. She may see him as a stable and rational influence on her capricious, volatile lifestyle. While it's generally a mistake to go into a marriage with the expectation of changing your partner, people often use marriage as a vehicle for changing themselves. Yet if partners are pulled to opposite extremes, tension may result. The carefree fiancee may seem irresponsible and childish after years of marriage, and the responsible, protective boyfriend may turn into a boring, overcautious husband. While it may be true in romance that "opposites attract," they also require accommodation in the long term.

Others are attracted to partners similar to themselves. People who are affectively sensitive and somewhat anxious, for instance, may be more comfortable with a spouse who shares these qualities.

In Chapter 3 I touched on the phenomenon of assortative mating, the tendency of people with psychiatric disorders to marry people with the same disorder more often than would be expected from random pairings. Assortative mating has a strong effect on the resulting children's genetic inheritance. Two parents with affective disorder are much more likely to produce a child susceptible to depression than if each had married someone without this predisposition. A marriage between a sociopathic, alcoholic father and an impulsive, affectively unstable mother with borderline personality disorder is likely to produce children with a genetic tendency toward impulsivity. The family environments in both of these marriages increase the likelihood that these genetic tendencies will be expressed.

Other variations may occur. People may find spouses with different, "complementary" disorders. A drug-abusing man may marry a passive, withdrawn, schizophrenic but not unattractive woman whose detachment from reality enables her to tolerate his abusive, neglectful behavior when no one else would. For her part, after having gone through a number of affairs in which men finally lost interest in her impenetrable passivity, she may value his investment, however negative, in the relationship. Their marriage might ultimately rest on the conviction that each is the other's only alternative to solitude. In addition to the handicap of growing up in an unstable environment, the offspring of such a marriage may carry genetic susceptibilities to both schizophrenia and impulsive, addictive, and aggressive behaviors—susceptibilities that may put them at risk even if they are adopted into other families at an early age. Such marriages also increase the chance of interactions between dimensions of psychiatric disorders. A child of these parents may have long-term problems with compulsive, antisocial, or aggressive behavior as well as occasional psychotic episodes that bring him to the hospital.

Assortative mating affects the child's family environment in other ways as well. Couples sometimes develop a tightly regulated relationship, based on mutual vulnerabilities or the fit of their personality styles, that does not easily tolerate the intrusion of a demanding presence in the form of a newborn child. Martin and Susan's marriage, molded by their anxieties into a strict regime of restrained and cautious formality, was severely jolted by Julia's arrival. In such families, children may feel like distractions from their parents' real lives; they may grow up with a sense of being unloved and unwelcomed. Some studies have suggested that many patients with borderline personality disorder fit this pattern. In other situations, a couple may look to the child to rescue their deteriorating marriage. If the compulsive husband above begins to look at his mildly histrionic wife's flirtatiousness as erratic emotionality, and she starts to think of his caution less as stable good sense and more as petty rigidity and jealousy, their child may become the one important thing they have in common and may as a result be burdened by excessive emotional demands in the guise of loving attention, often resulting in narcissistic problems in the child.

Even in the most optimal situations, a newborn infant begins life with more than a set of genetic predispositions. There are also the accommodations, wishes, compromises, disappointments, and fantasies of his or her parents. In fact, these fantasies and wishes may precede the infant's birth and may even be passed down from generation to generation. Parents give their children particular temperamental traits, which are passed on genetically, as well as particular attitudes and coping strategies, which are passed on in other ways. Besides providing the earliest and most important venue for the interaction of genes and environment, family life also provides a key entry point for psychiatry's interest in nonpathologic variations of innate temperament. As we saw with Martin, Susan, and Julia, a family may contain no member with any diagnosable psychiatric illness, yet as a whole be clearly dysfunctional and need therapy. Temperamental styles contribute greatly to these mismatches, and understanding these styles can contribute to their treatment.

❧

Mixing of temperamental traits occurs, of course, within individuals as well, and the dimensions of impulsivity, anxiety, affective instability, and cognitive disorganization that we have explored in this book do not rigidly align themselves with their correspondent personality disorder clusters. Assortative mating would lead us to expect that many people might suffer from more than one personality disorder or have disturbances related to more than one dimension. This is precisely what I do see in many of my patients.

Affective sensitivity, for instance, may occur in both anxious and impulsive individuals, although they manage their feeling states quite differently. The affectively sensitive person will respond readily and painfully to changes in his or her environment, such as separations, losses, or frustrations. People with dramatic cluster personality disorders tend to be disinhibited and to take action in response to their problems: they are likely to do something provocative, in order to manipulate the responses of others, to manage their internal states. Anxious people, on the other hand, are more likely to withdraw from others and to shy away from potentially painful situations to forestall anxiety. In the anxious cluster personality disorders, we see rejection sensitivity and an increased prevalence of depressive episodes. Dramatic cluster patients often show affective instability combined with impulsivity—in self-directed aggression such as suicide attempts when they are depressed, and in outward-directed violence and fighting at other times. Many borderline patients show alternations of inward- and outward-directed rage that may in some ways be analogous to the bipolar states of manic depressive illness.

Affective instability and impulsivity may in turn be combined with a third element, cognitive disorganization. The borderline patient who is enraged at being abandoned may develop paranoid ideas about a conspiracy among those who have "made me suffer." The wild gyrations of these people's emotional states—their euphoria when entering a new relationship, their terrible, self-punitive rages when they feel once again abandoned—may distort their rational processes as well. Sometimes these distortions reach the point of breaking with reality, a phenomenon we term mini-psychotic episodes. They can even include outright hallucinations, such as the small, gremlin-like alien creatures an infuriated borderline woman saw in the dimly lit hallway outside her apartment shortly after she separated from her boyfriend. Although she knew they weren't real, they seemed physically present to her. Being affectively driven, these brief episodes are quite different from the persistent cognitive disorganization seen in people with schizophrenia-related disorders. Moreover, people with strong affective sensitivities tend to be profoundly engaged with their environment and are less likely to have the social withdrawal, constricted emotions, and poor rapport common to the odd cluster disorders.

Impulsivity and anxiety may also be combined, even though they are in some ways opposites. Impulsive people act as a consequence of hurt feelings and don't anticipate future punishments, while anxious people do anticipate future punishment and rejection and act to forestall them. They avoid situations that offer the possibility of hurt feelings. In some people, however, impulsive and anxious features combine in a context of profound affective instability. After a disappointment such as losing out in a relationship or failing to get a coveted job, they may feel a deep rage, yet these feelings may be suppressed, even unacknowledged, until the inhibitory effects of an initial anxiety give way to impulsive action. Such people rarely grow physically violent, but when they do they can be quite destructive. When this combination of inhibition, impulsivity, and affective instability is further combined with the distorted world view of the schizophrenia-related personality disorders, the result may be dangerous or even criminally insane behavior. While chronic schizophrenic patients are usually too passive to be dangerous, the more functional schizotypal individual with gaps in his organization of reality, as well as the ability to hold back, for a time, his aggressive rages, may have just the combustible set of ingredients needed for the bizarre destructive acts of serial killers.

These extremely dangerous expressions of temperamental abnormalities are rare. For every mass murderer whose newspaper descriptions suggest the isolated, eccentric picture of a schizotypal personality, there are many, many quiet, isolated schizotypals who wish nothing more than to be left alone. In the vast majority of cases, multiple vulnerabilities bring only painful distress to an individual who finds himself unable to cope adaptively with his life. These simplified examples cannot come close to doing justice to the enormously varied and nuanced strengths and weaknesses each person possesses, but they illustrate ways in which the dynamics of personality may be understood from an interactive approach.

The environment's impact on a developing child must in some way be biologically encoded in the brain, in the subtle connections and adjustments in reactivity that underlie our memories and coping strategies. When environmental events are catastrophically horrendous, as in cases of child abuse, we may expect the physical effects on the brain to be correspondingly grave. More and more we are finding that abuse has not only profoundly serious psychological consequences but significant biological ones as well—that it may have enduring physical effects on the brain. It thus serves to illustrate, tragically, how environmental and biological influences ultimately merge.

While child abuse is not new, in recent years people have grown more aware of both its substantial prevalence and its long-lasting destructive effects. It has many underlying factors, most famously the abusing parent's own history of having been abused as a child. Alcohol or drugs may play a role in lifting the parent's inhibitions against sexual or violent behavior. While a tendency toward impulsive aggressive behavior in the parent may make him or her more likely to strike or batter a child, there is an element of interaction here as well. Sometimes, as I mentioned above, a parent may become enraged at traits in the child that he hates in himself, and some instances of abuse occur at the hands of anxious parents who feel threatened by the seemingly uncontrollable activity of an aggressive/impulsive child. These biological and psychological risk factors are exacerbated by socioeconomic stresses such as poverty, unemployment, or sudden downward mobility.

Given that these stresses are increasing at the same time that the resources for monitoring and intervening in cases of abuse are shrinking, it is easy to see why public concern about the problem has become polarized. There are those who see abuse as the proximate cause of a host of psychiatric problems, from eating disorders to personality disorders to the perpetuation of abuse itself in future generations. Others argue that the whole problem has been blown up out of proportion. They point to well-publicized instances in which mental health professionals, obsessed with recovering repressed memories, have suggested—and gotten their patients to believe in—bizarre, nightmarish events that never actually occurred. People arguing for greater attention to the problem sometimes charge that those who would minimize it are simply looking for excuses to spend less money on social interventions at a time when intervention is expensive and politically unfashionable. At times, the debate moves beyond the realm of verifiable fact or constructive opinion. It is possible to consider abuse an extremely serious problem even while remaining skeptical of the wilder claims made about it. For my discussion here, perhaps it is best to stick to what is known about the biological impact of abuse and neglect.

ॐ

The effects of abuse on the developing child at both the biological and psychological levels can be profound. A history of abuse has been statistically associated with anxiety disorders, substance abuse disorders, eating disorders, and personality disorders, particularly borderline personality disorder and multiple personality disorder. Some of the symptoms of borderline personality disorder, such as low self-esteem, impulsivity, and difficulties in interpersonal relationships, are easier to understand in the context of a history of abuse. If the abuser is an authority figure and an object of love and respect, the victim's shame and rage combine with a feeling that there is no one to turn to and that this treatment is somehow deserved. We are now learning that extreme trauma such as this can be understood from a neurobiological perspective as well: it has long-lasting physical effects on the brain. The trauma itself need not be exclusively physical. Sustained social stress has been shown to cause degeneration in the hippocampal neurons of monkeys; psychological trauma has been shown to affect learning and memory storage through long-term effects on the amygdala, hypothalamus, and brainstem. Repeated sexual, verbal, and physical abuse over years may be as detrimental to the brain as a blow to the head.

One of the systems on which this trauma acts is the norepinephrine system, whose alarm/arousal function (the "fight-or-flight" response) we looked at in Chapter 2. A physical attack on a child mobilizes this system, and repeated attacks (or one very severe episode) may induce changes in the receptors or even in the expression of the genes controlling this system, altering its trigger point so that it may be more easily activated by subsequent traumas. In effect, the system automatically adjusts itself for the world of danger the child faces. As these adjustments fail to prevent further attacks, the system makes itself more responsive still. In more primitive regions of the brain such as the limbic system, the resulting hyperresponsiveness can cause hyperactivity, exaggerated vigilance, sleep disturbances, and impulsivity. These behavioral changes—which have their evolutionary origins in responses to extreme danger from predators and other large, dangerous enemies— are not well suited to situations where the danger comes from within the family. Some of them may increase the likelihood of further abuse. To protect herself emotionally, the terrorized child may become withdrawn and psychologically numb.

These effects do not end when the abuse stops; they are self-sustaining. As the child thinks and dreams about the traumatic events, the same brain regions are activated, further sensitizing the noradrenergic pathways so that these regions are triggered at an even lower threshold. Severe, sustained abuse leads to a syndrome not unlike what we see in combat veterans with post-traumatic stress disorder, in which the slightest, almost imperceptible trigger can bring terrible memories flooding back with surreal vividness. In PTSD patients we can see evidence of chronic disturbances of the norepinephrine system in the high levels of catecholamine metabolites we sometimes find in their blood and other body fluids. As I write this, no similar studies have been reported on victims of childhood abuse.

The serotonin system may also be altered by trauma. While reduced serotonergic activity is generally associated with impulsivity, there are hints—from studies of adolescents done at other research centers as well as studies of female personality disorder patients done at our own center—that the serotonergic system may actually become *more* sensitive following trauma. While these studies are only beginning and have yet to be convincingly interpreted, they point toward an understanding of how the plasticity of the serotonergic system may be initially set by genetic factors and then altered by the environment. (These studies also argue against the suggestion that trauma itself causes reduced serotonergic activity. While there are many mechanisms by which abusive behavior may be passed on from one generation to the next, environmental effects on brain chemistry could be a mitigating rather than an aggravating factor if they cause abnormally diminished serotonergic activity to be increased.)

In the last chapter I mentioned Rachel Yehuda's studies of the hypothalamic-pituitary axis (HPA), a crucial neuromodulator system for responding to stress. Environmental stresses activate a number of brain systems and cause the pituitary gland to release adrenocorticotropic hormone (ACTH), which in turn stimulates the adrenal glands to release cortisol. Cortisol provides a brake on body defense mechanisms, such as inflammation, that are helpful over the short term but that ultimately damage tissues.

But cortisol itself may affect tissues as well, including those in the brain. Some investigators, such as Bob Sapolsky of Stanford and Bruce McEwan at Rockefeller University, have suggested that a persistently high level of circulating cortisol may damage a key part of the brain, the hippocampus, one of the important centers of memory. In MRI studies of PTSD patients, a group at Yale found a significantly smaller average hippocampal size, particularly among patients with a history of child abuse. Another recent study suggests reduced hippocampal size in women with a history of sexual abuse—who also show reduced suppression to dexamethasone, just like PTSD patients. Could their trauma have brought on hippocampal degeneration? Much more research is needed on this question, but it is certainly not far-fetched to state that trauma is likely to affect brain function in ways we can measure.

One of the differences between depression and PTSD appears to be the way the body has reacted to chronic stress. In depression the HPA is chronically overactive, cortisol secretion is abnormally high, daily rhythms are muted or lost, and the system is generally less able to respond to environmental changes. It is stuck in overdrive. This is a classic example of a failure of feedback control due to receptor dysfunction. Trauma or abuse victims, like PTSD patients, show precisely the opposite picture: very low baseline levels of cortisol secretion along with very high reactivity. Yehuda demonstrated this difference using dexamethasone, a drug that stimulates glucocorticoid receptors in the pituitary so that, in healthy subjects, cortisol secretion is suppressed. It is well known that this effect is blunted in depressed patients—the depressed patient's cortisol "escapes" from suppression. In fact the dexamethasone suppression test was once considered as a possible diagnostic test for depression. In PTSD patients, this suppression response is greatly exaggerated—the HPA is hyperreactive to suppression and, we think, to stimulation as well.

Why should this be? One answer may lie in the nature of the stress. The overproductive, underresponsive system seen in depression may be a sign that the body has acclimated itself to a relatively continuous irritant that falls below the level of emergency. In trauma victims, on the other hand, the stress is less frequent but far more threatening. Supersensitive cortisol receptors, yielding enhanced feedback inhibition, an abnormally low baseline level, and a very strong response to stimulation, may reflect a system that is primed to react to sudden physical emergencies.

Recently Yehuda and a colleague, Heidi Resnick of the University of South Carolina, found that victims of rape who also had a history of previous rape or assault were more likely to show symptoms of PTSD and to demonstrate low cortisol levels than rape victims who did not have such a history. Moreover, rape victims who had low cortisol levels at the time of their initial evaluation were more likely to develop PTSD. In the case of child abuse victims, this finding suggests how environmental influences may *become* biological ones: these women responded to a traumatic event in ways that were encoded in their bodies by earlier events.

This encoding may take place at a level even deeper than neural receptors. Some researchers are now looking at the impact of environmental events on the expression of genes themselves. Stressors may not only activate stress hormones and neurotransmitters that fine-tune the responsiveness of brain systems; some of them can also act directly on the genome to regulate the transcription of genetic information into proteins. As Steven Hyman, current director of NIMH, Eric Nestler of Yale, and colleagues have demonstrated, specific transcription factors activated by stress-induced mediators as well as drugs can change the expression of genes in nerve cells and so affect the chemical composition of key pathways in the brain. These factors are known to be affected by drugs of abuse, such as cocaine or amphetamine, as well as by antidepressant medications. Steroid stress hormones, such as cortisol, also modulate these transcription factors and thereby encode the effects of stress on future cell responses. Effects at this level open up the possibility of long-lasting structural changes in the nerve cell. Rather than simply stimulating or blocking receptors, a change in gene expression could perhaps change the number of receptor sites at a synapse or alter the cell's ability to form new connections. Ultimately, the modulation of gene expression may be the key to understanding how trauma causes the damage it does and why its effects are so long-lasting.

These effects may even transcend a single generation. While trauma may reach so deeply into our biology as to modify the expression of genes, it may also be passed to the next generation environmentally. Holocaust survivors, as discussed in Chapter 6, demonstrate the same circadian rhythm abnormalities and exaggerated feedback control of the HPA axis that combat veterans with PTSD do. What is intriguing is Yehuda's finding that the *offspring* of Holocaust survivors show similar abnormalities, even though they never directly experienced the trauma their parents did. Perhaps the sense of danger and uncertainty associated with living through such a time is passed on in the family milieu and primes the biologic systems of the children as well.

CHAPTER EIGHT

FROM THE INDIVIDUAL TO THE COMMUNITY

*Human personality is generally considered a gratuitous and more
or less private concern. It is supposed to have something to do with
how one impresses others, how one can "put himself over." This is
an American stereotype that has little to do with personality as
a vehicle for human interaction. It fails to recognize that the
personality and its inner organization are the supreme implements
for adaptation in its widest sense. It is not a matter to be dismissed
lightly. It is of the highest social importance.*

— ABRAM KARDINER AND LIONEL OVESEY

They are the same people
　　　　　　　　only further from home
　　on freeways fifty lanes wide
　　　　　　on a concrete continent
　　　　　　　　　spaced with bland billboards
　　　　　　illustrating imbecile illusions of happiness
The scene shows fewer tumbrils
　　　　　　　　but more maimed citizens
　　　　　　　　　　in painted cars

— LAWRENCE FERLINGHETTI

THE BIOLOGICAL REVOLUTION in psychiatry must inevitably change our view of how the person who has a psychiatric disorder fits into the community. Our culture's notions about people with these disorders—who is a responsible citizen and who is not, what behavior is a threat and what is not, and what is an appropriate response and what is not—continue to evolve. Although we lack a strong empirical base from which to discuss these subjects, we may be permitted to speculate.

If you compare statistics on the prevalence of various psychiatric diseases across societies and across decades, it becomes immediately clear that some diseases depend more heavily on social context than others. The incidence of schizophrenia, for instance, remains relatively constant throughout the world. But conduct disorder in children has become more common in America in the last twenty years, and depression seems to have increased over the same period. Mania, on the other hand, may have decreased in this century. Emil Kraepelin, writing about manic depressive disorder in the early part of this century, noted that roughly half of his patients experienced depression only, about a sixth mania only, and most of the rest showed what we would now call bipolar disorder. Today the ratio of depression to mania is closer to ten to one.

If mental diseases have biological and genetic roots, clearly time, place, and circumstance play an important role in their expression. Highly structured societies with deeply ingrained traditions tend to suppress the expression of individual differences and even of psychiatric symptoms. Communities consisting of interlocking networks of large extended families do not tolerate deviant or aggressive behavior to the same extent that modern American society does. These communities also offer children a much wider range of adults with whom they can form attachments. If the "goodness of fit" between child and parents is inadequate for the growing child's needs, grandparents, aunts and uncles, or older siblings and cousins can provide role models. In America today these people (except for the siblings) are apt to live too far away and see the child too infrequently to offer an enduring alternative adult relationship.

Immigrant families often carried this community with them to the New World. It was not uncommon for a small shopkeeper to have his apartment above the family's store and for the mother and children to work in the store with him. Other family members might have lived in the same building or nearby, especially if they needed the original couple's help in order to emigrate, and they might have worked in the store or for businesses in the neighborhood. The physical and emotional distance between work and home or between nuclear family and extended family was less than it often is today. The workplace was the family workplace, and children had frequent daily contact with mother and father, aunts, uncles, and cousins, usually centered around chores that contributed to running the business or household. In this structured, task-oriented, extended-family community, dramatically deviant, antisocial, or eccentric behavior was discouraged or shielded from the neighbors. Most such behavior was quickly noticed and constrained by punishment, peer pressure, and increased scrutiny. Other temperamental differences were sometimes tolerated and even indulged if they did not disturb the community's day-to-day life. Still other eccentricities, if shared by enough family members, became part of the community's tradition. An outgoing, independent person might have found this environment too restrictive, but for others it probably prevented vulnerabilities from developing into crises.

For instance, imagine a woman with schizotypal traits living in this setting. She might live her entire adult life without marrying, making a new friend, leaving her neighborhood, or having a single intimate conversation. Yet if her mother and two married brothers live nearby, she has a place to go for dinner, people to be near who tolerate her aloofness, and a way to participate in the holidays and festivals that give comfort and variety to our lives. If her brothers own a business, she could work there. If she has acquaintances whom she has known since childhood, she might see them now and then without causing herself undue stress. This sense of belonging to a family, a place, a set of responsibilities, and by extension a community provides a mooring that prevents her from drifting into more eccentric lifestyles. There is not sufficient cultural diversity or even much opportunity for such eccentricity to be expressed. The chance to entertain paranoid or referential ideas is limited—and if she expresses them, it will most often be to people who feel close enough to her to find them unthreatening and tell her she is wrong. Her brothers might be patronizing but no worse than that, and her suspiciousness will not endanger her place in a community that already knows to allow for it.

Take away the family and the neighborhood, put her in a two-bedroom suburban cottage with peeling paint and an unkempt lawn, and this woman's existence becomes much more precarious. With no one to see and no place to go, even to be a silent figure on the living room sofa while three generations chatter around her, she might develop increasingly bizarre habits and appearance as her isolation continues. Working for strangers whom she is incapable of turning into friends, she will be less secure in her job, especially if her ideas and behavior begin to disturb her coworkers. The chance of a crisis is much greater—a severe depression, a psychotic episode, or a descent into poverty—and recovery is apt to be slower and less complete. Yet with increased mobility, the rise of the nuclear and even "subnuclear"—single-parent—family as the dominant family unit, the growth of suburbs and the diffusion or even breakup of many extended families, this scenario is increasingly the more likely of the two.

Close-knit communities discourage antisocial behavior as well. Individual acts of violence and aggression are more likely to be prevented or punished in this setting, and children with a tendency toward hyperactivity or impulsivity are more likely to be consistently monitored and contained. A glib con man quickly becomes known as untrustworthy, and in a society of similar communities he would find it difficult, as an outsider, to gain the trust of strangers. Because life in these communities follows predictable routines, many of the stimuli for anxious, avoidant behaviors may never arise; other anxieties may be more difficult to sustain simply because the stimulus is inescapable.

Over the past fifty years, powerful social and economic forces have caused a decline in close-knit communities, from fishing villages to small rural towns to urban immigrant neighborhoods. Most Americans now live in suburbs surrounding large urban centers. With the adults' workplace far removed from the home, children now spend the majority of their time either at home or in school; they have little chance to interact with adults other than their teachers, their mother, and her circle of friends. Instead of helping out with tasks, children have *become* the task—a task that, with the rise of two-income households as well as single-parent households, is increasingly either assigned to hired workers or left undone while the parents work at paying jobs. As children become less central to the economic survival of the family, they are more likely to become a focus of their parents' unfulfilled personal or economic aspirations. Children are less likely to feel appreciated for themselves and more likely to see themselves as vehicles for assuaging their parents' disappointment with the way their own lives have turned out.

These changes may put added stress on vulnerable people. A child with a detached, schizoid temperament may be susceptible to the intrusions of parents seeking to fulfill themselves through their child, as well as more conscious of his inability to fit in with his peers. Impulsive, aggressive behavior may meet less consistent limits—needlessly harsh punishment alternating with neglect—in more impersonal settings. Anxious children may find these unfeeling settings more regularly threatening. Teenagers maturing in an increasingly anonymous world may escape the traditional checks and monitors that have always helped them shape their personalities and develop needed coping strategies. In a society that does not care about them and does not intervene in their development, these children may grow up unhappy and suffer mental illness at high rates. Vulnerabilities that might have been contained may blossom into serious disorders.

⑤

Why do these vulnerabilities survive the evolutionary process at all? My theme throughout this book has been that genes confer certain basic temperamental traits, and the physical means for expression of these traits is often the regulation of certain neurochemical systems. But genes are, of course, subject to natural selection, and genes that confer maladaptive traits should die out. Why don't they?

First, mental diseases are defined and identified by society, not biology. From an evolutionary point of view, there is nothing intrinsically wrong with being depressed, anxious, or even psychotic: what matters, broadly speaking, is the ability to reproduce and for one's offspring to do the same. Organisms that live long enough to reproduce will pass on their genes for another generation, and those that don't, won't. The first category of diseases that survive natural selection is those that are maladaptive only in a social, not an evolutionary, sense. The syndromes in the dramatic cluster, for instance, need not hinder reproduction at all. A promiscuous, impulsively violent, sociopathic individual may be very effective at producing offspring. So may a self-absorbed narcissist, a seductive histrionic person, or a borderline person who is terrified of abandonment. For that matter, one can easily imagine settings in which these traits could enhance social success. While impulsive antisocial behavior causes problems, an action-oriented, ruthlessly decisive, physically courageous personality may be an asset to a community, which may decide for itself at what extreme this temperament becomes undesirable. Many such genetic "liabilities" persist, despite the unhappiness they bring, because they have no strong impact on a person's reproductive potential.

Other psychiatric diseases appear to exaggerate traits that evolution has preserved because they are useful. The anxiety disorders probably offer the clearest example. In *Why We Get Sick,* Nesse and Williams point out that some capacity for fear is necessary as a safeguard against predators, starvation, and other dangers. So, they ask, why aren't we fearful all the time? It turns out that the fear response is bad for the body—it uses extra calories (unnecessary energy use is always risky) and damages tissues. These dangerous responses to danger "are bundled into a emergency kit that is opened only when the benefits of using the tools are likely to exceed the costs." At the same time, the inhibitions against opening this emergency kit must not be too great: "The cost of getting killed even once is enormously higher than the cost of responding to a hundred false alarms." What we have, therefore, is a finely tuned system with many intricate components. It is easy to imagine how a small neurochemical malfunction could put it out of adjustment, generating far too many false alarms. We have anxiety disorders because we have anxiety, and we cannot do without some level of anxiety. Donald Klein's suffocation alarm theory, which I discussed in Chapter 6, offers a sophisticated and plausible argument that is largely compatible with this overall view. Instead of Nesse and Williams's vague general anxiety mechanism, Klein posits a specific neural monitoring system with clear physiological functions and logical behavioral consequences.

Similar reasoning, applied to depression, is less convincing. Essentially the same argument appears in both *Why We Get Sick* and

Robert Wright's *The Moral Animal.* The capacity for sadness and discouragement has many useful effects: it makes us stop overestimating our capacities, hold off from current activities that may be maladaptive, and disengage emotionally from our surroundings in order to make changes easier to contemplate. If one is pursuing an effort that turns out to be hopeless, a sense of hopelessness may be highly conducive to survival. In a time of intense grief, the ability to disengage oneself emotionally may serve as a protective mechanism. As in anxiety, if this mechanism becomes dysregulated, we may become mentally ill.

But the complexities of depression cast doubt on this argument. The relation between depression and grief, discouragement, or any other emotion is less straightforward than that between anxiety and fear. First, we are not talking about a single emotion but a tangled cluster of them; and second, the reduced capacity in depression for any emotional engagement with the world forces us to respect a certain qualitative difference between depression and the normal emotional states it most closely resembles. Moreover, unlike panic disorder, there is not a unique, clear-cut physiological mechanism, even a hypothetical one, whose dysregulation would invoke a depressive response. The neurochemical evidence implicating both norepinephrine and serotonin (at least) in the disease suggests that a single mechanism may be unlikely. Depression is more probably a common pathway for the expression of disturbances in a number of systems interacting with environmental influences to a greater or lesser extent, depending on the degree and kind of vulnerability the disturbances confer.

This complex physiology suggests an equally complex genetic picture that is borne out by our difficulties so far in definitively locating genes for depression through gene linkage studies. Different families may carry different liability genes for depression. For example, some recent evidence implicates a linkage with depression on chromosome 18 in a subset of depressed patients' families. But this location may be only the most important of several. When families pass on a propensity for depression, they may be passing on particular profiles of large numbers of genes rather than one specific variation on one spot on the genome. Depression may be much like diabetes, which, as we saw in Chapter 4, can be directly influenced by some ten different genes. Given that the brain takes up such a large share of the genome (about one-quarter of all human genes are devoted to neural structure and function), the number of genes contributing to depression may be even more than ten, and each single gene's relative contribution proportionately less. It seems likely that there are perhaps three or four major genes predisposing to depression, with some—perhaps many—minor ones having a small influence. Such a genetic picture makes it hard to see depression as a straightforward exaggeration, in inappropriate circumstances, of a normal capacity. The capacity for depression may be more comparable to physical attractiveness or unattractiveness: a large number of genes makes possible a practically infinite variety of phenotypes, of which some make their owners unhappy, others are socially disadvantageous, and still others are reproductively maladaptive. But because many genes that contribute to ugliness in one person may contribute to beauty in another, they may persist in the population for a very long time.

Kay Jamison has examined the relationship between manic depressive illness and creativity in a remarkable book called *Touched with Fire*. She shows not only that people in artistic careers suffer depression at a higher rate than the general population, but that many features of the "artistic temperament" closely resemble those of manic depression. Depressed individuals and many artists both undergo extremes of emotion unknown to most people, yet must struggle to reconcile these extremes, and the experiences they bring, with an everyday, rational world. The intense, passionate frenzy of a creative outburst often alternates with long periods of unproductive despair. (Jamison actually charts the relation between mood and output over the life of the composer Robert Schumann.) While this link has been widely noted and even demonstrated statistically in a group of poets and writers, no one knows why it exists.

One possibility is that people who experience the world with more intense emotion are more aware of emotional nuances and able to make unusual connections between inner and outer experience, a condition that could both draw people to the arts and allow them to produce subtler, more original work. A painter who tries to communicate his vivid emotional experiences in colors on canvas may be driven to greater heights of creativity than a person who has been spared such experiences. The manic-like capacity of a comedian to energize an audience and a scientist's ability to synthesize many pieces of disparate information into a grand, unifying scheme may both draw on the energy and striving for connections that in extreme forms constitute mania. Could genetic susceptibility to bipolar disorder survive because it is linked to a positive trait, creativity?

Perhaps. And relatives of depressed patients, in whom the propensity to affective disorder may be more weakly expressed, may be highly successful artists, scientists, and businesspeople. But it's important to recognize that the experience of having a mood disorder is profoundly debilitating and that it interferes with an individual's success more often than it enhances it. While the susceptibility to mood disorder, coupled with talent and the ability to channel these affective tendencies into constructive pursuits, may contribute to some people's success, it's still very hard to argue that this link turns depression into an adaptive trait. Fortunately there's no need, in speculating on such a link, to argue that it is *causal*. Both qualities could arise from a common origin. For instance, one of the effects of upright posture in humans is that it freed the forelimbs to adapt themselves for purposes other than walking, such as tool use. Another effect was to change the mechanical forces exerted on the spine, making us susceptible to back strain. It explains very little, however, to note that people who use tools a lot suffer an above-average rate of back strain. While there may be a superficial causal relationship, in a deeper sense both the tool use and the back strain are independent products of long-term evolutionary adaptations. Similarly, the capacity to create art and the capacity for depressive illness could both arise from some fundamental logic of the brain's organization, which in turn may exist for reasons having little to do with either one. In evolutionary terms, they could be overlapping, accidental (though profoundly influential) by-products.

Schizophrenia is another widespread disease whose genes' presence needs explaining. We know that this disease has a genetic component and that schizophrenic adults reproduce at below-average rates. Why, then, have the genes predisposing to schizophrenia not disappeared from the population, rather than remaining constant, as all evidence suggests they have done? Short of coma, it's hard to imagine a less adaptive mental state in any environment than a delusional psychosis. It may be that these genes also confer some adaptive trait or traits that, in the absence of the disease, cause them to produce more offspring, but as to the nature of those traits we can only speculate.

One mitigating factor could be the age of onset. The later in life a disease strikes, the less effect it has on reproduction, and so the less its predisposing genes are subject to natural selection. Schizophrenia, which typically arrives between the late teens and mid-thirties, today affects many but not all of most sufferers' reproductive years. During most of human prehistory, when the average life expectancy seldom rose above the thirties, schizophrenia may have been largely a disease of "middle" age. Another factor could be that the modern practice of shunting the insane to the margins of society, either as residents of institutions or as paupers, is a recent innovation that is lowering these people's reproductive rates. In tribal and village cultures, where schizo-phrenic people tended to remain with their families, opportunities to father or bear children may have been greater. These two factors, the change in human life expectancy—with its consequent delaying of par-enthood—and the change in society's treatment of people with schizo-phrenia, may be lowering the incidence of the predisposing genes at a rate too slow to be detected as yet. Finally, schizophrenia itself is only the extreme end of a spectrum of related disorders. Some of the under-lying symptoms of schizophrenia, taken by themselves, may have been adaptive traits during much of human prehistory. Paranoia, fear of strangers, and an us-against-them world view may have contributed to survival in a world of small tribes surrounded by rival tribes. Adherence to a rigid routine may have served to maintain strict territorial bound-aries. Even psychosis may have brought with it a shamanic status, as suggested by the number of traditional American cultures that use psy-choactive drugs in religious rituals to induce a psychotic-like state. In modern cultures, a mildly eccentric creativity may be advantageous.

This interplay of social forces and psychological factors has not stopped: it continues to influence both individual fates and broad social movements. In my study of eye tracking in college-student vol-unteers, several of the students with poor tracking (associated with schizotypal personality traits) were members of the same local charismatic group. These groups may provide an attractive haven for people susceptible to mood disturbances or cognitive disorganization. They offer inspiration, support, a high degree of structure to help members regulate their feelings and thoughts, and guaranteed acceptance as long as members accept the credo of the group and its clearly defined rules. People who are otherwise unable to bring any focus or purpose to their lives, who desperately lack a sense of belonging, or who feel they cannot survive emotionally without this kind of support, may become fanatically attached to these groups. In the worst cases, as in the Charles Manson and Jim Jones cults, such people may endure terrible conditions, commit crimes, and even willingly die to stay close to their leader. These leaders' own psychological profiles may mirror the vulnerabilities of their followers, yet they may present a charismatic front that seems to promise salvation. Some may be manic depressive, as Jim Jones appears to have been; others may be psychopathic or schizophrenic.

Just as ideologic or religious cults tend to favor certain temperamental types over others, so do societies. Different historical periods encourage different styles of coping in the population at large and different traits in their cultural and political leaders. Instability, economic uncertainty, a sense of national humiliation or threat can bring to the fore demagogic leaders who feed on these insecurities and who may themselves suffer from mood or impulse disorders. Calmer times also have their characteristic leadership styles. The decade of the 1950s in America was known as the Age of Anxiety not only because of the continuing crisis of the Cold War and the remembered trauma of World War II, the largest war ever fought, but also because of the social upheaval brought on by rapid economic expansion and the creation of a new suburban culture. Political leaders tended either to inflame anxieties, as Joe McCarthy or Richard Nixon did, or to be tranquilizing elder figures like Dwight Eisenhower. Similarly, the culture seemed split between the bland, calming surfaces of Ozzie and Harriet and the terrible misgivings of the beat poets or the photographer Robert Frank, whose landmark 1957 book, *The Americans,* was rejected by every American publisher who saw it because it was too disturbing. The sixties, by contrast, were played out with manic intensity: idealism and expansiveness, rebellion and an intolerance of contrary views characterized the culture. Our government began dozens of ambitious new social programs; our political leaders were youthful and energetic—the Kennedy brothers, Martin Luther King, Jr.—and if you weren't part of the solution, you were part of the problem. (On the other side, if you didn't support the war in Vietnam, you were anti-American.) The most notable cultural development was rock-and-roll music.

By the 1980s, the historian Christopher Lasch was decrying what he called the Culture of Narcissism, in which an obsession with image, a hunger for novelty, and a shallow, insatiable consumerism mask a deep insecurity and lack of purpose. An unusually large generation reaching young adulthood combined with an economic expansion to create huge numbers of *nouveaux riches,* too many of whom seemed to draw their values from the popular T-shirt slogan "He who dies with the most toys wins." Our political leader was a soothing "communicator" offering reassuring homilies while delegating to others the day-to-day tasks of running the country; popular culture was dominated by the shape-shifting Madonna and the surgically altered Michael Jackson. The fine arts featured few new artists of lasting stature but many record-breaking auctions.

These caricatures are, of course, oversimplified; the style of a decade is a complex thing. But in each of these periods, it seems to me, leaders emerged who reflected the character of the culture as much as they shaped it. Each period may be said to have selected leadership styles from the diversity of temperamental styles available in the population.

Is there a dominant personality style of the nineties? I sometimes wonder if a schizoid temperament, fragmented and adrift from its moorings, might provide the best fit with the discontinuous and often unintegrated experience of modern life. The person with cognitive disorganization who lacks a sense of connectedness to others and the world, or even a sense of continuity within himself, seems a good match with a culture in which large segments of the population are not on speaking terms with each other and probably could not understand each other if they were. What has the average Internet user to say to the average migrant farmworker? What has a gay white New York advertising executive to say to a black minister in a storefront mosque less than half a mile away? In a world of constantly widening disparities in culture, income, technological capacities, and political and moral values, it should not be surprising that national leaders can remain popular (as our flirtations with Ross Perot and Colin Powell demonstrated) only as long as we can convince ourselves that we don't know what they stand for. At the same time, the dominant critical movement of our time, postmodernism (a movement that declares with its very name that it can define itself only by what it is not), repudiates not only the principles of modernism but the very idea that there can be any valid aesthetic principles. What is the validity of anything in a culture without consensus on what is important, and what is the point of trying to fix your values, your direction in life, or your own identity?

§

For all of the disease groups discussed in this book, the genetics is complex and poorly understood. Moreover, one of my themes throughout has been that a psychiatric disease stems partly from the patient's position on a spectrum of variation along a dimension of temperament. The temperamental quality, not the disease, is innate. There is, in fact, a long hierarchy of levels between genes and psychiatric diagnoses that should make us suspicious of glib statements about how they are connected.

- First, genes are the physical stuff that we actually inherit from our mothers and fathers. Not only are the genes' effects suppressed or enhanced by other genes, but the expression of a gene—whether its code is ever translated into a protein, when, and how often—is influenced by a number of biochemical factors, some of them environmental.

- Genes provide the basic blueprint for our neurochemistry and anatomy, but as we develop in the womb and afterward, neurochemistry and anatomy may also be affected by such factors as nutrition, trauma, infection, and exposure to chemicals. Brain development also responds to environmental stimuli, and the brain may be permanently affected by environmental events such as childhood abuse.

- Brain systems provide the physical basis for temperamental traits. These traits may be shaped not only by the physical factors that influence the brain but also by psychodynamic factors such as the growing child's family relationships.

- Temperamental traits set the broad outlines of the personality. But the personality is affected not only by physical factors and family relationships but by chance events, learning, and social context as well. Moreover, we can exercise some control over our personalities: with effort, we can accentuate certain aspects and suppress others, and we can replace old habits for responding to situations with new habits. Much of psychotherapy is aimed at giving patients the insight and self-control needed to make these changes.

- Psychiatric crises result from disordered reactions that take in all these levels at once. When we encounter life situations in which we temperamentally are prone to feel stress, and we lack the personality characteristics to deal with them successfully, then if we are susceptible, the stress may cause dysfunctions in our neurochemistry that result in disordered thoughts and behavior—which in turn may lead to a worsening situation and more stress.

It's worth bearing these different levels in mind when we hear talk in the media of how the Human Genome Project will allow us to genetically engineer personality. Since personality is only partly genetic, we can in the best circumstances only partly control it by genetic means. Even that presupposes a degree of knowledge that is orders of magnitude more sophisticated than we now possess. On a more modest scale, however, our increased knowledge of the human genome is already creating hard ethical dilemmas. Already insurers are requiring access to genetic information (such as pedigrees, if available) regarding susceptibility to mental illness. As specific genes associated with susceptibility for specific mental disorders are discovered, this issue will undoubtedly emerge even more strongly; legislation limiting insurance companies' access to this genetic information has been proposed.

What about using drugs to "fine-tune" and "transform" our basic nature? Are we entering an era of "cosmetic psychopharmacology," as Peter Kramer puts it—an era of using "mood brighteners" to mask the blemishes and idiosyncrasies of personality? Will we soon have available to us "designer medications" that let us tailor our personalities to our own specifications? In my view, they are not on the horizon. There is no clear evidence that even the newest antidepressants brighten mood in people who are normal at baseline. The possibilities (or dangers) have been somewhat oversold. Drugs that have worked for dampening mood swings, containing excessive impulsivity, or improving impaired information processing, for example, have shown little evidence of effectiveness in making healthy people happier, wiser, or sharper. These drugs, as best we can determine, work by normalizing imbalances or dysregulations in particular brain chemical systems. They cannot make an already correctly balanced or regulated system *more* correct. In this way these drugs are comparable to aspirin. Aspirin can lower your temperature if you have a fever or relieve pain or headache caused by inflammation. But if you don't have a fever, taking aspirin will not lower your temperature below normal, and if you have no headache, it will not make your head feel unusually good. In the same way, if you are not suffering from biologically based emotional difficulties, there is no evidence that taking an antidepressant or antipsychotic medication will make you feel "better than well." (In fairness, however, I must point out that the question has not been well studied. From a public health standpoint, there is little reason to study antidepressants' effects in people for whom they are not intended. A few pilot studies hint at increases in well-being among volunteer subjects receiving SSRIs, but it is unclear how many of these had mild depressive symptoms.) But any drugs will create side effects in a predictable percentage of people who take them, even if there is no significant emotional or psychological benefit.

What accounts for these drugs' reputation as personality-change pills is the pervasive effect of depression on personality. Depression can undermine a person's self-esteem, interest in new activities, assertiveness, and ease in social situations, all of which may be improved when the depression is lifted. Antidepressants that work primarily on the serotonergic system can also dampen excessive impulsivity and calm erratic mood swings in a person with affective instability. These changes can have a dramatic impact on a person's day-to-day mood and interactions with others. But the effect is most dramatic only when the neurochemical imbalance was most severe. There is no evidence that the kind of disinhibited aggression (whether directed toward oneself or others) associated with decreased serotonergic activity has any biological relationship to the nonaggressive kinds of impulsivity we associate with a "carefree" or "footloose" personality style. Nothing suggests that the serotonergic drugs have any effect on personality quirks such a penchant for a spur-of-the-moment shopping spree.

For people with profound disturbances in personality, I've found that the effect of these medications usually resembles moving a ship out of stormy seas. Their lives become less filled with suicide attempts, fights, and temper tantrums, and they become able, through psychotherapy or other therapies, to focus on the long-term personality changes they need to make in order to become happier and more successful. They can build on their strengths without being so vulnerable to continual setbacks brought on by a quick fuse or heedless action. They "feel more like themselves."

This line, to me, sums up the benefits of these drugs. Even people with severely imbalanced neurochemistry have some occasional feeling or memory of how it feels not to have such a condition, just as a person with asthma knows how it feels to breathe freely or one with angina remembers being able to run for a bus without fear. By helping to restore their neurochemical regulation, antidepressants move these patients closer to what most of us take for granted—health. The statement that they "feel more like themselves" strongly suggests that, rather than inducing some artificial state, these drugs are restoring a normal, if unaccustomed, balance.

Some instances of "mood brightening" occur because the drugs may induce hypomanic symptoms in patients predisposed to bipolar affective disorder. It is not unheard of for a depressed patient with no known history of mania to develop a manic episode shortly after starting antidepressants. For instance, I once had as a patient an art student who had been depressed and unable to paint for several months. A course of antidepressants quickly made him feel unburdened—but two months into his treatment he was painting furiously into the night with boundless enthusiasm and energy and was so talkative, with so little need for sleep, that he and his friends became alarmed. After I learned of this, I quickly prescribed lithium, and the episode came under control. It is interesting to note that this student had a family history of manic depressive disorder that he had not revealed to me during his initial evaluation.

Far from being universal mood brighteners for the healthy, the truth is that these drugs don't always work in patients who *do* have psychiatric symptoms. In people with sustained unhappiness or depression that stems from social or economic factors they can't control, the biological state of depression cannot easily be reversed by medication. Instead of feeling "better than well" after they begin to take antidepressants, they simply remain depressed. We cannot yet predict with certainty who will respond to antidepressants and who will not, although the somatic symptoms offer the most reliable indicator. Such bodily symptoms as sleep and appetite disturbances, which correlate most strongly with disturbances in neurotransmitter-related biologic measures such as the growth hormone response to clonidine, are most characteristic of depressions that will respond well to medication. This observation is consistent with the idea that antidepressants work to correct imbalances. Lithium, the best example of such a mode of action, stabilizes mood in both directions: it not only alleviates depression but also dampens the euphoria and irritability of mania.

Another factor in the widespread perception that these drugs would make *anybody* feel better is the improvement in the drugs themselves. Antidepressant drugs are now more precisely targeted toward specific brain chemical systems, and this refinement has greatly cut down on side effects, which in turn has made physicians less hesitant to prescribe them. Once given only to patients with very severe depressions usually requiring hospitalization, antidepressant drugs are now being used, often successfully, in much milder cases. This widespread use has revived a question that, for severe disorders, had been well settled: at what point does seeking mental health care become something akin to a moral failing?

Again, for severe disorders this is becoming less of an issue. Few now believe that a suicidally depressed person is to blame for failing to straighten up and fly right, any more than a person with kidney disease is to be blamed for needing dialysis. Similarly, few people now take seriously the idea that schizophrenia is "a sane response to an insane society" or that we are victimizing and oppressing the severely psychotic by trying to get them off the streets and into psychiatric care. But is there a point at which symptoms should be considered not severe enough to warrant medical treatment, because they are simply a part of the ups and downs of everyday life? As one letter writer to *Newsweek* commented in response to its cover story on Prozac in 1994, "I wonder what will become of the time-honored virtue of overcoming one's own problems through personal effort and self-determination."

Psychiatrists prescribe medications after they have made diagnoses according to standard criteria published by the American Psychiatric Association in its *Diagnostic and Statistical Manual of Mental Disorders,* the latest version of which is *DSM-IV.* Patients who meet the criteria for major depressive disorder or dysthymia may be successfully treated with antidepressants. Patients who don't meet these criteria or the criteria for other psychiatric disorders are not usually put on medication. In my experience, anyone who is sufficiently troubled by depression to see a doctor about it probably meets criteria for a depressive disorder and is a candidate for antidepressant treatment. People are almost always reluctant to admit they need psychiatric help, and few do so lightly.

Because of the stigma associated with depression, however, it is not uncommon to hear of people who brag about how much better they're feeling on Prozac or Zoloft and how much more efficient they are, at the same time that they minimize the severity of the depression that led their doctor to prescribe it in the first place. Moreover, some people whose depression is less than debilitating are very good at masking its effects (recall the quotation from Hugo Wolf in Chapter 1). They may seem relatively untroubled to their coworkers, yet come home from work and collapse into bed for a fifteen-hour sleep or spend a long weekend lying morosely on a sofa. Others may spend their lunch hours and all their evening hours washing their hands and showering because of a severe obsessive-compulsive disorder. Such people may encourage others to believe they are using antidepressants lightly even though they in fact suffer from a serious illness. They have the psychiatric equivalent of "walking pneumonia." No one has done any research to investigate how widespread this phenomenon is.

Certainly there is an issue of where to draw the line between when treatment is indicated and when it is not. This problem is in principle little different from determining a cutoff point for treatment of high blood pressure. There is an increasing consensus that even people with blood pressure just below the traditional cutoff points—140 mm Hg systolic and 90 mm Hg diastolic—may be at greater risk for complications such as heart disease or stroke than people who are at, say, 110/70. But where do we draw the line? Should a person with a blood pressure of 120/80 be given antihypertensives to lower their risk still further? I think most of us would say no. On the other hand, if a doctor with high blood pressure prescribes antihypertensives for himself and deliberately adjusts the dose to yield a blood pressure of 110/70, is this an abuse of medication? While the guidelines continue to shift, it is clear that as diastolic pressures fall into the 80–85 mm Hg range, nonpharmacologic interventions such as diet, exercise, and stress management become much more desirable than drugs. Similarly, a person's cholesterol levels can be reduced by either drug treatment or lifestyle changes. Although our idea of what is an acceptable level, and thus our threshold for drug treatment, has grown lower over the years, still everyone agrees that the smaller the adjustment that needs to be made, the better it is to do it through lifestyle changes rather than medication.

The spectrums of severity we see in many psychiatric diseases are very comparable to ranges of hypertension, cholesterol level, or blood sugar, but they are impossible to quantify. The major consideration in both deciding whether to prescribe medication and assessing its effectiveness—the degree of suffering or impairment a person experiences—cannot with any precision be put on a numerical scale. Two people's levels of distress vary greatly even when they report identical symptoms. These decisions have to be made by the doctor and patient together, with full knowledge of the risks—side effects, long-term effects—and potential benefits, in a way that balances the patient's needs and wishes with the general guidelines for these drugs' use. The risks are not trivial. Even the newest antidepressants, which carry far fewer side effects than previous generations of drugs, may still cause nausea, reduced sex drive, delayed orgasm, or restlessness. Further, we still don't know what long-term changes in the brain may result from chronic use of these drugs, though no adverse effects are now suspected. Just as with hypertension, atherosclerosis, and diabetes, however, the smaller the adjustment that needs to be made, the stronger the *medical* argument for accomplishing it through lifestyle changes.

One group of patients to whom Peter Kramer devoted considerable attention in *Listening to Prozac* were people who had had serious depressive episodes in years past and now were bothered by mild or residual symptoms that they couldn't quite get rid of—such as trouble getting up in the morning or a tendency to brood guiltily. If medications will relieve these symptoms, why not use them? I confess I am unable to see a great moral issue here or any compelling virtue in telling these people they must solve their problems through personal effort and determination alone, without the benefits of effective medication. Far better to make these decisions by balancing the expected gains against the risks.

What about people with milder forms of anxiety or depression, who do not meet the full criteria for either an anxiety-related or depressive disorder? Should these people be prescribed antidepressants if their symptoms are seriously disturbing to them? The list of syndromes constituting a recognized disorder is not immutable, and mixed symptoms of anxiety and depression have been proposed for inclusion in *DSM* as an official diagnosis. Other "nonsyndromal disorders" are sure to be proposed in the future. If they are approved, it will lend many people's symptoms a medical validity that can then provide a basis for studying the effectiveness of antidepressant drugs in such cases. We will then be able to "legitimately" treat these patients. We will also be creating another instance of what critics of psychopharmacology call bracket creep, the increasingly broad definition of psychiatric disorders that is driven (say the critics) more by available technology than by understanding. Disorders are defined by validating criteria such as laboratory data, clustering of specific symptoms, and family histories, as well as their response to particular treatments including drug treatment. The use of the last criterion is what raises concerns about bracket creep. But when it becomes clear that a group of symptoms causes significant distress, forms a unified and cohesive entity, and responds to psychopharmacologic treatment, why should we balk at treating it just because it wasn't previously recognized as a legitimate psychiatric disorder? The goal of psychiatry, after all, is not to prevent bracket creep but to improve people's mental health.

Ultimately, these questions will be resolved on a pragmatic basis: we will learn under what circumstances these drugs can be shown to help, and we will come to understand their long-term risks as well as their short-term side effects. Guidelines based on established diagnoses for which the medications have proved effective will provide norms around which physicians will make individual treatment decisions, balancing in any one case the risks, the benefits, and the patient's interest in receiving the drugs as part of an overall treatment.

§

Are antidepressant drugs overprescribed, as many commentators in the media seem to feel, or underprescribed, as many experts believe? There is no doubt that the amount of psychopharmacologic medication being prescribed has increased dramatically, and one of the reasons is the increasing recognition, diagnosis, and treatment of psychiatric symptoms. What is less well appreciated is the extraordinary prevalence of these symptoms in the general population. If we include history of depression, anxiety, phobias, and personality disorders as well as psychoses and other major psychiatric syndromes, the proportion of individuals who have met the criteria for a psychiatric disorder, according to a recent epidemiologic study, appears to be as high as 48 percent. This figure begins to resemble the incidence of parasitic infection in some tropical communities. It is sometimes offered as a reason for skepticism of the basic premises of psychiatric diagnosis, as if such a high incidence were unbelievable on the face of it and therefore must indicate a psychiatric community run amok. But why should it be unbelievable? Other major disease categories, such as infection or cardiovascular disease, affect comparable fractions of the population. When people say that Prozac makes them feel "better than well," maybe we should think carefully about what we mean by "well."

There is also growing evidence that the prevalence of some psychiatric disorders has increased over the past few decades. Depression is an example. While it is very difficult to control for such factors as age of onset and changes in diagnostic practices, careful epidemiologic studies consistently suggest an increasing incidence of depression over the past century, particularly in adolescents and young adults. Although it's almost impossible to establish the cause of the increase, the one factor that can be definitely ruled out is a change in genetic susceptibility to depression, because the time scale is much too short for this. But the vulnerability to depression is more likely to translate into an overt depressive episode than it was two or three decades ago. We can see this in the rising rate of suicide among younger people, as well as in their widespread identification with suicidal entertainment figures like Kurt Cobain. (The romance of suicide, it must be noted, is not a recent development. Goethe's great eighteenth-century bestseller, *The Sorrows of Young Werther,* set off such a wave of suicides among German-speaking youth that the author felt compelled to insert a foreword in later editions admonishing readers not to follow Werther's example.) This epidemiologic trend is partly responsible for the increase in antidepressant use.

Another factor in this increase is the expanding set of indications for psychotropic medications. Drugs that once were reserved for the major affective disorders and psychoses are now known to help in obsessive-compulsive disorder, dysthymia, personality disorders, social phobias, and impulsivity. The reduced side effects of the newer medications are also encouraging psychiatrists to prescribe them not only for milder ailments but for many different ones. In fact, these drugs have so many other uses that the term *antidepressant* is getting to be a misnomer.

Finally, the stigma associated with having a psychiatric disorder has been greatly lessened. Partly this is due to the recognition of the role biology plays in these illnesses. Many well-known people have come forward to speak about their depression and have sometimes talked about their pharmacologic treatment. These people have contributed to the increasing public acceptance of the view that psychiatric disorders are ill-nesses to be treated rather than personal failings to be hidden at all costs.

There are, however, some real concerns about the use of these med-ications outside the usual treatment setting. One common occurrence is what happened to a biologist of my acquaintance who often felt anx-ious and depressed about her research. Although she wasn't distressed enough to seek formal treatment, her brother, a doctor, had read about Prozac and prescribed it for her. One day after starting the medication, she found herself giggly, talking to strangers in line at the grocery store, and feeling unusually cheerful. This made her uncomfortable, so she stopped the medication. She probably was going through the first stages of hypomanic symptoms brought on by the drug. In any case, it's not clear that she needed antidepressants in the first place—but it's not clear either that she wouldn't have been helped by formal treatment.

A more widespread danger is that, as antidepressants become more successful, insurance companies may become even more restrictive than they are now in paying benefits for psychotherapy. They may begin to deny benefits altogether. This would be cost-effective for the insurers but unfortunate for patients. As I have said repeatedly in this book, medication is not a substitute for psychological therapy but rather a biological stabilizer that enables therapy to be productive. Such an action by health insurers would accelerate the already evident trend of primary practitioners overprescribing these medications without the advice of an experienced psychiatrist and in the absence of any con-comitant psychotherapy. This happened with Valium over the past two decades, and it is clearly happening with SSRIs today. It is an abuse of these medications that can be countered by increasing internists' aware-ness of the role they play in psychiatric treatment and the need to have a trained professional prescribing them in a collaborative therapeutic setting. Ideally, primary practitioners should work in teams with men-tal health professionals and consulting psychiatrists to confront the many aspects of depression and anxiety they see in their daily practice. It would be a loss for patients if, as physicians became more aware of the need for teamwork, they were prevented from employing it by the reimbursement guidelines of insurance companies.

Another concern that has been raised is that by masking rather than alleviating psychological symptoms, antidepressants may make people less able to deal with the social problems at the core of their psychological problems. This was a valid concern with a tranquilizer such as Valium—people had the same problems; they just weren't as bothered by them—but the newer drugs tend to improve coping skills. The real concern here is that the people with the greatest social problems often have the least access to antidepressants. Poverty, job loss, lack of options for improving oneself, and a general anxiety about one's future may all precipitate depression, and the conditions of poverty may even contribute to a predisposition to psychiatric disorders, just as they do to infant mortality. Unlike the affluent, however, when less well-off people self-medicate, they are apt to do it with less trendy drugs: alcohol or street narcotics.

The newer antidepressants seem much less susceptible to this kind of street abuse than drugs such as Valium, amphetamines, or barbiturates. Those drugs produce a noticeable high—a blissful relaxation with the barbiturates, energy and euphoria with the amphetamines—and they do it reliably in almost anyone who takes a large enough dose. Except for the occasional and unpredictable triggering of a hypomanic state, the new psychotropic drugs produce no immediate high at all and are less attractive to abusers than the current street pharmacopoeia. Still, some of the new antidepressant medications can be bought on the street.

Set against these concerns are many signs that psychopharmacologic medications are still underprescribed. The signs and symptoms of psychiatric disorders, especially depression, often go unrecognized in primary care settings. This may happen because the patient, either out of shame at appearing weak or from lack of insight into his own moods, voices his distress in terms of vague physical complaints rather than a direct statement about his psychological state. Psychiatric illnesses continue to be stigmatized much more than other medical disorders, to the point that most people are loathe to consider them even as possible explanations for their own behavior or unhappiness. The inability to get up each morning with positive spirit and optimism, full of energy to face the day's challenges, is often construed as a personal fault for which the appropriate solution is to pull oneself up by one's own bootstraps. When this effort fails, people are left with a variety of puzzling and disturbing symptoms that impair their capacity to function. Since medical problems are not usually looked on as a sign of weakness but rather as a reflection of a disease process that is out of our personal control, these people may visit many doctors with multiple complaints, none of which can be tied to a specific "physical" (i.e., nonpsychiatric) disease. Instead of tacitly acquiescing in this self-deception, physicians need to consider depression as a possible contributing influence. Several studies have shown that appropriate treatment of psychiatric conditions can lead to markedly reduced utilization of medical services—which suggests that much of this utilization was unnecessary to begin with. Not only do psychiatric disorders often go unrecognized, even when they are recognized, the lack of expertise in psychopharmacology in the average medical setting means that the best treatments are not always prescribed.

§

The debate over "cosmetic psychopharmacology" clearly shows the pervasive double standard to which psychiatric disorders are subjected. We condone medically unnecessary cosmetic surgery without question, despite the well-known risks of anesthesia and the operation itself, yet are very critical of individuals who seek help for depression or anxiety if they are not so severely ill as to require hospitalization. A person who smilingly announces to acquaintances that her life has been transformed by a medication like Prozac immediately invites skepticism, resentment, or the suspicion that, after all, she must be a very shallow person. But who knows what misery she was going through before, which she may have kept completely hidden?

One of the first patients I ever treated, during my rotation through Stanford's Internal Medicine department as a third-year medical student, was a man who had complained for months of increasing listlessness and fatigue. No one could figure out what was wrong with him until finally he was diagnosed as having subacute bacterial endocarditis, an infection of the inner wall of the heart. We gave him intravenous penicillin, which brought a dramatic cure. He "felt like a new man." Who in their right mind would think to question his sincerity or the moral and social wisdom of giving him the penicillin? Now suppose the cause of his fatigue were not a bacterial infection but depression and that it could be relieved, equally dramatically, with a different drug. Would his treatment meet with the same universal approval?

Precisely because depression and personality disorders involve aspects of ourselves over which we feel we should have some voluntary control and which involve the means by which we experience and affect the world, it is unsettling to think that such a profound change could be brought about by a mere chemical. It is another loss of human uniqueness, a reminder that we are not separate from the rest of creation but are made of the same stuff and subject to the same effects as the rest of the world. But from a medical point of view, the understanding and chemical treatment of mental disorders is no more surprising or unsettling than our modern understanding of ulcers—once thought to be purely a badge of "excessive stress"—as arising from a combination of stress, acid secretion, and bacterial infection, treatable with antibiotics.

For all that ours is called a pill-popping society, most people in my experience are reluctant to take a medication unless they are in considerable pain. They have to be convinced that it will help them. Few of my patients either discount the risks of psychotropic drugs or expect miracles from them. When they are used appropriately, in combination with psychotherapy, the results are not immediate or dramatic. But the combination may, in time, profoundly change the way a person experiences and relates to the world and permit a more satisfying life.

§

The mind-body split in psychiatry, which has existed since the time of Descartes, is close to being healed. In this book I have sketched the outlines of a science of the mind and mental disorders that encompasses genetics, the anatomy and chemistry of the brain, child development, family dynamics, social factors, and ideas from traditional psychoanalytic theory. It is a psychiatry that counts among its intellectual influences such people as Charles Darwin, James Watson, and Francis Crick as well as Sigmund Freud. It promises to explain both severe mental diseases and healthy personality within the same framework, in a manner that makes sense equally in terms of biochemical data, clinical observation, and our everyday experience. These are exciting times in psychiatry.

Unfortunately, they are also troubled times. Whether those outlines will ever be filled in—whether we will continue to make significant strides in learning how to alleviate the suffering of mental disorders and in exploring their causes and prevention at both the biological and psychosocial levels—remains in doubt. Increasingly powerful research tools, used with insight and imagination, could open new and more effective preventive measures and treatments. At the same time, however, the continuing stigma of these disorders, the sense that mental health has a lower priority than physical health, and the curtailment in federal spending for research jeopardize our progress. Proposed changes in Medicare and Medicaid may make it more difficult for the medical centers that foster this research to survive, since most depend on these reimbursements for education and training. Research money is becoming scarcer, and agencies such as the Veterans Administration, which provides care for many of the chronically mentally ill patients where I work, are cutting back personnel. Mental health funding often suffers because the idea persists, still, that even the severely mentally ill are somehow to blame for their illness.

The truth is, as always, more subtle and difficult. While no one is to blame for their own mental illness, neither are most people completely at its mercy. Learning how to fight these afflictions—or, when fighting fails, how to live with them—is a pathway to self-knowledge. If you have read my book this far, I would leave you with one thought. The new psychiatry lies before us like an unexplored wilderness full of treasures as well as dangers. Given the choice between knowledge and ignorance—between the ability to relieve the often agonizing distress of mental disorders on one hand, or increasing helplessness in the face of that distress on the other—who would not choose knowledge?

NOTES

CHAPTER ONE

p. 1. Epigraph: William Styron, *Darkness Visible* (New York: Random House, 1990), 46–47

p. 7 ff. Patient accounts of depression: F. K. Goodwin and K. R. Jamison, *Manic-Depressive Illness* (New York: Oxford University Press, 1990), 22–41

p. 7. Sylvia Plath, *The Bell Jar* (New York: Harper & Row, 1971).

p. 8. Suicide rates in depressed patients. Goodwin and Jamison, *Manic-Depressive Illness,* 228. The authors write, "Findings from our more recent review of 30 studies of completed suicide in manic-depressive patients . . . do not differ significantly from those of Guze and Robins. We found a range, 9 to 60 percent, of manic-depressive deaths secondary to suicide, with a mean of 19 percent." One of the standard psychiatry texts gives a rate of one in six. (Max Hamilton, "Mood Disorders: Clinical Features," in H. I. Kaplan and B. J. Sadock, eds., *Comprehensive Textbook of Psychiatry,* 5th ed. (Baltimore: Williams & Wilkins, 1989), 897.)

pp. 13–14. Accounts of Robert Lowell's manic episodes. Paul Mariani, *Lost Puritan: A Life of Robert Lowell* (New York: Norton, 1994), 310–311, 441.

p. 15. Ratio of depressed patients who have unipolar disorder. Goodwin and Jamison, *Manic-Depressive Illness,* 161.

p. 17. "Melancholy...an hereditary disease." R. Burton, *The Anatomy of Melancholy* (1652; reprint, London: Thomas Tegg, 1845), 137.

p. 17. "Hereditary taint . . ." E. Kraepelin, *Manic-Depressive Insanity and Paranoia.* R. Mary Barclay, trans., and George M. Robertson, ed. (Edinburgh: E. & S. Livingstone, 1921), 165.

p. 17. The extent to which depression runs in families. E. S. Gershon et al., "A family study of schizoaffective, bipolar I, bipolar II, unipolar, and normal control probands," *Archives of General Psychiatry* 39 (1982): 1157. Described in E. S. Gershon et al., "Mood Disorders: Genetic Aspects," in Kaplan and Sadock, eds., *Comprehensive Textbook of Psychiatry,* 5th ed., 880.

p. 18. Danish twin study. E. S. Gershon, "Genetics," in Goodwin and Jamison, *Manic-Depressive Illness,* 377.

p. 19. Study by Price. Ibid., 376.

p. 19. Personality similarities in twins. A. Tellegen et al., "Personality Similarity in Twins Reared Apart and Together," *Journal of Personality and Social Psychology* 54 (1988): 1031.

p. 19. "And that which is more to be wondered at." R. Burton, *The Anatomy of Melancholy,* 137.

p. 20. Gamow's declaration. D. Frank-Kamenetskii, *Unraveling DNA* (New York: VCH, 1993), 17.

p. 24. Gene linkage studies. W. H. Berrettini et al., "Chromosome 18 DNA Markers and Manic-Depressive Illness: Evidence for a Susceptibility Gene," *Proceedings of the National Academy of Sciences* 91, vol. 13 (1994): 5918–5921.

CHAPTER TWO

p. 27. Epigraph: E. Canetti, *The Agony of Flies: Notes and Notations.* H. F. Broch de Rothermann, trans. (New York: Farrar, Straus and Giroux, 1994), 7.

p. 27. Szasz and Laing arguments. See, for example, R. D. Laing, *The Divided Self* (London: Tavistock Publications, 1960); R. D. Laing, *The Politics of Experience* (New York: Pantheon Books, 1968); and T. S. Szasz, *The Myth of Mental Illness: Foundations of a Theory of Personal Conduct* (New York: Harper & Row, 1961).

p. 28. "Diagnostic bracket creep." P. D. Kramer, *Listening to Prozac* (New York: Viking, 1993), 15. See also p. 35: "In clinical pharmacology, contemporary technology plays a dominant role in shaping ideology. What we look for in patients depends to a great degree on the available medications."

p. 35. Actions of norepinephrine. G. Aston-Jones and F. E. Bloom, "Norepinephrine-Containing Locus Ceruleus Neurons in Behaving Rats Exhibit Pronounced Responses to Non-noxious Environmental Stimuli," *Journal of Neuroscience* 1 (1981), 887–900.

p. 36. Julius Axelrod, "The Fate of Noradrenaline in the Sympathetic Neuron," *Harvey Lectures* 67 (1973): 175–197.

pp. 37–38. The catecholamine hypothesis and supporting evidence. J. J. Schildkraut, "The Catecholamine Hypothesis of Affective Disorders: A Review of Supporting Evidence," *American Journal of Psychiatry* 122 (1965): 509–522. See also W. E. Bunney, Jr., and J. M. Davis, "Norepinephrine in Depressive Reactions," *Archives of General Psychiatry* 13 (1965): 483–494 and D. L. Murphy et al., "Regular Induction of Hypomania by L-Dopa in 'Bipolar' Manic-Depressive Patients," *Nature* 229 (1971): 135–136.

p. 40. Increasing interest in receptor function. L. J. Siever et al., "Norepinephrine in the Affective Disorders and Their Treatment: II. Receptor Assessment Strategies" in C. R. Lake and M. G. Ziegler, eds., *The Catecholamines in Psychiatric and Neurologic Disorders* (Boston: Butterworth Press, 1985), 235–268. See also D. S. Charney et al., "Noradrenergic Neural Substrates for Anxiety and Fear" in F. E. Bloom and D. J. Kupfer, eds., *Psychopharmacology: The Fourth Generation of Progress* (New York: Raven Press, 1995), 971–981.

pp. 44. Roth Yalow studies. Roth Yalow and S. A. Berson, *Journal of Clinical Investigation* 39 (1960): 1157. Yalow et al., *Annals of the New York Academy of Sciences* 131 (1965): 357.

p. 46–47. Redmond study. E. Redmond, "New and Old Evidence for Involvement of a Brain Norepinephrine System in Anxiety," in W. E. Fann et al., eds., *The Phenomenology and Treatment of Anxiety* (New York: Spectrum, 1979).

p. 48. Study with Tom Uhde. L. J. Siever and T. W. Uhde, "New Studies and Perspectives on the Noradrenergic Receptor System in Depression: Effects of the Alpha-Adrenergic Agonist Clonidine," *Biological Psychiatry* 19 (1984): 131–156.

p. 49. Dysregulation hypothesis of depression. L. J. Siever and K. L. Davis: "Overview: Toward a Dysregulation Hypothesis of Depression," *American Journal of Psychiatry* 142 (1985): 1017.

p. 53. Nemeroff study. P. M. Plotsky et al., "Neuropeptide Alterations in Mood Disorders," in *Psychopharmacology: The Fourth Generation of Progress,* 971–981.

p. 54. S. F. Maier and M. E. P. Seligman, "Learned Helplessness: Theory and Evidence." *Journal of Experimental Psychology,* 1 (1976): 3–46. J. M. Weiss and P. E. Simpson, "Neurochemical and Electrophysiological Events Underlying Stress-Induced Depression in an Animal Model," *Advances in Experimental Medicine and Biology* 245 (1988): 425–440.

p. 59. Schemas. M. J. Horowitz et al., "Cyclical Patterns of States of Mind in Psychotherapy," *American Journal of Psychiatry* 151, no. 12 (1994): 1767–1770.

CHAPTER THREE

p. 63. Epigraph: E. Canetti, *The Agony of Flies,* 47.

pp. 67–68. A. Tellegen et al., "Personality Similarity in Twins Reared Apart and Together."

p. 68. Costa and McCrae study. R. R. McCrae and P. T. Costa, *Personality in Adulthood* (New York: Guilford Press, 1990).

p. 72 ff.: The dramatic cluster in *DSM-IV* diagnoses. D. N. Jackson and W. J. Livesley, "Possible Contributions fro Personality Assessment in the Classification of Personality Disorders," in W. J. Livesely, ed., *The DSM-IV Personality Disorders* (New York: Guilford Press, 1995), 459–481.

p. 83. Silverman and Torgerson studies. J. M. Silverman et al., "Affective and Impulsive Personality Disorder Traits in the Relatives of Patients with Borderline Personality Disorder," *American Journal of Psychiatry* 148 (1991): 546–554.

p. 84–85. Kretchmer's classification of personality types. E. Kretschmer, *Physique and Character* (London: Kegan Paul, 1925).

p. 85. Sigmund Freud on character. S. Freud, "Analysis Terminable and Interminable," in *The Complete Psychological Works,* vol. 23 (London: Hogarth Press, 1964), 240.

pp. 85. Problems with psychoanalytic theories of character. Many of the ideas presented here, including the paper by Glover, the identification of over 800 different personality types, and the Moore and Fine definition of character, come from E. L. Auchincloss, and R. Michaels, "Psychoanalytic Theory of Character," in J. P. Frosch, ed., *Current Perspectives on Personality Disorders* (Washington, D.C.: American Psychiatric Press, 1993), 2–17.

p. 86. Eysenck's theory of personality factors. H. J. Eysenck, *The Biological Basis of Personality* (Springfield, IL: Charles C. Thomas, 1967).

p. 86. Cloninger's theory of personality factors. C. R. Cloninger, "A Systematic Method for Clinical Description and Classification of Personality Variants," *Archives of General Psychiatry* 44 (1987): 573–588.

CHAPTER FOUR

p. 89. Epigraph: Sigmund Freud, "Mourning and Melancholia," in P. Gay, ed., *The Freud Reader* (New York: Norton, 1989), 588.

p. 90. Jacobs study. B. L. Jacobs and C. A. Fornal, "Serotonin and Behavior: A General Hypothesis," in *Psychopharmacology: The Fourth Generation of Progress,* 416–469.

P. 91. Meltzer study. H. Y. Meltzer and R. C. Arora, "Platelet Serotonin Studies in Affective Disorders: Evidence for a Serotonergic Abnormality," in M. Sandler et al., eds., *5-Hydroxytryptamine in Psychiatry: A Spectrum of Ideas* (New York: Oxford University Press, 1991), 50–89.

p. 92. Asberg study. M. Asberg et al., "Psychobiology of Suicide, Impulsivity, and Related Phenomena," in H. Y. Meltzer, ed., *Psychopharmacology: The Third Generation of Progress* (New York: Raven Press, 1987), 655–668.

p. 92. Delgado study. P. L. Delgado et al., "Serotonin Function and the Mechanism of Antidepressant Action Reversal of Antidepressant-Induced Remission by Rapid Depletion of Plasma Tryptophan," *Archives of General Psychiatry* 47 (1990): 411–418.

p. 94. Important studies at NIMH. G. L. Brown et al., "Aggression, Suicide, and Serotonin: Relationships fo CSF Amine Metabolites," *American Journal of Psychiatry* 139 (1982): 741–746. See also M. Linnoila et al., "Low Cerebrospinal Fluid Concentration Differentiates Impulsive from Nonimpulsive Violent Behavior," *Life Sciences* 33 (1983): 2609–2614.

p. 94. Coccaro's research program. E. F. Coccaro et al., "Serotonergic Studies in Patients with Affective and Personality Disorders Correlates with Suicidal and Impulsive Aggressive Behavior," *Archives of General Psychiatry* 46 (1989): 587–599 and *Correction* 47 (1990): 124.

pp. 95–96. Coccaro's later work. E. F. Coccaro et al., "Physiological Responses to d-Fenfluramine and Ipsapirone Challenge Correlate with Indices of Aggression in Males with Personality Disorder," *International Clinical Psychopharmacology* 10 (1995): 177–179.

p. 96. Study by the group in Ireland. V. O'Keane et al., "Blunted Prolactin Response to d-Fenfluramine in Sociopathy: Evidence for Subsensitivity of Central Serotonergic Function," *British Journal of Psychiatry* 160 (1992): 643–646.

p. 97. Roy and Linnoila's studies of pathological gamblers. A. Roy et al., "Extraversion in Pathological Gamblers Correlates with Indexes of Noradrenergic Function," *Archives of General Psychiatry* 46 (1989): 679–681.

p. 100–101. Cholinergic system and mood regulation. L. J. Siever et al., "Central Cholinergic-Adrenergic Imbalance in the Regulation of Affective State," *Psychiatric Research* 4 (1981): 108–109.

p. 101. Cholinergic challenge in depressed patients. S. C. Risch et al., "Differential Mood Effects of Arecholine in Depressed Patients and Normal Volunteers," *Psychopharmacology Bulletin* 19 (1983): 696–698.

p. 106. Kernberg's theory of schemas. O. F. Kernberg, *Object-Relations Theory and Clinical Psychoanalysis* (New York: Jason Aronson, 1976).

p. 108. Phineas Gage. A. Damasio, *Descartes' Error: Emotion, Reason and the Human Brain* (New York: G. P. Putnam's Sons, 1994), 3–10. Hanna Damasio's computer reconstruction, pp. 22–23.

p. 109–110. Animal studies of serotonin dysregulation and aggression. M. J. Raleigh and G. L. Brammer, "Individual Differences in Serotonin-2 Receptors and Social Behavior in Monkeys," *Society for Neuroscience Abstracts* 19 (1993): 592. M. D. Botchin et al., "Low Versus High Prolactin Responders to Fenfluramine Challenge: Marker of Behavioral Differences in Adult Male Cynomologus Macaques," *Neuropsychopharmacology* 9, no. 2 (1993): 93–99.

p. 110. PET studies of borderline patients and violent offenders. P. F. Goyer et al., "Positron Emission Tomography and Personality Disorders," *Neuropsychopharmacology* 10, no. 1 (1994): 21–28. A. Raine et al., "Selective Reductions in Prefrontal Glucose Metabolism in Murderers," *Biological Psychiatry* 36, no. 6 (1994): 365–373.

p. 111. Concordance of aggression in identical twins. E. F. Coccaro et al., "Heritability of Irritable Impulsiveness: A Study of Twins Reared Together and Apart," *Psychiatry Research* 48 (1993): 229–242.

p. 112. Tryptophan hydroxylase studies. D. A. Neilson et al., "Suicidality and 5-Hydroxyindolacetic Acid Concentration Associated with a Tryptophan Hydroxylase Polymorphism," *Archives of General Psychiatry* 51 (1994): 34–38. See also D. A. Neilson et al., "Association of Tryptophan Hydroxylase Genotype with Suicidal Behavior in Finns: A Replication Study." Lecture, American College of Neuropsychopharmacology 34th annual meeting, San Juan, P.R., 1995.

p. 115. D. Nelkin and S. Lindee, *The DNA Mystique* (New York: W. H. Freeman, 1995), 128.

p. 116. Epidemiology of antisocial disorder. R. C. Kessler et al., "Lifetime and 12-Month Prevalence of *DSM-III-R* Psychiatric Disorders in the United States: Results from the National Comorbidity Survey," *Archives of General Psychiatry* 51 (1994): 8.

p. 118. Todd diabetes study. S. T. Bennett et al., "Susceptibility to Human Type 1 Diabetes as IDDM2 Is Determined by Tandem Repeat Variation at the Insulin Gene Minisatellite Locus," *Nature Genetics* 9 (1995): 284–292.

CHAPTER FIVE

p. 127. Epigraph: Vladimir I. Nabokov, "Signs and Symbols," in *The Stories of Vladimir Nabokov* (New York: Knopf, 1996), 595–596.

p. 134. Psychodynamic theories of schizophrenia. T. Lidz, *Schizophrenia and the Family* (New York: International Universities Press, 1965).

p. 134. Bateson and Jackson's double-bind theory. G. Bateson et al., "Toward a Theory of Schizophrenia," *Behavioral Sciences* 1 (1956): 225.

p. 135–136. Dutch Hunger Winter. Susser, Ezra, et al., "Schizophrenia After Prenatal Famine: Further Evidence," in *Archives of General Psychiatry* 53 (January 1996): 25.

p. 137. Weinberger study of ventricular size. D. R. Weinberger et al., "Evidence for Dysfunction of a Prefrontal-Limbic Network in Schizophrenia: An MRI and rCBF Study of Discordant Monozygotic Twins," *American Journal of Psychiatry* 149 (1992): 890–897.

p. 139. Weinberger and Berman studies. D. R. Weinberger et al., "Physiologic Dysfunction of Dorsolateral Prefrontal Cortex in Schizophrenia I Regional Cerebral Blood Flow Evidence," *Archives of General Psychiatry* 43 (1986): 114–124. See also D. R. Weinberger et al., "Physiological Dysfunction of Dorsolateral Prefrontal Cortex in Schizophrenia: A New Cohort of Evidence for a Monoaminergic Mechanism," *Archives of General Psychiatry* 45 (1988): 606–615.

p. 140. Other studies of frontal and temporal lobe dysfunction. R. E. Gur et al., "Laterality and Frontality of Cerebral Blood Flow in Schizophrenia: Relationship to Symptom Specificity," *Psychiatry Research* 27 (1989): 325–334. See also R. McCarley et al., "Auditory P300 Abnormalities and Left Posterior Superior Temporal Gyrus Volume Reduction in Schizophrenia," *Archives of General Psychiatry* 50 (1993): 190–197.

p. 141. Discovery of Thorazine's antipsychotic properties. J. Delay and P. Deniker, "Le traitment des psychoses par une méthode neurolytique dérivée de l'hibernotherapie," in *Congrès des médecins aliénistes et neurologistes de France* (Luxembourg, 1952), 497–502.

p. 141–142. The dopamine hypothesis. I. Creese et al., "Biochemical Actions of Neuroleptic Drugs: Focus on the Dopamine Receptor," in L. L. Iversen et al., eds., *Handbook of Psychopharmacology*, vol. 10 (New York: Plenum, 1978). See also P. Seeman et al., "Antipsychotic Drug Doses and Neuroleptic/Dopamine Receptors," *Nature* 261 (1976): 717.

p. 142. Measurement of HVA in blood plasma. D. Pickar et al., "Longitudinal Measurement of Plasma Homovanillic Acid Levels in Schizophrenic Patients," *Archives of General Psychiatry* 43 (1986): 669–676. See also M. Davidson et al., "Changes in Plasma Homovanillic Acid Concentrations in Schizophrenic Patients Following Neuroleptic Discontinuation," *Archives of General Psychiatry* 48 (1991): 73–76.

p. 143–144. Interaction between dopamine and structural abnormalities. P. S. Goldman-Rakic and H. R. Friedman, "The Circuitry of Working Memory Revealed by Anatomy and Metabolic Imaging," in H. S. Levin et al., eds., *Frontal Lobe Function and Dysfunction* (New York: Oxford University Press, 1991).

p. 146. Epigraph: N. Gogol, "The Overcoat," in D. Magarshack, trans., *The Overcoat and Other Tales of Good and Evil* (New York: Norton, 1965), 252.

p. 157. Studies by Ken Kendler. K. S. Kendler et al., "The Roscommon Family Study: III. Schizophrenia-Related Personality Disorders in Relatives," *Archives of General Psychiatry* 50 (1993): 781–788. See also R. E. Straub et al., "A Potential Vulnerability Locus of Schizophrenia on Chromosome 6p24-22: Evidence for Genetic Heterogeneity," *Nature Genetics* 11 (1995): 287–293.

p. 161–164. Eye-tracking studies. P.S. Holtzman et al., "Eye Tracking Dysfunctions in Schizophrenic Patients and their Relatives," *Archives of General Psychiatry* 31 (1974): 143–151. See also L. J. Siever et al., "Impaired Smooth Pursuit Eye Movement: Vulnerability Markers for Schizotypal Personality Disorder in a Volunteer Population," *American Journal of Psychiatry* 141 (1984): 1560–1565. See also M. S. Buchsbaum et al, "Attentional Dysfunction and Psychopathology in College Males," *Archives of General Psychiatry* 42 (1985): 354–360.

CHAPTER SIX

p. 169. Epigraph. W. H. Auden, *The Age of Anxiety* (New York: Random House, 1946), 8.

p. 175. Sigmund Freud, "Little Hans: Analysis of a Phobia in a Five-Year-Old Boy," in *The Complete Psychological Works*, vol. 10: 3–149.

p. 176. Nesse and Williams's ideas on anxiety as an environmental disease. R. Nesse and G. Williams, *Why We Get Sick* (New York: Times Books, 1994), 212–214.

pp. 183–184. Jerome Kagan's studies of inhibited and anxious children. J. Kagan et al, "Childhood Derivatives of Inhibition and Lack of Inhibition to the Unfamiliar," *Child Development* 59 (1988): 1580–1589.

p. 184–185. Steven Suomi's studies of fearful monkeys. S. J. Suomi, "Primate Separation Models of Affective Disorders," in J. Madden, ed., *Neurobiology of Learning, Emotion and Affect* (New York: Raven Press, 1991).

p. 186. Carbon dioxide and panic attacks. J. M. Gorman et al., "Ventilatory Physiology of Patients with Panic Disorder," *Archives of General Psychiatry* 45 (1988): 31–39. See also J. M. Gorman et al., "Anxiogenic Effects of CO_2 and Hyperventilation in Patients with Panic Disorder," *American Journal of Psychiatry* 151 (1994): 547–553.

p. 187. Donald Klein's suffocation alarm theory of panic attacks. D. Klein, "False Suffocation Alarms, Spontaneous Panics, and Related Conditions: An Integrative Hypothesis," *Archives of General Psychiatry* 50 (1993): 306.

p. 188. The noradrenergic system in panic disorders. T. W. Uhde et al., "Blunted Growth Hormone Response to Clonidine in Panic Disorder Patients," *Biological Psychiatry* 21 (1986): 1081–1085. See also D. S. Charney et al., "Neurobiological Mechanisms of Panic Anxiety: Biochemical and Behavioral Correlates of Yohimbine-Induced Panic Attacks," *American Journal of Psychiatry* 144 (1987): 1030–1036.

p. 189. Autonomic dysfunction in PTSD. R. Yehuda et al., "Lymphocyte Glucocorticoid Receptor Number in Posttraumatic Stress Disorder," *American Journal of Psychiatry* 149 (1991): 499–504. See also R. Yehuda et al., "Hypothalamic-Pituitary-Adrenal Dysfunction in Post-Traumatic Stress Disorder," *Biological Psychiatry* 30 (1991): 1031–1048; R. Yehuda et al., "Dose-Response Changes in Plasma Cortisol and Lymphocyte Glucocorticoid Receptors Following Dexamethasone Administration in Combat Veterans with and without Posttraumatic Stress Disorder," *Archives of General Psychiatry* 52 (1995): 583–593; R. Yehuda et al., "Cortisol Regulation in Posttraumatic Stress Disorder and Major Depression: A Chronobiological Analysis," *Biological Psychiatry* 40 (1996): 79–88.

pp. 191–192. The serotonin system in obsessive-compulsive disorder. J. Zohar et al., "Serotonergic Responsivity in Obsessive-Compulsive Disorder: Effects of Chronic Clomipramine Treatment," *Archives of General Psychiatry* 45 (1988): 167–172.

p. 193. Study on social phobias. M. E. Tancer et al., "The Hypothalamic-Pituitary-Thyroid Axis in Social Phobia," *American Journal of Psychiatry* 147 (1990): 929–933.

CHAPTER SEVEN

p. 195. Epigraph: T. Sejnowski and S. Quartz, *The Intelligent Brain* (New York: Harper Collins, in press).

p. 210. Sadistic murderers. M. H. Stone, "Sadistic Personality in Murderers," in T. Millon et al., eds., *Psychopathy: Antisocial, Criminal and Violent Behaviors* (New York: Guilford Press, in press).

p. 214. Hippocampal volume. J. D. Bremner et al., "MRI-Based Measurement of Hippocampal Volume in Patients with Combat-Related Posttraumatic Stress Disorder," *American Journal of Psychiatry* 152 (1995): 973–981.

p. 215. PTSD symptoms in rape victims. H. S. Resnick et al., "Effect of Previous Trauma on Plasma Cortisol Level Following Rape," *American Journal of Psychiatry* 152 (1995): 1675–1677.

p. 216. Stress-induced changes in gene expression. S. E. Hyman and E. J. Nestler, "Initiation and Adaptation: A Paradigm for Understanding Psychotropic Drug Action," *American Journal of Psychiatry* 153, no. 2 (1996): 151–162.

p. 216. HPA abnormalities in offspring of Holocaust survivors. R. Yehuda et al., "Phenomenology and Psychobiology of Intergenerational Response to Trauma," in Y. Danieli, ed., *Intergenerational Handbook: Multigenerational Legacies of Trauma* (New York: Plenum, in press).

CHAPTER EIGHT

p. 217. Epigraph: A. Kardiner and L. Ovesey, *The Mark of Oppression* (New York: Meridian Books, 1962), 10.

p. 217. Epigraph: L. Ferlinghetti, "A Coney Island of the Mind," in *A Coney Island of the Mind* (New York: New Directions, 1958), 9.

p. 218. Kraepelin's report of relative frequencies of mania and depression. E. Kraepelin, *Manic-Depressive Insanity and Paranoia*, 133.

p. 218. Modern ratio of depression to mania. Goodwin and Jamison, *Manic-Depressive Illness*, 161–184.

pp. 221–222. Evolutionary psychologists' explanations for depression. Nesse and Williams, *Why We Get Sick*, 216–218. See also R. Wright, *The Moral Animal: Why We Are the Way We Are, The New Science of Evolutionary Psychology* (New York: Pantheon Books, 1994), 271–272.

p. 224. K. R. Jamison, *Touched With Fire: Manic-Depressive Illness and the Artistic Temperament* (New York: Free Press), 1993.

p. 234. Letter to *Newsweek*, 28 February 1994, 14. The article that provoked the letter ran in the issue of 7 February 1994, 36–43.

pp. 236–237. Epidemiology of psychiatric disorders. R. C. Kessler et al., "Lifetime and 12-Month Prevalence of *DSM-III-R* Psychiatric Disorders in the United States: Results from the National Comorbidity Survey," *Archives of General Psychiatry* 51 (1994): 8.

INDEX

A

Abraham, Karl, 85
Acetylcholine, 36, 100
Aggression
  in borderline personality
    disorder, 81
  serotonin and, 89–125
Aggressive-impulsive disorders
  noradrenergic system in, 190
  serotonin and, 92
American Psychiatric
    Association, 234
  classification system, 15
*Analysis Terminable and
    Interminable* (Freud), 85
Anatomy of Melancholy
    (Burton), 17, 118–19
Antidepressant drugs, 5
  Clorgyline, 42
  Deprenyl, 42
  monoamine oxidase
    inhibitors (MAOIs), 38,
    55, 56, 121
  for personality disorders, 121
  prescription, 237–42
  reputation, 232–33
  side effects, 236
  tricyclic antidepressants, 38,
    55, 56
Antisocial personality disorder,
    78–80, 103–4
  assortive mating and, 82
  response to emotional
    stimuli, 114
  treating difficulty, 113–17, 124

Anxiety, 183
  combined with impulsivity,
    210
  fear different from, 172–73
  in psychological theories,
    174–75
Anxiety disorders, 169–78
  case study, 169–71
  child abuse and, 212
  noradrenergic dysfunction,
    92, 190
  See also Generalized anxiety
    disorder; Obsessive-com-
    pulsive disorder; Panic
    disorder; Post-traumatic
    stress disorder (PTSD)
Anxiety personality disorders,
    178
  affective sensitivity in, 209
  biology of, 191
  psychological treatments,
    192–93
  See also Avoidant personality
    disorder; Dependent
    personality disorder;
    Obsessive-compulsive
    personality disorder
Archives of General Psychiatry,
    187
Asberg, Marie, 92, 94
Assortive mating, 82
  and family environment,
    207–8
Auchincloss, Elizabeth, 85

Avoidant personality disorder,
    179–80
  and panic disorder, 186
Axelrod, Julius, 36
Axial system of evaluation, 178

B

Barrett Impulsivity Scale, 95
Bateson, Gregory, 134
Behavior, brain chemicals
    and, 69, 102
Berman, Karen, 139, 140
Berritini, Wade, 24
Berson, Solomon, 44
Biological model of
    disease, 29–30
Bipolar affective disorder
  in A.P.A. classification
    system, 15
  case studies, 1–6, 9–10,
    36–37, 40–41, 58–59,
    60–61
  catecholamine hypothesis,
    37–39
  chromosome linkage,
    23, 24, 223
  creativity and, 224–25
  psychotic symptoms, 11–12
  See also Depression; Mania
Borderline personality disorder,
    80–82, 104, 105, 122
  cholinergic system, 101–2
  PET scans, 110
  physostigmine and, 106–7

Borderline personality
disorder *(cont'd)*
and state-dependent
memory, 107
Bouchard, Jack, 19, 67–68
Brain, 32–34, 229–30
cerebral cortex, 108–10
hippocampus degeneration,
214
in schizophrenia, 135–41
Brodie, Keith, 38
Brown, Gerald, 94
Brown-Goodwin Life History
of Aggression, 95
Buchsbaum, Monte S., 110,
139, 161, 162
Bunney, William, 37, 38,
40, 42
Buproprion (Wellbutin), 56
Burton, Robert, 17, 19, 118
Buss-Durkee Hostility
Inventory, 95, 112

C
Carbamezepine (Tegretol), 121
Charney, Dennis, 188
Child abuse, 211–13
Cholinergic-adrenergic balance
theory, 101
Cholinergic system, 101
in personality disorders,
101–2
Cleckley, Hervey, 79, 113
Clomipramine, 191
Clonidine, panic disorders
and, 188
Clonidine/growth hormone
test, 47–48
depression, 47–48
personality disorders, 97
Clonidine/MHPG test, 48, 50
Cloninger, 86
Clozapine (Clozaril), 145
Coccaro, Emil, 94, 111
Cognitive behavioral
therapy, 123
Cognitive disorganization, 132
Cognitive psychotherapy, 5
anxiety personality
disorders, 192

Community
close-knit communities and
personality disorders,
218–20
psychiatric disorders in, 217–43
Conduct disorder, 78
Continuous Performance Task
(CPT), 163
Cornblatt, Barbara, 163
Cortisol, 53–54
Costa, Paul, 68, 86
Coursey, Bob, 161
Criminal behavior, 115–16
Cyclothymia, 15–16, 104

D
Damasio, Antonio, 108
Damasio, Hanna, 109
Davidson, Michael, 142
Davis, John, 37, 40, 101
Davis, Ken, 49, 142
Delay, John, 141
Delgado, Pedro, 92
Deniker, Pierre, 141
Deoxyribonucleic acid
(DNA), 20–23
Dependent personality
disorder, 180–81
Depression, 1–12, 16
and adrenergic receptor, 48
catecholamine hypothesis, 91
environmental factors, 20
genetics and, 17–20
increase, 238
indoleamine hypothesis, 91
neurotransmitters dysregulation as cause, 49–50
and norepinephrine, 52
personality disorders
distinguished, 72
physical symptoms, 10–11
reaction to chronic
stress, 215
role of hypothalamic-
pituitary axis (HPA), 53
Descartes' Error (Damasio), 108
Desipramine, 57
Dexamethasone, 215
effect on PTSD patients, 189
suppression test, 54

Diabetes, 43–45
genetics of, 118
glucose tolerance test, 47
*Diagnostic and Statistical
Manual of Mental
Disorders (DSM-IV)*, 16,
72, 155, 159, 234, 236
Dialectic behavioral therapy
(DBT), 124
DNA. *See* Deoxyribonucleic
acid (DNA)
DNA Mystique, The (Nelkin
and Lindee), 115–16
Dopamine, 35, 36–37
agonists, 144
Dramatic cluster personality
disorders, 63–87, 107
affective sensitivity in, 209
biological reasoning and, 103
case study, 63–66, 71–72,
80–81, 82–83, 97–98, 122
genetic factors, 83–84
psychotherapy, 124
See also Antisocial personality disorder; Borderline
personality disorder;
Histrionic personality
disorder; Narcissistic
personality disorder
Drugs
antidepressant. *See*
Antidepressant drugs
benzodiazepines, 190
neuroleptics, 135, 141, 145
and psychotherapy, 239
psychotropic, 238
and treatment of personality
disorders, 121
use for diagnosis, 28
See also specific drugs
*DSM-IV. See Diagnostic and
Statistical Manual of
Mental Disorders
(DSM-IV)*
Dysthymia, 16

E
Eating disorders
child abuse and, 212
serotonin and, 92

Electroconvulsive shock
  therapy (ECT), 146
Environmental impact
biologically encoded in
  child's brain, 211
encoded on the genes, 216
Eye-tracking, 160–61
in schizotypal personality
  disorder, 163
social impairment
  correlation, 161–62, 163
Eysenck, Hans, 86

F
Family, 195–216
case study, 195–202
Fenfluramine, 93–94
aggression and, 95–96
borderline disorders and, 102
depression and, 94
personality disorders and, 94
PET scans and, 111
Fluoxetine (Prozac), 55, 91, 191,
  234, 238, 239, 241
Fluvoxamine (Luxox), 55
Freud, Sigmund, 85, 175

G
Gamow, George, 20
Generalized anxiety
  disorder, 176
drugs for, 190–91
Genetics
correlation with neurochemical results, 111
depression and, 17–20
of diabetes, 118
in dramatic cluster, 83–84
gene amplification, 24
markers, 23
misuse of studies, 116, 119
molecular genetic
  analysis, 24
multigenic inheritance, 118
normal personality variation
  vs. personality
  disorders, 117
and personality, 67
and psychiatric diagnoses,
  229–30

in schizophrenia, 135, 225–26
schizophrenia-related
  personality disorders, 157
survival of mental
  diseases, 221–27
Gershon, Elliot, 24
Glover, E.G., 85
Goodwin, Frederick, 7, 8, 9,
  38, 94
Gorman, Jack, 186
Goyer, Peter, 110
Grey, Sir Jeffrey, 86
Grur, Raquel, 140
Grur, Ruben, 140
Gunderson, John, 105

H
Harlow, Harry, 184
Heart disease, biological
  model, 29–30
Histrionic personality disorder,
  73–75, 104, 105, 122
assortive mating and, 82
Hollander, Eric, 192
Holzman, Philip, 161
Human Genome Project,
  118, 119
ethical dilemmas, 230–31
Huntington's disease, 24, 120
Hyman, Steven, 216
Hypomania, 12, 15

I
Imipramine, 28
Impulsive-aggressive disorders.
  See Aggressive- impulsive
  disorders
Impulsivity
in antisocial personality
  disorder, 79
combined with anxiety, 210
dopamine and, 102–3
in personality disorders,
  103–4
Innate temperament, child
  development and, 203–6
Intrator, Joanne, 114

J
Jackson, Donald, 134

Jacobs, Barry, 90, 99
Jamison, Kay, 7, 8, 9, 224
Janowsky, David, 101

K
Kagan, Jerome, 68, 183, 185
Kendler, Ken, 30, 157
Kernberg, Otto, 106
Klein, Donald, 186, 187, 222
Kraepelin, Emil, 17, 218
Kramer, Peter, 28, 231, 236
Kretchmer, Ernest, 84

L
Lactate infusion test, 186
Laing, R. D., 27
Lasch, Christopher, 228
"Learned helplessness" model,
  54–55
Lesch, Klaus-Peter, 103
Liebowitz, Michael,
  186
Lindee, Susan, 115
Linehan, Marcia, 123
Linnoila, Markku, 94, 97
Listening to Prozac (Kramer),
  28, 236
Lithium, 39, 56, 57, 233
and personality disorders, 121
as treatment for mania,
  12, 233
Lost Puritan (Mariani), 13–14
Lowell, Robert, 13–14

M
Mania, 12–15, 25
paranoia and, 14–15
Manic depression. See Bipolar
  affective disorder
Manic-Depressive Illness
  (Goodwin and Jamison),
  7, 8, 9
Manic Depressive Insanity and
  Paranoia (Kraepelin), 17
Mariani, Paul, 13
Mask of Sanity, The
  (Cleckley), 79
McCarley, Robert, 140
McCrae, Robert, 68, 86
McEwan, Bruce, 214

Meltzer, Herbert, 40, 91
"Metapsychology or
    Metaphysics" (Glover), 85
Michels, Robert, 85
Moral Animal, The
    (Wright), 223
Murphy, Dennis, 38, 40, 92,
    103, 161, 191

N

Narcissistic personality
    disorder, 75–78, 104, 105
  assortive mating and, 82
  therapy and, 124
Nelkin, Dorothy, 115
Nemeroff, Charles, 53, 91
Nesse, Randolph, 174, 222
Nestler, Eric, 216
Netazadone (Serzone), 55–56
Neurons, 32–33
Neurotransmitters, 33–35
  biogenic amines, 91
  interaction of, 98
  personality traits and, 84
Noradrenergic system, 46–47,
    52, 97, 188–91
  in panic disorder, 188
Norepinephrine system, 35, 36
  and depression, 49, 51
  effect of abuse on, 213
  serotonin interaction, 98–100

O

Obsessive-compulsive disorder,
    99, 176
  and obsessive-compulsive
    personality disorder, 186
  serotonin and, 91, 191
Obsessive-compulsive person-
    ality disorder, 181–83
  and obsessive-compulsive
    disorder, 186
Odd cluster personality
    disorders, 146–68
  case study, 146–50, 165–67
  See also Paranoid personality
    disorder; Schizoid person-
    ality disorder; Schizotypal
    personality disorder
Olanzepine (Zyprexo), 145

P

Panic attacks, 173–74
  theory of, 187
Panic disorder, 171–74, 175
  link with avoidant
    personality disorder, 186
  noradrenergic system, 188
  serotonin and, 91
Paranoia, mania and, 14–15
Paranoid personality disorder,
    154–55
  schizotypal personality
    disorder overlap, 158
Parasympathetic nervous
    system, 36
Paroxetine (Paxil), 55
Personality
  components of, 86–87
  constancy, 68–69,
    183–84
  generation styles, 227–28
  genes and environment in
    development of, 69–71
  genetic factors of, 67–68
  groups' styles, 227
  theories of development,
    86–87
  traits correlated to
    neurotransmitters, 84
  unstable, 67
Personality disorders
  affective sensitivity, 103–5
  child abuse and, 212
  cholinergic system, 101–2
  depression distinguished, 72
  drugs and, 121–22
  multiple disorders in same
    patient, 209
  talking therapies, 122
  See also Dramatic cluster;
    Odd cluster; and specific
    disorders
PET. *See* Positron emission
    tomography (PET)
Phobias, 171, 173, 174, 187
Physostigmine, 101
  given to borderline patients,
    106–7
Pickar, Dave, 41, 142
Plomin, Robert, 68

Positron emission tomography
    (PET), 110
  use on borderline
    patients, 110
  use with Wisconsin Card
    Sort Test, 139
Post-traumatic stress disorder
    (PTSD), 177–78
  autonomic dysfunction
    in, 189
  hypothalamic-pituitary
    axis in, 189
  reaction to chronic
    stress, 215
Price, J., 19
Prozac. *See* Fluoxetine (Prozac)
Psychoanalytic theory,
    anxiety in, 174–75
Psychodynamic therapy, 123
  anxiety personality
    disorders, 193
Psychotherapy
  drugs facilitating, 239
Psychotic symptoms
  in bipolar affective
    disorder, 11–12
  in borderline personality
    disorder, 81–82
  in schizophrenia, 131

R

Raine, Adrian, 110
Raleigh, Michael, 109
Receptors, 45–46
  binding of chemicals to, 45
  in noradrenergic
    system, 46–47
  regulation of, 42
Redmond, Gene, 46
Reserpine, 38
Resnick, Heidi, 215
Risch, Craig, 101
Risperidone (Risperdal), 145
Roth, Jesse, 44
Roy, Alec, 97

S

Sacks, Oliver, 37
Sapolsky, Bob, 214
Schemas, concept of, 58–59

Schildkraut, Joseph, 37
Schizoid personality
    disorder, 155–57, 159
Schizophrenia, 127–46
  brain function
    disorders, 138–41
  brain structure abnormali-
    ties, 135, 136–38
  case study, 127–31, 132–34
  dopamine hypothesis, 141–45
  environmental factors,
    135–36
  genetics and, 135, 225–26
  noradrenergic dysfunction,
    92
  psychodynamic models,
    134–35
  serotonin and, 91–92
  symptoms, 131–32
Schizotypal personality
    disorder, 151–54, 167
  paranoid personality
    disorder overlap, 158
Seamans, Philip, 141, 142
Selective serotonin reuptake
    inhibitors (SSRIs), 55, 91,
    121, 239
Seligman, Martin, 54
Serotonin, 53, 108
  and aggression, 89–125
  effect of abuse on, 214
  fenfluramine used
    as probe, 93–94
  level determination, 92–94
  norepinephrine interaction,
    98–100

obsessive-compulsive
    disorder, 191
  receptors, 100
  suicide and, 95
Sertindole (Serlect), 145
Sertraline (Zoloft), 55, 234
Shelton, Richard, 84
Shenton, Martha, 140
Shyness
  genetic element in, 185–86
  lifelong trait, 183–84
Snyder, Solomon, 141, 142
SSRIs. *See* Selective serotonin
    reuptake inhibitors
    (SSRIs)
State-dependent learning,
    59–60, 61
State-dependent memory,
    105–6
  in borderline disorder, 107
Suicide, 67
  depression and, 8–9
  serotonergic activity and, 95
Suomi, Stephen, 184
Sympathetic nervous system,
    35–36
Szasz, Thomas, 27

T
Tellegen, Auke, 19, 67–68
Thorazine, 141
Todd, John, 118
Touched with Fire
    (Jamison), 224
Twin studies, 18–19, 67–68
  harm avoidance, 184

schizotypal personality
    disorder, 157
Tyramine, 42
Tyrosine, 36

U
Uhde, Tom, 48
Unipolar major depressive
    disorder, 15

V
Valium, 190, 239, 240
Valproate (Depakote), 121
Venlafaxine (Effexor), 55
Violence, biological
    bases of, 120

W
Weinberger, Daniel,
    137, 139, 140
Weiss, Jay, 54
Why We Get Sick (Nesse and
    Williams), 174, 222
Williams, George, 174, 222
Wisconsin Card Sort Task,
    139–40, 144, 166
Wolf, Hugo, 9
Wright, Robert, 223

Y
Yalow, Rosalyn, 44
Yehuda, Rachel,
    189, 214, 215, 216

Z
Zohar, Yosi, 191